INVISIBLE CITY

INVISIBLE CITY

Poverty, Housing, and New Urbanism

JOHN INGRAM GILDERBLOOM

Foreword by Neal Peirce

UNIVERSITY OF TEXAS PRESS, AUSTIN

COPYRIGHT © 2008 BY THE UNIVERSITY OF TEXAS PRESS

All rights reserved

Printed in the United States of America

First edition, 2008

Requests for permission to reproduce material from this work
should be sent to:
    Permissions
    University of Texas Press
    P.O. Box 7819
    Austin, TX 78713-7819
    www.utexas.edu/utpress/about/bpermission.html

♾ The paper used in this book meets the minimum requirements
of ANSI/NISO Z39.48-1992 (R1997) (Permanence of Paper).

LIBRARY OF CONGRESS CATALOGING-IN-PUBLICATION DATA
Gilderbloom, John Ingram.
    Invisible city : poverty, housing, and new urbanism /
John Ingram Gilderbloom ; foreword by Neal Peirce. — 1st ed.
        p. cm.
Includes bibliographical references and index.

ISBN 978-0-292-71710-7 (pbk. : alk. paper)
    1. Low-income housing—United States—Case studies   2. Urban poor—
United States—Case studies.   3. People with disabilities—Housing—United
States—Case studies.   4. Older people—Housing—United States—Case
studies.   I. Title.
HD7288.85.U6G54   2008
363.50973—dc22
2007007186

This book is dedicated to academic freedom—
may it live forever and may we fight all those
who try to end it.

With grateful appreciation to my mentors
on my Zen journey of learning. They taught me
how to think, to be brave, and to have fun doing it:
Richard P. Appelbaum, Howard Becker, Stella Capek, Greg Davis,
Mark Dowie, Richard Brautigan, Allen Ginsberg, Henry Cisneros,
William Domhoff, Andres Duany, Joe Feagin, Richard Flacks,
Roger Friedland, Bill Friedlander, Mary Ann Gilderbloom, Max
Gilderbloom, Murray Gilderbloom, Chester Hartman, David
Harvey, Maureen Dowd, Tom Hayden, Christopher "Sandy" Jencks,
Dennis Keating, Ron Larsen, Dennis Leung, Dave Lewis, Harvey
Molotch, Kathryn Newman, Kenneth Rexroth, Mark Rosentraub,
Donovan Rypkema, Herb Segal, Derek Shearer, Twyla Tharp,
Don Terner, and Russell Weaver. This book is lovingly dedicated
to them.

CONTENTS

FOREWORD

BY NEAL PEIRCE

It's possible to be deeply caring, as John Gilderbloom is in this book, about the poor, the distressed, the homeless of his "Invisible City." But can one also be pragmatic, rigorous in analysis, and focused unflinchingly on demonstrated results?

It's no easy stretch, but Gilderbloom comes close in this book. He dismisses ideological nostrums about housing, whether they come from the interventionist left or the do-nothing free-market right, and he faults self-interested analyses of the real estate industry. Decent and desirable housing, he suggests, should be an inalienable right for each human in the one life he or she has to lead. It *matters*.

The social concern expressed here comes as a fresh breeze in an America alarmingly focused on such trivia as gilded bathrooms, multi-car garages and bloated square footage, citizens ready to wreak political revenge on anyone who interferes with the sanctity of the middle to upper classes' federal housing tax breaks. (And in fact, with the home mortgage deduction, they do garner the huge majority of federal housing subsidies each budget year.)

The real question isn't whether government plays a role in Americans' housing. It's *how* it can unlock the fiscal and policy doors to decent housing for our disadvantaged, impoverished, and elderly, in the interest of equity, shared community, and the general welfare writ large. Showing the relevance to more people, perhaps, we should take note of the recent years' poignant stories of how teachers, police, firefighters, and government workers are often literally priced out of the places they serve.

Refreshingly, Gilderbloom does not push for some single, magic, nationally applied housing solution. Indeed, one of the most interesting questions he poses is why some cities seem able to provide affordable housing for a broad swath of their population while others cannot. He raises uncomfortable questions for us to consider. Should we welcome, he asks, the success of such cities as Chicago, Boston, and San Francisco that have added stunning numbers of downtown housing units in the past several years? The price to pay, he alleges, is such broad inflation of all a city's housing costs that the lower-income classes are seriously disadvantaged and "priced out" of their own neighborhoods.

On a similar tack, Gilderbloom faults some of the HOPE VI housing projects of recent years because they do, in fact, create fewer total housing units for very poor people than may have existed before. I'd start on the positive: HOPE VI projects may represent imperfect or incomplete efforts, but they *have* succeeded in a total remake of some of America's most dangerously blighted neighborhoods, in the process creating quite healthy, new, mixed-use communities.

For too long, we had to worry deeply about the future of our great cities. Their new success in drawing middle-class residents, their use of HOPE VI–like devices to dismantle some of the most socially poisonous concentrations of the very poor ever known, represent a heartening social turn I'd prefer to celebrate, not denigrate.

But Gilderbloom does us an immense favor by suggesting sensitive, customized, city-by-city evaluations, based on real-world social and housing market conditions, with a focus on just what steps each community (and I would say citistate region) needs to do to assure satisfactory housing for all income groups among its residents.

In a sense, this relates to a troubling dilemma of American society as a whole. Those who suggest that "the poor have always been with us," that their plight is beyond constructive engagement and change, do us a tremendous disservice. The result of our failure to guarantee correct housing, back-up services for hard-pressed mothers, day care for children, community recreation and social services and good schools is a weakening of our nation. It creates enormous burdens—burdens for the deprived families, burdens for all of society in stunted lives, unrealized income and tax yields, and social and criminal system costs.

It may be easier to argue that investment in social services and education will help such families reach a critical turning point. But housing is a critical, indispensable part of the equation; where people live *is* immensely important; to ignore the quality of their shelter is to undercut every other possible investment we make in them, from the federal low-income tax credit to local recreational programs.

Gilderbloom raises the critical question: Why are some cities able to provide affordable housing while others fail in the effort? How can elected and appointed government officials, developers, landlords, and banks work *together* to create the optimal set of policies, ranging from code enforcement to subsidy?

I think he's right in saying extensive research is necessary to find the right—and often elusive—customized answers, community by community, region by region. We need research that encompasses (and balances) existing market forces, the impact of existing government codes and regulations, the roles and potentials of nonprofit, community development groups, and much more. And research that does search out, and check the local applicability of, programs that show a proven track record elsewhere.

Does such research need to be objective, undistorted by self-interested, industry-financed analysis? Well, yes. But who can do this? Certainly competent, disinterested university-based research can be extremely helpful. But perhaps we need to go a significant step further—to create independent panels, government-supported but broadly representative of civic organizations, community groups, and (yes, but only one player from) the real estate organizations. Their job should be to analyze, systematically and regularly and in an academically rigorous way, evolving local and regional housing conditions—to compare local steps with those being undertaken in other cities and states. And then to suggest, to policy-making bodies ranging from their local governments to their state legislatures and executive departments, the mix of specific place-relevant policies and steps that they are convinced can move that city, region, and state closer to adequate housing for all.

The long-range goal—controversial but consistent with John Gilderbloom's vision—should be a mix of types of housing, price points, and decent availability of supply in *every* community. Call that approach, if you will, idealistic, probably expensive, hard to implement. But just consider the alternative—the status quo, the fraying of community, the serious American housing dilemma that we've allowed to develop and fester. Reforming it will be challenging *and* expensive. But inaction, lack of imagination in finding (and funding) new approaches, may prove the most disastrous course of all.

ACKNOWLEDGMENTS

I would like to thank the following people who were helpful in putting this book together over the past few years: Max Gilderbloom, Neal Peirce, Muthusami Kumaran, the late Joseph Stopher, Bill Friedlander, and Jim Davis of the Gheens Foundation, as well as my dogs, Snoopy and Dexter. We would like to thank the co-authors of this book for collaborating with me on several chapters: Richard Appelbaum, Anthony Campbell, Zhenfeng Pan, Tom Lehman, Stephen A. Roosa, Mark Rosentraub, Michael Brazley, Roger Lewis, Steven Hornburg, Patrick Smith, and Richard Layman. Our special thanks also go to Lin Ye and Shannon Pratt. Shannon Pratt helped gather information for Chapter 2. Tess Arkels, in particular, contributed greatly to the revisions made in Chapter 1 and the acknowledgments. We would also like to thank George Darnell for his excellent contributions to Chapter 6. Additional thanks to Cynthia Cooke, whose conversations were always stimulating and thoughtful. Rick Bell gave us good ideas on Chapter 7.

My thanks also go to my amigos—Larry Muhammad, Tom Donovan, Gary Sayed, Dick Vreeland, Andres Duany, Richard Appelbaum, Steven Cohn, and Kiki Harmon. Special thanks to Krista Salerno, who heard many of these ideas and provided a means for me to meet some of the most successful landlords in the business. Finally, special thanks to the various listserves that often got the first draft of these ideas and helped to correct them: American Urban Sociological Association (special thanks to Herb Gans, Stella Capek), Pro-Urban Listserve/Congress of New Urbanism (special thanks to David Brain, Charles Bohl, Andres Duany, John Hooker, John Massengale, Donovan Rypkema, Emily Talen, and of course Lucy Rowland "Snow White"), Urban History Forum (Mark Peel), Urban Geography Forum,

New York American Planning Association Forum, Urbanist Listserv, and R21 Forum (Terry Nichols Clark). Special thanks to the Kentucky and Indiana Real Estate Investors Associations, Urban Land Institute, and my late mother's real estate company, Lauder Properties, which taught me a great deal about landlording in practice, with gold stars going to Mary Martin, Joe Hampton, Dutch Trading Company, Neighborhood Development Corporation, Kimberly Stephenson, Debbie Terry, Mark Wright, Beth Medina, Bill Weyland, Steve Wiser, Craig Hollman, National City Bank, and Eric Landis.

I would like to thank my beloved Original Highlands neighborhood and the local restaurants that gave me space to work through some ideas and eliminate some bad ones: Lynn's Paradise Café, O'Shea's, Molly Malone's, Jack Fry's, Monkey Wrench, and Stevens & Stevens. My neighborhood nonprofit Lakeside Swim Club and volleyball leagues, along with my twice-yearly visits to Hotel San Luchesio in Amsterdam and North Shore in Oahu (*Mahalo* to Hawaii International Conferences in Honolulu for financial support and housing), were great opportunities to reflect on making the connections among the various chapters—thanks to Todd Swanstrom, Belinda Glockler, the Gelderbloms of Holland, Pieter Rings, Leon Deben, and Manuel Aalbers for the great times in Holland. Consequently, four chapters that were ultimately not a good fit for this book are being held for another publication. As usual, background music was an inspiration during the hot summer days of writing this, especially: Beatles (including David Harvey's favorite album, *Abbey Road*), Zombies, Clash, Animals, Yardbirds, Tess Arkels (*Orphan of the Heart* CD!), Paul McCartney, Joe Jackson, Inmates, George Harrison, Tom Petty, Ryan Adams, Fleetwood Mac (*Kiln House, Then Play On*), Santana, Alfredo Rodriguez, Polo Montanez, Elvis Costello, Joni Mitchell, and Chucho Valdes.

We would like to thank the fine people at the University of Texas Press, including Jim Burr, Mary J. LaMotte, Nancy Bryan, and Lynne Chapman. University of Texas Press believed in this book and put together the resources to make this the best book possible. Copyeditor Tana Silva raised the book another notch with her suggestions. All in all, they are the best book publishers I have ever had pleasure of working with during my career.

We would like to also thank the organizations that provided generous financial support for this book, including the Center for Sustainable Urban Neighborhoods (SUN) at the University of Louisville, the Houston Housing Authority, the City of Houston, the U.S. Department of Housing and Urban Development (HUD), the Center for Environmental Justice sponsored by the U.S. Environmental Protection Agency (EPA), HUD HOPE VI Evaluation, HUD Community Outreach Partnership Center, and Department of Education Community Service Grant.

Special thanks to Kris Rengert of Housing Policy Debate, Sylvia Lewis of the American Planning Association (APA), and Micah B. Kleit at Temple University Press for allowing us to draw portions from my 1988 book with Richard Appelbaum, *Rethinking Rental Housing*, especially Chapters 2 and 3. Thanks to several academic presses that expressed a strong interest in the book and gave me some good direction on the theme of the book. More thanks to Chris Peveler at the University of Louisville for his technical expertise, as well as my graduate students in my housing, Netherlands, and historic preservation courses at the University of Louisville. I would also like to thank the Kentucky Institute for Environment and Sustainable Development (KIESD), which supports my research at the Center for Sustainable Urban Neighborhoods (www.louisville.edu/org/sun) run by the Office for the Vice President of Research.

We would like to thank the following people who read the entire manuscript: Allison Houlihan, Amy Staebler (twice), Anthony Campbell, Sam Bell, Alice Willett, Carrie Beth Lasley, Matt Hanka, and Ben Creech. Special thanks to Rita Hazlett and Ben Creech for doing an extraordinary job of checking references for the manuscript. Also, thanks go to my graduate research assistants at the university, Anthony Campbell and Matt Hanka, who worked tirelessly to gather data and complete the important edits and revisions throughout the whole process. Conventional wisdom says that writing is supposed to be painful, but Matt Hanka, Liz McConnell, Ben Creech, and Max Gilderbloom made it fun and relaxing and made sure we met our deadline by spending the final two weeks going over changes in the manuscript, editing, deleting, adding, updating, and checking references. My son, Max Gilderbloom, was usually the first person to hear some of my thoughts and in the end was the last person to see this manuscript before it went to the publisher.

I remain solely responsible for any errors or omissions in the content and the interpretations. While I used many suggestions and ideas from my coauthors, some of them I did not use because of my writing style or because I simply thought they were wrong.

Conducting research is not a popularity contest. Research, as Max Weber said, is saying what "is" rather than what "ought to be." Academic institutions should not be in the business of trying to suppress academic freedom, intimidating professors, or politicizing research. Rather, universities should be in the business of telling the truth, not telling "feel-good lies" for the rich and powerful. I do not apologize for my criticism of the former Kentucky Democratic Governor Paul Patton, of the University of Louisville's disastrous retreat from its urban mission, or of President George W. Bush or for my research, which seems to have upset, at one time or another, tenants, landlords, and government interests. I am hopeful that our department's moving from the College of Business to the College of Arts and Sciences will end one of the most shameful periods in the University of Louisville's history, in which professors doing urban policy research were harassed both within and outside the university. I am thankful to several legal experts and administrators who lent me assistance in the fight for academic freedom: Herb Segal, Carrie Donald, Russ Weaver, Edwin Render, Jeffrey Segal, Steven Paul Cohn, Dean Blaine Hudson and Associate Dean John Ferre of the College of Arts and Sciences, and Provost Shirley Willihnganz.

We have received funding for a DVD to accompany this book. The DVD will be available at a minimum cost to cover shipping and handling only and will provide a larger gallery of color photos to illustrate my points. We have included several film clips that complement the book as well. To order the DVD, visit one of my websites: http://www.louisville.edu/org/sun or http://www.gilderbloom.org.

INVISIBLE CITY

CHAPTER 1

INTRODUCTION AND OVERVIEW

In *The Sociological Imagination*, C. W. Mills (1959) asserts that social scientists should document the problems of society, find the causes of these problems, and advocate for policy changes. *Invisible City* refers to the people in our society whom we walk past every day and never truly see: the poor, disabled, elderly, and homeless. This book looks at the unseen forces that shape the location, design, and cost of housing and neighborhoods that impact disadvantaged populations. *Invisible City* moves past the front stage of a city (Michigan Avenue in Chicago, Times Square in New York, South Beach in Miami) and looks at the backstage of cities. It's a term that calls out to document the invisible city that moves past the grandeur to the unseen elements of the city. After Katrina, the term "invisible city" took on another kind of meaning with the disappearance of cities and neighborhoods in the Gulf Coast area. More importantly, *Invisible City* refers to viable solutions to housing and neighborhood problems that are not on the radar screen. We want to bring solutions to people and to generate a debate in our neighborhoods and cities. My view of the invisible city is shaped by a sociological perspective that integrates economic, historic, social, and political forces that are largely unseen to the casual observer.

Place matters. But place is not just about location in a city or a neighborhood (see Dreier, Mollenkopf, and Swanstrom 2004) but also about the kind of housing in which we live and how it shapes us as people. Life chances are structured by place, such as the country, city, neighborhood, and house in which one lives. Our homes shape us in significant ways. Along with place, power and poverty shape the lives of the invisible classes. Inequality and poverty are not just created between the capitalist and the worker within the workplace—they are also created by the inequality of housing. In this book we hope to shed new light on these invisible forces and to challenge many of the conventional assumptions of how cities function.

This book represents twenty-five years of work on the invisible city and its inhabitants. Much of this material came out of work that my consulting company has performed along with university-funded research focusing on hidden classes of people. Much of this work has been done in collaboration with my numerous graduate students and several respected academics. All of the chapters in this book are updates, elaborations, and revisions of many of the themes of my work. The focus of this work has always been on attractive, affordable, and accessible housing.

A central concern of urban studies is to develop an understanding of the social and spatial constraints on basic necessities (e.g., housing, jobs, health care, and transportation) that are distributed on a non-random basis. British sociologist and neo-Weberian Ray Pahl (1975) states that a person's opportunities to secure adequate schooling, jobs, health care, and a safe neighborhood are shaped by the spatial and social allocation of housing and transportation services. Pahl further asserts that an individual's life opportunities are powerfully influenced by "managers" (the government, banks, developers, landlords, and tenants) who determine the use of space. A person's life is not determined solely by his or her relationship to the means of production, but by spatial location in the urban system.

Inequalities are generated within and among cities. Why is it that certain cities can provide affordable housing and others cannot? What is the role of government, banks, developers, and landlords in the allocation of housing needs? While an economist might explain the cause of homelessness as a supply-and-demand problem, progressive urban scholars consider the institutional constraints such as the allocation of accessible, attractive, decent, and affordable housing. A critical examination must be made of how essential human needs are distributed within and across urban systems.

The Weberian analyst attempts to understand how access to fundamental needs varies among urban areas and attempts to identify why certain urban places have difficulty allocating necessities while others do not. In *Whose City?*, Pahl argues that "access to resources is systematically structured in a local context" (1975, 203). Concerning housing, Pahl believed that urban scholars should focus on the key actors who manage the urban housing system (property owners) and the recipients of their housing ("those who must rent") (Pahl 1975, 244–246). Pahl writes:

> It is evident that I have taken as my starting point the fact that the whole society is urban, but that, since people's life chances are con-

strained to a greater or lesser degree by the non-random distribution of resources and facilities, urban sociology is concerned with the understanding of the causes and consequences of such distribution for relevant populations. The Weberian analysis is concerned with the understanding of the causes and consequences of such distribution for relevant populations. The values and ideologies of those in the distributing, organizing and care-taking professions, and the relations between the formal and informal patterns of social relationships, are of central concern to Weberian analysis. (206)

Pahl's argument that the Weberian analyst should attempt to explain the causes and consequences of resource allocation provides a new direction and meaning for urban studies. An urbanist, according to Pahl, examines those resources that are "fundamental" (necessary to survive) and have a "spatial" dimension. The urbanist argues that "housing and transportation are elements in my view of the city, family allowances and pension schemes are not" (10). Pahl argues that since the allocation of space is inherently unequal (no two persons can occupy the same space), Weberian analysis must examine how these spatially distributed resources are dispersed. The progressive urbanist should also focus on the "gatekeepers" and "urban managers" as conscious social forces molding the urban environment. Progressive urbanists must abandon the assumption that subsocial urban forces compete against one another, a theory often called "human ecology." In *Invisible City* we have used Pahl's framework as a starting point for our research on cities.

Because of the collapse of socialism, Marxism as both a tool of analysis and a policy solution seems increasingly irrelevant. Housing problems need to be repaired within the capitalist structure. This is something of interest not just to a Marxist but to neo-Weberians and others as well. Pahl has argued that the best way to examine the success or failure of a city is through the distribution of basic necessities to its citizens.

Pahl argues that urban sociology must tightly focus on how basic needs such as housing, education, recreation, transportation, safety, and employment vary by city and that we must come to understand how urban managers and gatekeepers can increase or decrease these basic necessities for living in the city. Elected leaders, nonprofits, bureaucrats, social movements, and community organizers change, remake, rebuild, revitalize, and destroy the pattern and infrastructure of the city, which can have an impact on the life chances of all citizens. The gatekeepers allocate resources, make policy, and enforce police actions (building-code enforcement and planning approvals, along with the criminal justice system). Pahl has argued against those who thought that anything and everything that happens within a city is urban, since countries have become largely urban. Urban sociology, in order to survive, must have a focus that examines the allocation of basic resources. This is why the success of a city depends on social class and should not be defined only by the very rich. Social justice is still important even if you are not under the spell of a Marxist framework.

With that said, it is surprising that some would take an economist position that the "success" of a city is measured by how high the rents have grown (the usual suspects such as New York, Boston, San Francisco, Los Angeles, and, increasingly, Chicago fall into this category). In other words, if people are able to pay relatively high rents, the city must be better at providing the good life. But if we use the framework of Pahl, these cities are failures, not successes, because they are not meeting the needs of a large number of people who lack affordable, attractive, and safe housing. As Michael Stone (1980, 1983) has argued, "shelter poverty" is the result of housing prices being so high that there are few resources left for other basic necessities. By using the criterion of meeting the basic necessities of poor and working-class citizens, I think we need to look elsewhere. In the United States, I think smaller and midsize cities like Louisville do a better job in this regard. However, they still fall short, and their leadership is not under the rubric of a "progressive agenda." Joe Feagin's book on Houston highlights the many problems and challenges of a city that adopts a "free market" and limited government response to urban needs. Policy, planning, capital, government, and social movements play a role in shaping our cities. People and place matter in shaping our life chances.

Ray Pahl's thinking on city was problematic because it focused only on basic human needs. It never explored or embraced the importance of cultural, creative, and personal freedoms (including sex and drug experimentation). In this case, the Soviet, Cuban, and Chinese socialist cities fail miserably. My twenty-five visits to Havana over a six-year period caused me more alarm than elation. Indeed, compared to cities in other nearby developing countries, Havana supplies at the bare minimum the basic necessities of life—shelter, food, health care, education, and transportation—but its lack of democratic governance provides very little space to debate or to access and express ideas of good and bad. Cuba's lack of tolerance for dissent from the norm is chilling and oppressive to the people. This kind of oppression cannot be justified or supported by simply blaming Cuba's state of emergency on early U.S. attempts to support violent overthrow of the country and later creating an economic blockade against it. Freedom exists only for those who support the government and its policies rooted in the Soviet system of the 1950s. Much of socialist Havana (we are not talking about the greatest collection of Spanish Colonial architecture outside of Spain or the wonderful people, who are kind, gentle, and loving) is rooted in the architecture and planning mistakes of the Soviet Union. In fact, since the early 1960s nearly all the schools, hospitals, housing projects (other than homes), and government buildings were based on Soviet blueprints. (In other words, if you ever want to get a taste of what Siberia looked like, go to the outskirts of Havana, where it is replicated in perfect detail—without the snow, ice, and frigid winds.) Soviet worker houses had no style, personalization, flair, or symbols of self-identification. In this they are not unlike the "brutal" projects in South Chicago, which were bland, boring, and unhappy places for residents. The only way you could tell the difference between your place and your neighbors' was the number on the door.

Havana also called on a car-dependent transportation system that fed growth outside, rather than inside, the city. Socialist Cuban cuisine is a dismal mush of rice, beans, and occasionally some meat thrown in. If we embrace the notion of the creative city that embraces gay sexual freedom, Havana fails in this sense. There is no such thing as a gay bar, and regular roundups of gay citizens do occur. Prostitutes are routinely arrested and sent to work farms. Internet access is either monitored or restricted by costs. Foreign newspapers are nearly impossible to obtain, except for the ones left behind by tourists and resold. Hotels and architecture outside the confines of Soviet style can be counted on one hand. Newer forms of artistic expression, even without a political angle, are frowned upon and censored. Cuban socialism is more about homogeneity and sameness than greatness and freedom. The point of all this is to show that the way we measure a city's greatness should include not only meeting the essential needs of citizens, but also providing them with freedom and creativity.

Following the collapse of Soviet and Chinese forms of socialism, I don't think we can look to their cities as beacons of enlightenment or models for creating social justice. I think about cities outside of the United States and am inspired by places like Amsterdam, which has a large ethnic mix, a relatively low homeless population, and better housing in terms of rent, condition, and attractiveness. Amsterdam employs excellent transportation and education systems and encourages a sustainable lifestyle. In contrast to the bland Soviet version of housing projects, the Amsterdam school of socialist architecture believed that all housing should have ornamentation, be attractive, and provide privacy for the inhabitants. Amsterdam, at this moment in history, might be the world's greatest city because of its ability to ensure basic necessities, freedom, and creativity. In my mind, great cities provide for all, work to enhance the lives of all, and ensure as much freedom as possible. With the recent election, Amsterdam is now governed by a coalition of socialists, greens, and progressives. My own impression is that people living in Amsterdam seem more tolerant, more secure, kinder, warmer, happier, and healthier than citizens in other cities around the world. It is an exciting time in Amsterdam, just as Santa Monica and Burlington were exciting places twenty years ago (see Clavel 1987, *The Progressive City*, and Capek and Gilderbloom 1992, *Community Versus Commodity*).

While there is much that is great about New York, Boston, Chicago, and my hometown, San Francisco, these cities fall far short with regard to social justice for the lower classes. As a nation, we should look to America's "unhip" smaller and midsize cities (small can be beautiful!) or to Amsterdam for greatness. Greatness is never permanent, though. From my perspective, Chicago was a great city twenty years ago when rents were affordable and lofts could be purchased at a fraction of the cost of New York lofts, while the city still provided a cutting-edge cultural environment.

CHAPTER OUTLINES

The following paragraphs present an overview of each chapter and the book in general. Chapter 2, "Economic, Social, and Political Dimensions of the Rental Housing Crisis," frames our study by exploring the dimensions of the housing crisis and by asserting why this fundamental need for housing can have such an important impact on our lives—from our sense of esteem, to our politics, to our health, to crime, to the quality of our urban lives. America, along with the rest of the world, will see a reversal of housing fortunes if energy costs continue to soar, interest rates climb, and zoning laws that reduce affordable housing options are put into place.

Chapter 3, "Why Rents Rise," presents a sociological view of housing that sheds new light on some of the assumptions of mainstream economic analysis in relation to renting. Housing markets fail to function according to traditional economic theory. Conventional housing analysis is incomplete because it ignores a number of critical variables that explain variations in rent across cities. This study extends the inter-city rent differentials investigation Richard Appelbaum and I (Gilderbloom and Appelbaum 1988) conducted in somewhat isolated housing markets. We draw on that earlier work to briefly examine Edgar Olsen's (1973) seven conditions for a free market to operate for rental housing and show that these needed conditions cannot be met in the real world of rental housing.

Utilizing U.S. Census data from the years 1990 and 2000, we test our 1970 and 1980 models in Chapter 3 with the addition of several key variables that measure the impact of rental landlord professionalization, changes in housing quality, age of rental housing stock, and their impacts on inter-city rent price differentials. We find that both the cost of homeownership and the level of household income remain critical factors in explaining the levels of median rent across cities. The theory we developed is largely confirmed in the larger rental housing market. However, several key differences and trends deserve attention from planners and policy makers in the effort to provide affordable housing options for urban residents. This chapter gives a new understanding of why a rental housing crisis exists and what needs to be done to solve it.

Chapter 4, "Pros and Cons of Rent Control," examines the impact of rent control. Because of the moderate nature of rent control regulations, most cities that have enacted rent control laws have been unsuccessful in lowering overall rents. The successes of strong rent control laws, such as Santa Monica's, are the exception rather than the rule. This chapter gives an overview of the impacts of moderate rent laws in the United States upon both landlords and tenants and assesses the impact of these laws on the supply, condition, and value of rental units. The passage of a rent control law is not enough to assure long-term success. Without a strong grassroots organization, rent control becomes only a symbolic response to the crisis.

Chapter 4 also explores a liberal public policy program of rent control by seeing how it is co-opted into a toothless policy. This chapter explores how public policy is influenced, created, and disseminated by organizations that have a major financial stake in a particular outcome. Urban policy analysis is not often a neutral field of study; rather, it is dominated by researchers whose conclusions are determined by those funding their studies. As we will show in this chapter, real estate–sponsored studies of urban housing policy are often riddled with questionable methodological approaches, inaccurate data analyses, and conclusions based more on ideology than fact. The dominance of these highly ideological and biased studies demonstrates why professors with tenure should be challenging these studies and providing unprejudiced information. More surprising is how influential these studies are in compelling the media, politicians, and even academics to take positions on urban policy issues based on conclusions that are biased and lack merit.

Most studies on rent control utilize economic models based on either computer simulations or case studies. Some studies have utilized economic modeling and concluded that rent control lowers rents. Other studies have used economic modeling and suggested that rent control ordinances cause reductions in maintenance and increases in the proportion of undesirable tenants. It is obvious that the battle over rent control is often a battle over studies. Objective information is difficult to obtain because of the lack of support in both academic and government circles. Academic social science tends not to reward academic research when it is applied to real governmental policy. Government in an age of austerity prefers to obtain studies from industries to reduce costs and support the demands of their ideological partners. Power can be defined as the ability to identify, frame, and define issues of social concern. If real estate organizations are allowed to continue to frame, analyze, and define urban issues from their perspective, government will not be properly equipped to deal with the problems of homelessness, slum formation, unaffordable rents, abandonment, and arson for profit. Government has a responsibility to the public and must seek out studies that lack bias. My studies of rent control have frustrated and angered the real estate industry, yet the industry has been unable to challenge my research on any substantive level.

In Chapter 5, "Invisible Jail: Providing Housing and Transportation for the Elderly and Disabled," we talk about the invisible jail in which physical space structures the life chances of the disabled and elderly. The term "invisible jail" means that many people are locked into their homes or neighborhoods because architects and planners have failed to design a space that liberates them. For the elderly and disabled, space that creates self-reliance and that allows a wheelchair user or blind person to do highly personal activities like shower, cook, use the restroom, or travel without the aid of others is liberation, whether it is a simple rail in a bathroom or a curb cut on a sidewalk. This chapter carefully documents the housing preferences and needs of disabled, elderly, and low-income people. We begin with an examination of the quality of housing provided to special populations. We go beyond such traditional concerns as assessing the number of housing units with adequate plumbing and heating. This approach is too simplistic because it fails to consider concerns such as the unique needs of the elderly and disabled. We then explore the problems related to specific location and design needs that will help foster independent living.

When we did this research in Houston, it generated a vigorous public debate on addressing the housing needs of the elderly, disabled, and poor. The major Houston newspapers embraced this study with positive coverage, generating calls for better planning of housing, transportation, and work places. This research also was used as part of the debate to help pass the Americans with Disabilities Act (ADA) a few years later.

Little research has been conducted on the housing modification needs of the elderly, partly due to a lack of reliable data. Studies of these needs are often inconclusive, anecdotal, and unsystematic. Many rely on decennial census data, an approach that provides a limited and unsatisfactory portrait of the special housing needs of the elderly. Our research is intended to fill this void. This chapter was originally a report for the City of Houston and earned an American Institute of Architects Chapter Award.

An often-overlooked segment of any society is composed of those people who are relegated to assisted-living arrangements or nursing homes. As the U.S. population has grown older, a nursing home crisis has occurred. As 2020 approaches, it is predicted that there will be a need for an additional half-million nursing home beds. Besides the lack of beds, there is also a dire need to improve the overall quality of nursing home care. Utilizing available studies, suggestions are made regarding the optimum nursing home bed vacancy rate. As more and more Americans require assisted-living arrangements, decision makers will be forced to take a serious look at the worsening national nursing home crisis. Our research also calls for an increase in non-institutional nursing home arrangements such as house sharing.

Chapter 6—"HOPE VI: A Dream or Nightmare?"—explores the success of the federal HOPE VI project. So far, the HOPE VI project appears to be accomplishing its objectives: changing the physical shape of housing, reducing concentrations of poverty, providing support services, establishing and maintaining high standards of community and personal responsibility, and forming partnerships. When residents compared their HOPE VI homes and neighborhoods to their previous residences, levels of satisfaction were generally higher in almost every area. These attitudes were consistent for former residents of both public housing and non-public housing. However, these gains are not the whole story.

This chapter presents a case study of the Park DuValle Revitalization Project in Louisville, Kentucky, to evaluate whether the U.S. Department of Housing and Urban Development (HUD) HOPE VI program enhances residents' quality of life. The research implies that HOPE VI enhances the lives of about 25 percent of those who live in public housing. However, HOPE VI leaves more than three-quarters of the public housing residents without upgraded HOPE VI homes or without homes at all. In our case study, HOPE VI provides 75 percent of the new housing units at market rates to renters and homeowners. What happened to those who were displaced? Where did they go? These replacement housing units came at a cost of around $160,000, equivalent to upper-middle-class housing in Louisville. HOPE VI builds housing that is two to three times more costly per unit than competing non-profit community development groups. We also compare Louisville's HOPE vi program with a more successful HOPE vi program in Newport, Kentucky. Newport is a model plan for this program that integrates housing in middle-class neighborhoods instead of keeping it segregated.

Chapter 7, "Renewing and Remaking New Orleans," examines what happens when part or all of a city disappears, with a case study of Hurricane Katrina and its aftermath. In this chapter we investigate several approaches to reconstructing neighborhoods in New Orleans that were devastated by Katrina. This chapter looks at strategies for providing housing for the poor and minority residents whose homes were damaged or lost. Louisville, Kentucky, is cited as an example of how shotgun houses—both new and old—can provide affordable housing ownership for the poor. We argue that preserving, restoring, and building shotgun houses is an effective, affordable, energy-efficient, attractive, sustainable, and culturally sensitive approach that will aid the redevelopment of socially and economically viable neighborhoods. We find that shotgun houses complement architectural tourism and create value in ownership for residents. We argue against replacing shotguns with suburban-style housing or abandonment of the historic vernacular architecture that was rooted in the black community. This is not simply a defense of the shotgun type, but a concise and effective argument of an urban design philosophy that takes history seriously and seeks to make both historic preservation and social equity the twin bases for the reconstruction of New Orleans. The case of Katrina holds important lessons for the rest of the nation.

Chapter 8, "University Partnerships to Reclaim and Rebuild Communities," is a case study of how a partnership with a university can help revitalize, restore, and renew a poor neighborhood but not result in low-income people losing their homes. This chapter is an update of my work over a fourteen-year period in West Louisville, a once poor, black neighborhood filled with fear, hopelessness, and hardship. This is one of the few examples where the New Urbanist paradigm is applied to a poor, black neighborhood and illustrates some of the positive outcomes of such an effort by creating affordable homeownership for more than one hundred residents. In addition to the owner-occupied dwellings, 550 attractive, accessible, and affordable rental housing units were built. The revitalization led to new business and job opportunities, a reduction in crime, a neighborhood that has a true mixture of incomes from poor to rich, and what many have called the "miracle of West Louisville."

With 3,500 institutions of higher education around the United States, communities need to access the brain power of colleges and universities not only to figure out the economics or the design of homes, but to figure out strategies to empower the lives of the poor. In other words, if we know so much, then how come there are still so many unsolved problems in the invisible city?

Chapter 9, "Housing Opportunities for Everyone," explores the fundamental right of homeownership in America. We question why liberals and the left do not view homeownership as a top priority to support. Homeownership strategy is nearly invisible when it comes to housing policy advocacy, and instead programs like rent control and housing vouchers are given much more weight. The private market alone cannot provide affordable housing for all citizens, especially for minorities, the disabled, the elderly, and the poor. The conservative free-enterprise approach has worked against the economically disadvantaged. However, reliance on the traditional liberal strategy of providing massive tax breaks and subsidies to builders and landlords has proven to be too costly and inefficient for solving the housing crunch. New and bold measures must be used to combat the housing crisis. I will attempt to show that affordable housing is possible for low-income households through these different means.

More government, not less government, is needed to resolve the nation's housing crisis. However, this call for greater government involvement must be accompanied by the adoption of programs that have a proven track record. We must target programs that are not wasteful or ineffective. With a call for more government, there must also be a call for increased participation in government and the involvement of ordinary citizens. Examples such as the savings and loan and HUD scandals provide evidence that unmonitored government is problematic. This book raises questions on whether rent control and Section 8 are good housing policy choices. It is also clear that the economically disadvantaged are harmed most by this misuse of funds.

We have added an appendix that we consider useful in terms of discussing the housing crisis and developing possible solutions. The appendix is a revised and edited version of a report by the Housing Strategies for Houston Task Force, on which I served as an active member. The lead authors, Roger Lewis and Steven Hornburg, worked to build consensus among housing leaders on what Houston and other cities need to do to address the housing problem. It is a creative approach of how one task force addressed the housing crisis in a city.

Unlike so many stale reports that are produced by appointed city commissions, this document is fairly progressive and needs a wider readership. The Houston task force notes that there is a common misperception that Houston has no housing crisis because of its free-market policies. In fact, Houston's housing problems are similar to those in many other cities around the country, and the crisis continues to worsen with no end in sight. Moreover, the report calls for a partnership of city and university leaders, housing groups, developers, and corporations to address significant housing problems in a bold, innovative, and pragmatic fashion.

CONCLUSION

Can we have hope about the future of cities? Are ghettos inevitable? Can we make the invisible city a place that is visible to policy makers? Can we make the social problems of the poor, disabled, elderly, and renters visible again so we can properly address them? Is government intervention harmful to the workings of the market, or will economic democracy generate the "good city"? As we head into the new century, can a more comprehensive, more engaging, and perhaps more optimistic theory of the city be embraced? These are the kinds of questions we should be addressing as we seek to develop a new urban paradigm.

I believe cities can be remade for all to enjoy. Goodman (1956) observed that an individual "has only one life and if during it he has no great environment, no community, he has been irreparably robbed of a human right." Grassroots activist movements have created a public dialogue centering on human rights and what constitutes a fair and just society. They have rendered problems and social relations visible which are often hidden from the popular view that a free market unleashed can solve all problems. This question is symbolic of a much larger debate about democracy, community, and the economic riches that will determine what kind of society the United States will become in this century.

As an activist, consultant, and educator who has worked in a wide range of roles in revitalizing inner-city neighborhoods and building accessible, affordable, and attractive housing, I believe that contemporary urban scholars have failed to capture the dynamics of what is happening in our cities. It is my hope that *Invisible City* will shed new light on the forces that shape our cities and the often ignored, invisible people who toil and struggle in our cities. Whether it is our houses, our neighborhoods, or our cities, we must recognize how these places shape us and how we shape them. We must be able to see the home as a force that shapes us every day. But we need to move beyond the caveman notion of shelter that protects us against nature and turn the homes where we live into attractive, accessible, and affordable places.

CHAPTER 2

ECONOMIC, SOCIAL, AND POLITICAL DIMENSIONS OF THE RENTAL HOUSING CRISIS

WITH RICHARD P. APPELBAUM
AND MICHAEL ANTHONY CAMPBELL

Housing is one of the most important problems facing the United States. Affordable, attractive, and accessible housing remains a major concern for millions of citizens in the United States and elsewhere. This chapter documents the dimensions of the housing crisis from an economic, social, and political perspective. Because of record economic growth, many observers mistakenly believe that housing as a social problem has been resolved. Their understanding is based on a simplistic analysis that relies on one or two economic indicators. This chapter presents the hidden dimensions of the housing problem in a more nuanced and sophisticated manner. My hope is to illustrate more precisely the nature of the housing problem.

In western society, the home embodies much more than simply a structure for shelter. This is particularly true in the United States. The "American Dream" is a symbol of security, freedom, and self-sufficiency. The home as a "symbol of self" is prominent in a society that still glorifies its rugged individualists whose survival was dependent on their ability to house and provide for themselves. Sociologists and psychologists have long recognized that a house is an important symbol of self, reflecting the status of an individual:

> The house as symbol-of-self is deeply ingrained in the American ethos (albeit unconsciously for many), and this may partly explain the inability of society to come to grips with the housing problem, which is quite within technological and financial capabilities to solve and which [society] persistently delegates to a low level in the hierarchy of budgetary values. America is the home of the self-made man, and if the house is seen (even unconsciously) as the symbol of self, then it is small won-

der that there is a resistance to subsidized housing or the State providing housing for people. The frontier image of the man clearing the land
and building a cabin for himself and his family is not far behind us. To
a culture inbred with this image, the house-self identity is particularly
strong. Little wonder then that in some barely conscious way, society
has decided to penalize those who, through no fault of their own, cannot build, buy or rent their own housing. They are not self-made men.
(Cooper 1971, 12)

The post–World War II years brought a dramatic growth in homeownership rates. A boom of housing construction in the suburbs and increased federal expenditures for mortgage financing, combined with the expansion of
median real income, facilitated the escalation of homeownership. A steady
increase in homeownership also occurred in the 1990s.

More recent trends indicate that the record high homeownership rates in
the United States have hit a plateau. In some parts of the country, rates have
even begun to decline. The decline in homeownership rates is tied to rising
interest rates, prices, and affordability, fuel cost increases, and a reduction in
available building sites due to environmental regulations and homeowners'
associations. The result has been to more deeply divide the nation into two
camps: the haves and the have-nots.

Homeownership, not renting, is responsible for the increased level of
importance attached to owning, which is seen as a prize that rewards the
middle class. The 1992 Fannie Mae National Housing Survey reported that
by a three-to-one margin Americans would rather own a home than retire
ten years early. By the same token, living in a good neighborhood was more
important than living in a good house. This suggests that pushing homeownership out of reach has also contributed to declines in neighborhood
quality. This may also reflect a certain lowering of expectations concerning
the realistic chances of owning a home.

Another significant dimension of homeownership is conveyed when income is constant. Homeownership is considered one of the most important
long-term goals by 60 percent of those in the lowest income range, while
only 31 percent of those in the highest income range share this opinion
(Fannie Mae 1992). This suggests that those who do not own a home or those
for whom homeownership has traditionally been out of reach attach more
importance to owning a home than those who already own or those who
have the means to be homeowners.

Housing is more than shelter. Our dwellings shape our moods, how we
think, our economic opportunities, and social relations. In the American

mind, housing represents home and community as well as physical structure. Our housing is a symbol of self and a haven from the world outside. The house that is the American Dream is more than a square box and a roof. It combines shelter with the promise of security, peace, and independence. The American Dream is of comfortable living space for children and the disabled and couples and older people; it entails growth and nurturing, refuge and support.

Spatial relationships influence housing, and housing influences spatial relationships. Housing provides a framework for the structuring of economic, social, and political relationships. Housing inequality and segregation limit educational and employment opportunities for low-income and minority families, especially as they force the families to pay more of their incomes for declining services. Housing design and location patterns reinforce the traditional division of labor within the male-dominant family. These patterns foster unpaid work in the home and restrict opportunities for female labor-force participation (Hayden 1984; Rothblatt, Garr, and Sprague 1979; Saegert 1981). In this way, housing reinforces and perpetuates economic and social divisions that exist within the larger society. Housing also has a tremendous impact on one's mental and physical health.

For most middle-class Americans over the past fifty years, the promised security of homeownership appeared to be a realistic expectation—a part of the American Dream. The rapid development of suburban detached dwellings, the availability of federally insured long-term mortgage financing, and the postwar rise in average real income all contributed to that expectation. For more than a half-century, the proportion of renters steadily declined, and by 2000, two out of every three American households owned their own homes.

The poor never have had the opportunity to share in the American Dream. For minority households, elderly renters living on fixed incomes, female-headed households, and a significant number of working-class white families, ownership has been, at best, a distant promise, and a vague hope for one's children. As long as most middle-class Americans felt secure in the dream, national policy could ignore the needs of those who were denied it. These forgotten people have become the face of the invisible class of the city.

DIMENSIONS OF THE HOUSING PROBLEM

The Millennial Housing Commission (2002) describes the housing problems in the United States:

Affordability is the single greatest housing challenge facing the nation. In 1999, one in nine households reported spending more than half its income on housing, while hundreds of thousands went homeless on any given night. Wide gaps also remain between the homeownership rates of whites and minorities, even among those with comparable incomes. And while greatly reduced from generations ago, housing quality problems persist.

Federal programs define housing affordability in terms of the ratio of income to housing costs. Individuals or families who spend more than 50 percent of their incomes on housing are considered to have a severe housing affordability problem. Those who spend between 30 and 50 percent of their incomes on housing are considered to have a moderate affordability problem. According to the Millennial Housing Commission, low-income families who spend more than 30 percent of their incomes on housing face extreme hardships that diminish the opportunity to create savings or to pay for other necessities. Based on these definitions, 13.4 million renters and 14.5 million homeowners are facing an affordability problem. Renters may struggle to pay utility costs or other costs outside of their contract rent, while homeowners may struggle with property maintenance or home equity. Elderly and disabled homeowners in particular also struggle with the ability to maintain their properties.

There are several reasons households struggle to pay housing costs. For many households, incomes are too low to cover the most meager rents. Among households in areas with a high cost of living, even a moderate-income household cannot afford the housing costs. Other households have problems maintaining income to afford housing costs because of age, disability, or the lack of steady full-time work. Affordability problems reach across all income groups, but the problem is much more concentrated in low-income groups.

Having a full-time job does not exempt households from facing housing issues. In 1999, 11.3 million people faced severe housing affordability problems; almost one-fourth of them had full-time employment incomes based on minimum wage. At $5.15 an hour, this is the equivalent of making $10,712 yearly. Many of the jobs are seasonal, part-time, or temporary work. Many households that make at least half of the minimum wage yearly salary are considered underemployed. This group represents 13 percent of low-income households, which have a severe affordability problem.

Housing gaps between whites and minorities have become another challenge for America. After a period of stagnation in the 1980s, there was an increase in minority homeownership beginning in the 1990s: between

1994 and 2000 the number of low-income households that owned homes was about 2.5 million. Of the 2.5 million, approximately 1.2 million were African-Americans and 1.2 million were Hispanic.

One of the greatest barriers to homeownership for low-income families is the lack of funds for a down payment, but as a result of many lenders dropping or decreasing the down payment amount, many low-income families were able to purchase homes. In 2000 nearly 16 percent of all loans were made with a 5 percent or less down payment. Even with the relaxing of the lending criteria there is still a large gap in homeownership between whites and minorities. In 1999 the gap between African-Americans and whites was 27.2 percent, and the gap between whites and Hispanics stood at 28.6 percent. The minority gap continues to be a rising concern because minority households will account for two-thirds of household growth in the future. The housing problem that is facing our nation today is not as great as in the past, but it still represents a challenge.

QUALITY OF HOUSING

By most criteria, the average quality of American housing meets the highest standards in the world. Since 1940, there has been a sharp reduction in the number of units that are overcrowded, lack plumbing and sanitation, or show signs of structural dilapidation. The rate of crowded housing has decreased from 20.2 percent in the 1940s to 5.7 percent today. The rate of severely crowded rooms has changed from 9 percent in the 1940s to less than 3 percent in 2000. Lack of plumbing in rental units has decreased from 45.3 percent in the 1940s to less than 1 percent. Great strides have been made in the quality of housing, but along with these strides, there has been a drastic loss of affordable rental housing.

According to the Millennial Housing Commission (2002), the lack of affordable rental units is a critical housing problem. Available low-income housing is located in poor neighborhoods, and many of them are isolated from areas of opportunity and jobs. The commission reported that only 6.7 million rental units had costs in the range that 8.5 million families can afford. The problem of low-income housing will only continue to grow as the number of households headed by persons under age twenty-five or over age sixty-five continues to grow. These groups tend to have lower incomes, and as they grow in proportion to the population they will increase the demand for housing. The commission projected that nearly 250,000 low-income units would need to be constructed over the next twenty years to have enough rental units to close the gap of 1.8 million households.

There are several reasons that developers are not building more affordable housing. The Millennial Commission report identifies three of them. First, there is a lack of attractive financing options for developers. Developers want certain guarantees that will minimize risk before making their investments (e.g., fixed low-interest rates and long amortizations). Developing with government involvement means added risk that funding will be interrupted or temporary, risk that the subsidies will not be enough to cover operating costs, and risk that the government will not honor its contract.

Second, there are vast numbers of developmental restrictions in some areas on multi-family housing and manufactured housing. Many areas charge impact fees on these development types and enact zoning regulations that restrict or impede the construction of such units. All of these tactics and costs deter development of affordable multi-family housing.

Finally, there are barriers to preserving housing for low-income households. It is important not only to build new affordable housing units, but also to preserve the existing housing stock. In 1995 nearly 25 percent of privately owned federally subsidized units did not receive adequate funding for maintenance and renovations. Also, HUD did not keep the subsidies to levels of market rates, and therefore owners did not maintain their properties. The lack of preservation is caused by tax penalties applied to property sales because of increased value for improvements. Also, many housing construction codes favor new construction, which deters even moderate rehabilitation. There is a persistent gap between the insufficient subsidies that go to low-income families and the cost of maintaining the housing facilities.

Another argument is that affordability is not a function of the quality of the unit, but the result of individual shortcomings such as divorce or inadequate income (Weicher, Villani, and Roistacher 1981; see also Myers and Baillargeon 1985, 66). Thus the housing crisis is seen as a personal problem rather than a social one. Economists argue that "affordability" is a subjective notion that should be dismissed in favor of more objectively measurable ones such as quality (see Myers and Baillargeon 1985, 66). According to their reasoning, no support can be found for the existence of a rental crisis because of the steady improvement in the quality of the housing stock (Clemer and Simonson 1983; Hendershott 1981; Lowry 1981a,b).

Myers and Baillargeon (1985, 66) astutely point out that the rising-quality argument is irrelevant in light of a government mandate that all housing have adequate plumbing, heat, running water, toilet facilities, and so forth.

Local housing codes and federal policies have aimed to increase the quality of our housing stock, while poor renters occupy the most affordable housing left. Unless it can be shown that large numbers of lower-quality units have been left vacant by renters seeking luxuries elsewhere, it must be concluded that renters are forced to pay higher rents in markets with fewer low-cost opportunities. In this view, unless we decide it is good for lower-income households to carry excessive rent burdens, the appropriate policy choice is to either solve the affordability problem or else lower quality again (Myers and Baillargeon 1985, 66). Although housing quality has in the aggregate improved, this improvement is not shared equally by all consumer groups.

HOW HOUSING SHAPES HOW WE THINK AND SEE

As low-income families are facing more crowding in homes, higher transportation expenses, and high housing costs, it is necessary to design housing that provides the most benefits to humans. Research shows that housing designed to bring in more sunlight will improve the overall mood of humans. Natural light has also been credited with providing an overall improvement of mood, better test scores, decreased fatigue, and reduced eye strain (Edwards and Torcellini 2002, 17). In other words, public housing projects that look like barracks not only hurt one's sense of self, but they also make thinking "foggy." Studies have also shown that sunlight can decrease heating costs, which can help low-income families faced with tough economic decisions.

THE SOCIAL EXPERIENCE OF TENANTS

There are systematic and sociologically significant differences between the lives of tenants and homeowners in society. Despite a range of income and lifestyle characteristics in the United States, renters are disproportionately likely to be of low-income, elderly, and non-union status, as well as members of households headed by single women (Dreier 1982). Their housing is typically older and in poorer condition than that of homeowners, although tenants pay a greater proportion of their incomes for such housing. In terms of income, tenants are disproportionately poor compared to homeowners. Almost two-fifths of the nation's tenants can be classified as in poverty. In addition, tenants tend to be younger, have lower occupational prestige, live in multi-family structures, be unmarried, and live in integrated neighborhoods.

In *Tenants and the American Dream* (1983), Allan Heskin argues that tenants in the United States are considered second-class citizens. At the broadest level, the position of tenants is vitally influenced by a cultural value system that glorifies property ownership as a symbol of accomplishment, especially the American Dream of owning a home (Adams 1984; Halle 1984). Moreover, the concept of homeownership is underlined by its crucial linkage to other patterns of consumption, such as those relating to automobiles and durable goods (Gilderbloom and Markham 1995). Despite the difficulties of achieving homeownership, the tenant population in the United States is considerably smaller than it is in many other countries; thus, tenants are "the un-propertied in a society where property is central" (Heskin 1983, xi). The intense identification with private property ownership as a measure of character and as a component of freedom has been characterized as a "civil religion" (Robert Bellah, cited in Dreier 1982) in the United States, causing tenants to be perceived as an out group. This is reflected in everyday cultural practices such as the unfavorable portrayal of tenants in the media and in literature (Dreier 1982; Heskin 1983). Seen as more tenuously attached to the central value system, their power in society is measurably different from that of homeowners and landlords, and their self-image has tended to reflect this relationship.

Second-class citizenship is underscored by legal and governmental practices that take place on an everyday basis. Tenants are situated in a tax structure that vastly favors homeownership. In the United States, homeowners can deduct mortgage interest and local property taxes from what they owe in federal taxes, a privilege that increases with income. They pay no capital gains tax if their money is reinvested into a new home within two years. Landlords have traditionally possessed the additional benefit of depreciation write-offs as well as numerous other incentives for turning over property quickly and engaging in speculative purchases. Tenants bear the brunt of these "gifts" to other social groups, paying a larger percentage of their incomes for housing that is documentably worse than that of homeowners. As Barnes (1981, 16) points out, their rent pays not only for "profit for banks, insurance companies, real estate agents," but also for a parade of present and past landlords who have sold and engaged in refinancing. In 1990 the federal government provided homeowners with a $70 billion subsidy in the form of mortgage and tax write-offs as well as protection against capital gains taxes (Capek and Gilderbloom 1992).

The disproportionate financial burden carried by tenants has been matched by an inferior legal status. In the United States, laws regularly favor the landlord's right to make profits over the tenant's right to decent shelter. Indeed, some analysts have seen feudal remnants in the relationship between landlord and tenant (Heskin 1983). In Arkansas, the nonpayment of rent is still a criminal offense. Tenants are advised by the office of the attorney general that they have virtually no rights in the state (Capek 1989). Where tenant protections have been instituted, there has often been a considerable reluctance to enforce them (Lipsky 1970), and tenants frequently play no active role in the process (Morrissy 1987, 8).

The social experience of tenants is further shaped by the fact that, both formally and informally, a renter's living space is not treated in the same manner as that of other groups. Numerous theorists have pointed out that the need for a home does not stop with the need for shelter (Castells 1983; Cox 1981; Fried 1963). The need is also an expressive one (Dreier 1982; Saunders 1984) for a secure bounded space in which one is free to "be oneself" and to keep at a distance the capriciousness and intrusions of the outside world (Suttles 1972). However, the right to such a space is unevenly distributed. If one accepts Lyman and Scott's (1967, 238) definition of "home territories" as "those areas where the regular participants have a relative freedom of behavior and a sense of intimacy and control over the area," the vulnerable and often transient status of tenants disqualifies them from residing in "home territories." The rent may go up, the building may be converted, repairs may no longer be made, or the tenant may be evicted. All of these possibilities are usually beyond the control of tenants. Unlike the homeowner, the tenant's need for a dignified space does not materialize.

Until recently, tenants in the United States have been unable to appeal to a basic set of shelter-related rights that are equated with human rights. Instead, the law has counted the "risks" to be all on the side of landlords or investors, while those of tenants have been ignored. An apartment becomes less than a home, even though it is paid for with far less state assistance than that given to the homeowner. The problem is compounded by the pervasive attitude that real estate is a "cash cow" to be milked. While not all landlords are guilty of this, too many of them enter the business without considering their responsibility to tenants. Rather than a two-way relationship of responsibility between tenant and landlord, a frequent outcome is "blaming the victim" or resenting the tenant for asking for repairs or maintenance. For this reason, tenants have historically yielded their rights to decent shelter, fearing eviction or retaliation.

RISING COST OF RENTAL HOUSING

Renters with low to moderate incomes have high housing costs, which are one of the biggest expenditures in their budgets. Median gross rent as a percentage of household income stabilized nationwide from 1990 to 2000 (Table 2.1). However, for those renters who find themselves on the lower tiers of the economic hierarchy, housing costs continue to consume an unacceptable proportion of their incomes (Table 2.2).

As Table 2.2 illustrates, those who are classified as "extremely low-

TABLE 2.1. *Median Gross Rent as a Percent of Household Income, 1990 and 2000*

Location	1990 (%)	2000 (%)
United States	26.40	25.50
Northeast	26.70	25.50
New York City	25.70	26.60
Midwest	25.00	23.70
Chicago	26.30	24.80
South	25.70	24.90
Houston	23.20	23.80
West	25.70	25.90
Los Angeles	29.50	28.30

SOURCE: U.S. Census Bureau, Housing and Household Economic Statistics Division, "Historical Census of Housing Tables, Gross Rents" (revised December 2, 2004)

income" renters have an average housing cost almost 2.5 times greater than what would be considered affordable given their reported incomes. Two-thirds of our citizens are making unaffordable housing payments. As shown in Table 2.2, only those who reach $26,541 in household income are making affordable housing payments.

Unaffordable housing is a serious problem for all low-income Americans. However, the issue is particularly serious for black and Hispanic renters in the United States. From 1993 to 2003, the number of black households rose 16.9 percent, while the number of Hispanic households exploded to the tune of 92 percent (U.S. Census Bureau 2005). Table 2.3 shows that in 2003 the rent-to-income ratio for black and Hispanic households exceeded the national average: 22 percent of black households paid more than 50 percent of their incomes toward rent, and nearly 26 percent of Hispanic households paid more than 50 percent, while the national average was 21 percent. Hispanic immigrants who speak little or no English have by far the worst housing quality and affordability problems. Unscrupulous landlords often take advantage of their undocumented residency status, which renders them powerless (Gilderbloom and Markham 1993).

According to the National Association of Realtors, apartment rents in 2006 were expected to rise by 5.2 percent in one year because of rising home prices, higher interest rates, condo conversions, and Hurricane Katrina. In New York, rent in Manhattan takes about 65 percent of one income, followed by Los Angeles at 38 percent (Knox 2006). Others like mega housing developer Bob Toll estimate that Americans on average will put roughly half of their incomes into housing in the next decade (Gertner 2005).

TABLE 2.2. *Housing Costs and Renter Household Ability to Pay, 2002*

Renter Household Income Level	Number (Millions)	Share (%)	Median Reported Income	Monthly Housing Costs		Cost as % of Income
				Affordable	Actual	
Extremely Low	8.5	25	$ 7,000	$175	$426	58
Very Low	6.2	18	$17,000	$ 425	$509	35
Low	7.3	21	$26,541	$664	$565	25
Moderate	6.6	19	$40,000	$1,000	$643	19
High	5.3	16	$68,000	$1,700	$736	12
All	34.0	100	$24,400	$610	$560	25

SOURCE: Millennial Housing Commission (2002), Figure 5

The lack of affordable housing is not just a problem for single adults in the United States. With each passing year it becomes increasingly difficult for working families at the bottom of the economic strata to afford housing and other life-sustaining expenses. Ann B. Schnare, chair of the Center for Housing Policy, stated that "working a full-time job does not guarantee a family a decent, affordable place to live" (Center for Housing Policy 2005a, 5).

Families have critical housing needs when they pay more than half of their incomes on housing and/or live in severely dilapidated conditions. In 1997 roughly 3 million working families had critical housing needs. By 2003 that number had increased to 5 million, a 67 percent increase in just six years. In 2003 the Center for Housing Policy (2005a, 31) found that "working families were 2 to 3.5 times more likely to live in housing with more than one person per room." There were 43 million working families in 2003, and 4.2 million (9.8 percent) were deemed to have severe housing cost burdens. These 4.2 million working families with severe housing cost burdens represented a 76.4 percent increase since 1997, when there were 2.4 million. Immigrant working families are especially troubled by the cost of housing in the United States. Immigrant working families are 75 percent more likely than native-born working families to pay 50 percent or more of their incomes for housing (15).

Sociologists have examined housing in terms of the impact of rental costs on individuals and groups. They have concluded that rent levels exert a major impact on the lives of tenants. High rents are a major source of shelter poverty since they can influence the size of households, immediate social relations, schools, job opportunities, health care access, and other needs that

TABLE 2.3. *U.S. Monthly Housing Costs as a Percent of Income, by Race, 2003 (in thousands)*

	All	*Black*	*Hispanic*
Occupied Units	105,842	13,004	11,038
Renters	33,604	6,811	5,931
0–24%	11,449 (34.1%)	2,069 (30.4%)	1,599 (27.0%)
25% or more	18,676 (55.6%)	3,968 (58.3%)	3,887 (65.5%)
35% or more	12,284 (36.6%)	2,561 (37.6%)	2,679 (45.2%)
50% or more	7,189 (21.4%)	1,505 (22.1%)	1,513 (25.5%)
60% or more	5,462 (16.3%)	1,178 (17.3%)	1,077 (18.2%)

SOURCE: U.S. Census Bureau 2003, Tables 2–13, 5–13, 6–13

are spatially diverse. When rents rise, tenants have to pay the rent, move, or double up. Each of these alternatives has potentially negative social and economic consequences for tenants.

SHELTER POVERTY

What is meant by "affordable" housing? At what point is a tenant paying "too much" for rent? Obviously, any standard is somewhat arbitrary, depending on such factors as income, expenditures on food, health, and other necessities, as well as expectations concerning living standards. Typically, government policy has defined "overpayment" as anything in excess of a specified percentage of household income, a standard followed by the banking industry in determining loan eligibility for home mortgages. The government defines "gross housing rents" as all costs associated with housing, such as utilities, food, etc. The government defines "contract rents" as the rental amount in the signed lease agreement.

According to the Millennial Housing Commission (2002), people have an affordable housing problem when they are spending more than 50 percent of their income on housing. The report notes, though, that for many low-income families, 30 percent of their income devoted to housing costs is an extreme financial burden. Before the Reagan administration, the standard was 25 percent of household income. However, in a cynical attempt to downplay the housing crisis, the standard was raised to 30 percent, thereby reducing the numbers of people who were classified as having unaffordable housing payments.

When a low-income tenant pays a large portion of his or her income into rent, cutbacks often have to be made on other basic necessities, such as food, medical care, clothing, and transportation. Stone (1980) describes this as "shelter poverty," whereby the high cost of housing makes it impossible to afford other basic necessities of life. He offers this definition in lieu of the conventional "percentage of income" approach, on the grounds that paying even 1 percent of one's income into housing might be too great if it means forgoing other basic necessities.

The Bureau of Labor Statistics calculates a minimum budget necessary to afford "non-shelter necessities at a minimum level of adequacy" that allows one to reasonably calculate how much a person can afford for shelter as a percentage of income (Stone 1983, 103–105).

A national survey released June 1, 2005, by the Pew Research Center for the People and the Press found that Americans, especially those living in the West or the Northeast, felt that housing had become too difficult to afford in their communities. One in four Americans felt that they had more personal debt than they could afford. Less than half of the population believed that housing was affordable. Among households earning between $30,000 and $75,000, there was a 10 percent decrease in the belief that housing was affordable. According to the National Low Income Housing Coalition (2004), one-third of renters in all fifty states lived in unaffordable housing.

Even higher rents are expected in the near future. On the day we were completing the editing of this book, USA Today had this blaring headline on the front page: "Renters Will Dig Deeper in 2007" (Knox 2007). USA Today reports on a national survey by real estate brokerage firm Marcus and Millichap that breathlessly states, "Landlords are expected to raise apartment rents for a third-straight year in 2007, forcing tenants to turn over a growing chunk of their pay and making it harder to save for a home . . . [with] the projected rise of 5% this year, rents would be 14% higher than at the end of 2004." Hessam Nadji, a managing director of Marcus and Millichap, makes the following quote: "This is a national trend. We're seeing rents rise in the majority of markets, and we see this continuing for at least three more years" (ibid.). The report found the biggest increases in rent from 2004 through 2007 to be in rent-controlled Manhattan (23 percent) and San Francisco (20 percent)—in Chapter 4 we explore the reasons rent control can no longer hold rents down—and the fast-growing nonregulated cities of San Jose (23 percent), Orlando (21 percent), and Fort Lauderdale (21 percent) had rents going up an average of 7 percent a year—in Chapter 3 we show why fast-growing cities have higher-than-average rents. For some, 7 percent might seem small, but in real dollars this means a low-end apartment in San Francisco or Manhattan renting at $1,500 in 2004 would go up an average of $300 with a 20 percent increase in rents over a three-year period; a more typically priced apartment in these cities of, say, $2,000 would see rents going up an average of $400 in three years. The report blames the rent increases on homeownership being more difficult to obtain because of high interest rates, the inability to save money for a down payment, and tougher banking requirements to get a loan.

OVERCROWDING

High rents can also contribute to overcrowding. The U.S. Census Bureau defines "overcrowding" as any housing unit that has more than one person per room. The rate of overcrowding decreased throughout the 1980s but began to rise in the 1990s and rose again in 2000 to 5.7 percent (U.S. Census Bureau 2000). The Census Bureau defines "severe overcrowding" as any housing unit that has 1.5 or more persons per room. Severely crowded homes followed the same trend as overcrowded homes. In 1980 the rate of severely crowded homes was at a low of 1.4 percent but jumped to 2.7 percent, or 2.9 million housing units, in 2000 (ibid.).

The *New York Times* reported a steady rise—more than any other kind of housing arrangement—in "multi-generational households," those of three or more generations, which increased by 38 percent from 1990 to an all-time high of 4.2 million households for the year 2000 (Navarro 2006). The article cites real estate professionals who see this trend "accelerating" since 2000 and U.S. Census Bureau estimates that this kind of housing arrangement represents 4 percent of all types.

Research conducted by the Fannie Mae Foundation (1992) shows that overcrowding is more prevalent in the western and southwestern United States than in the rest of the nation. California is home to 1.7 million overcrowded households (U.S. Census Bureau 2000). Four demographic and geographic areas have high overcrowding: large multi-ethnic urban counties, counties in the West and Upper Midwest with high proportions of American Indians and Alaskan Natives, predominantly Latino counties in the Rio Grande Valley of Texas, and agricultural counties on the West Coast, in Texas, and in Florida (U.S. Census Bureau 2000).

Regions that have the highest increases in median gross rent also have the highest percentages of overcrowded housing units. The western regions of the United States saw an increase in median gross rents of 39.3 percent from 1990 to 2000 (Simmons 2002).

"The process of immigration has a clear and discernible impact on the consumption of housing space. In housing markets with high levels of recent immigration, overcrowding is higher than in non-immigrant metropolitan areas" (Clark, Devloo, and Dieleman 2000). Crowded housing disrupts the quality of life and has a negative impact on surrounding communities. Overcrowding causes classroom sizes to increase to unmanageable levels, increases traffic congestion, creates more waste, and decreases property values. Santa Ana, California, has the highest amount of overcrowding in the nation, with 37 percent of its households severely overcrowded, and the city has an immigrant population of 53 percent. As a result of the overcrowding situation, the mayor of Santa Ana created a task force to study the problem. The city decided to halt the construction of more apartment housing units and passed strict anti-crowding laws in the 1980s. The restrictions, however, failed to control the overcrowding problem. The city of Santa Ana added 45,235 more residents during the 1990s, but housing units only increased by 1,391. This pushed Santa Ana's average household size from 4.0 to 4.55, compared to the national average of 2.59 (Marquez 2002).

Pynoos, Schafer, and Hartman (1973, 4) report that "overcrowding may lead to increased stress, poor development of sense of individuality, sexual conflict, lack of adequate sleep leading to poor work and school performance, and interfamilial tensions." Schorr (1963) argues that overcrowding is responsible for more health problems than the actual quality of the unit. Baldassare's national survey of metropolitan areas found that overcrowding can lead to poor marital relations (1979, 110).

The most methodologically sound study on this issue is the work of sociologists Gove, Hughes, and Galle (1979). Using regression techniques to control for the intervening variables, they find that overcrowding within the home is "strongly related to poor mental health, poor social relationships in the homes, and poor child care; and [is] less strongly but significantly related to poor mental health, poor social relationships outside the home" (78). Taken together, the three overcrowding variables explain more of the variance than the combined impact of sex, race, education, income, age, and marital status. Research by Booth and Edwards (1976, 308) finds that "household congestion" has a small positive impact on the incidence of sibling quarrels and the number of times parents hit their children.

DISRUPTION OF SOCIAL NETWORKS

A report by the U.S. Census Bureau found that from 1997 to 2000, cheaper housing was an increasing motivator for people to move; 448,000 people cited cheaper housing as the reason for moving from 1997 to 1998. However, that number leaped by 414 percent to 2,303,000 from 1999 to 2000. While tenants are most vulnerable to being forced out of their homes, homeowners are increasingly threatened by mortgage foreclosures and loss of home. In 2002 the Mortgage Bankers Association of America reported that mortgage foreclosures were at their highest levels in thirty years. In the three-month period from April 1 to June 30, 2002, there were 134,855 new foreclosures. This is an astounding number because it represents nearly four of every thousand mortgaged homes in the United States (MBAA 2002). Mortgage foreclosures have become a very serious issue for those at the bottom of the economic ladder as "risk-based" pricing and sub-prime loans have been embraced by many banks. With rising interest and variable interest rates, there will be a steady rise in foreclosures.

Experts have long agreed that a person who is forced to move from his or her neighborhood can undergo considerable psychological stress from the loss of community or reference groups (Fried 1963; Harvey 1973, 82–86; Wechsler 1961). Children are intensely affected by moving, and it typically takes six to eighteen months for children to psychologically adjust to the move (Olkowski 1993). Depression is correlated with sudden shifts or changes in social support networks, and Harvey (1973, 85) finds that this may be particularly true in lower-income groups: "low-income groups . . . often identify closely with their housing environment and the psychological costs of moving are to them far greater than they are to the mobile upper middle class."

Fried (1963, 151) reports that a person's mental health is threatened, if not adversely affected, when he or she is forced to move from his or her dwelling unit. He catalogues this effect with such threats as "the feeling of painful loss, the continued longing, the general depressive tone, frequent symptoms of psychological or social or somatic distress, the active work required in adapting to the altered situation, the sense of helplessness, the occasional expressions of both direct and displaced anger and tendencies to idealize the lost place." He found that 46 percent of the women and 38 percent of the men he interviewed gave evidence of "fairly severe grief reaction or worse." In his interviews with displaced residents, Fried reports the following remarks: "I had a nervous breakdown . . . I threw up a lot . . . I felt like taking the gas pipe" (ibid.). Depressive disorders might result when an individual is forced to leave the community or home through which he or she acquires a sense of self-esteem, as described by Angrist (1974, 499):

> This critical link between relationships with people and well-being is
> also substantiated in other ways. Social interaction may be considered
> a pervasive source of reinforcement, and in situations relatively free of
> constraints, sustained interaction over time among one or more persons
> indicates satisfaction . . . When moving disrupts patterns of interaction,
> the result is a decline in satisfaction and hence in well-being.

More recently in New Orleans, we can see this effect in the suicide rates before and after Hurricane Katrina destroyed the city. Before this travesty, 9 in every 100,000 people committed suicide. Post-Katrina, the incidence of suicide nearly tripled, to a shocking 26 per 100,000. Dr. Jeffrey Rouse, who deals with psychiatric cases for the New Orleans coroner's office, reported this increase to have happened over the course of four months. The official number of suicides for 2006 in New Orleans was 12, in a drastically reduced city population of half its original size, but Rouse said this number was wrong due to many suicides being unclassified or wrongly classified as accidents (Saulny 2006).

Charles Curie, administrator of the City of New Orleans Substance Abuse and Mental Health Services Administration, said, "We've had great concerns about the level of substance abuse and mental health needs being at levels we have not seen before" (Saulny 2006). Many who are not about to kill themselves are still watching as their lives are worn down from persistent feelings of sadness, hopelessness, and stress-related illnesses. "The symptoms of depression have, at minimum, doubled since Katrina," said Susan Powell, a political scientist at the University of New Orleans. "These are classic post-trauma symptoms. People can't sleep, they're irritable, feeling that everything's an effort, and sad" (ibid.).

IMPACT ON FAMILY FORMATION

As the cost of housing and rents rises, along with cutbacks in government aid, family size and workforce participation are understandably affected. In 1984 Hohm argued that high housing costs increasingly required two incomes to afford homeownership. Consequently, many young couples are choosing to limit the size of their families and not having children at all. In *The Two-Income Trap* (2003), Harvard law professor Elizabeth Warren and her daughter Amelia Warren Tyagi demonstrate how having children is the best indicator of whether someone will end up in "financial collapse."

In an article in the *New Yorker*, James Surowiecki (2003) asserts that "over the past two decades, the cost of having children has risen much faster than the cost of being childless." Surowiecki argues that the increasing financial burden of offspring is attributable to housing and education costs. The Federal Reserve Board found that between 1983 and 1998 the price of housing for married couples with children rose 79 percent, nearly three times as much as it did for childless people (ibid.).

One very telling statistic of how reproduction makes people economically vulnerable is that between 1980 and 2000, the percentage of women between the ages of forty and forty-four who had no children doubled (Suro-wiecki 2003). Children are a consumer durable who return only a "psychic income," and as they become more expensive, people will accumulate fewer of them. Children can also easily be labeled as "public goods" in that every-one benefits from them even if everyone does not pay for them (Surowiecki 2003).

HOMELESSNESS

Efforts to get an accurate assessment of how many people are plagued by homelessness are complicated by problems of definition and methodology. As a result of constraints, most studies are limited to counting people who are in shelters or on the streets. Martha Burt, a principal research associate at the Urban Institute, asserts that "over the course of a year at least 2.3 mil-lion people and probably as many as 3.5 million people experience home-lessness at least for a short period" (Urban Institute 2000). Sue Marshall, executive director of the Community Partnership for Prevention of Home-lessness, asserts that the fastest-growing segment of the homeless popula-tion is women with children. Marshall estimates that "on any given day there are literally 7,500 to 8,000 people in the District of Columbia who are homeless." There have been estimates that 2.3 percent of D.C.'s population experiences homelessness in a year's time, nearly twice the national average (Urban Institute 2000).

According to the work of the Urban Institute and numerous other studies, homelessness is the extreme outcome of the combined effects of several fac-tors, among which the shortage of affordable rental housing plays a large and growing role. The Urban Institute (2000) study concludes that the increase in homelessness during the 1983–1985 economic recovery was the result of "the concordance of increased poverty and income inequality with housing market developments deleterious to the poor," including rising rents and diminishing low-income housing supply (20–21).

Estimates of the number of homeless are difficult to ascertain. The *Los Angeles Times* (2007) reported an estimate of 744,000 homeless in 2005. This number is conservative since the count was based mostly on home-less shelters, and many homeless do not use these services (Dreier et al. 1991). Actual counts have been done in only a few places, including parts of downtown Boston (Boston Emergency Shelter Commission 1983), Phoe-nix (Consortium for the Homeless 1983), and Pittsburgh (Winograd 1982), although the authors of such studies even acknowledge the impossibility of adequately defining and subsequently locating homeless people. Does one count only street people and those living in shelters as being homeless? What about persons who are forced to live temporarily with friends or relatives or persons who live in cars or vans? There are many homeless who are not readily visible, including those who simply want to be left alone. Those who seek to avoid authorities, such as undocumented workers, and most of those who have "lost" their housing wind up sleeping in cars or abandoned buildings or on friends' sofas.

Displacement, shortages of affordable rental housing, sluggish economic growth, and the deinstitutionalization of mental patients all contribute to the worsening problem. It is estimated that a "clear majority of the homeless are chronically disabled" by mental illness, alcoholism, or a combination of the two (Gilderbloom and Appelbaum 1988.) The remainder of the homeless population suffers from temporary personal distresses that include loss of employment, eviction or other loss of housing, and marital distress. In general, the homeless are now younger and more likely to be in families than was the case two decades ago.

The homeless also face significantly greater health problems. A New York City study by the National Ambulatory Medical Care Survey found that the homeless suffer from a considerably higher incidence of virtually all forms of ailments (*USA Today* 1985). For example, in comparison with the general population, the homeless experience:

- Twice the number of traumatic injuries (fractures, wounds, cuts)
- Four times the number of colds
- Five times the number of lung disorders
- Fifteen times the number of limb disorders
- Three times the number of skin problems
- Six times the number of nerve disorders
- Four times the number of nutritional disorders

HEALTH PROBLEMS AMONG THE HOMELESS

It is estimated that more than half of the homeless suffer from some form of mental illness, and an estimated 25 to 33 percent of the homeless who use shelters have been in a psychiatric hospital at least once (Walsh 1985, 3). A survey of homeless studies (Gilderbloom and Appelbaum 1988; Walsh 1985) provides the following summary:

- In Philadelphia, of 179 shelter users given psychiatric examinations, 40 percent were found to have major mental disorders.

• In Washington, D.C.'s House of Ruth shelter for women, 48 percent needed psychiatric treatment.

• Community Service Society studies of New York homeless in 1981 and 1982 indicated that as many as half had serious psychiatric disorders.

• In San Francisco, a study of 103 homeless people found that 57 "could recall" at least two visits to psychiatric hospitals or mental health facilities.

• In Phoenix, two studies of homeless food-line patrons found that 30 percent had at one time lived in mental institutions.

• In Boston, a study of Shattuck Shelter by Harvard Medical School professor Ellen Bassuk found that 40 percent suffered from psychotic mental illness and 33 percent had a history of psychiatric hospitalization. Bassuk termed the shelters "open asylums" or substitutes for the mental hospitals of old.

In the face of increasingly adverse housing conditions combined with the declining federal role in assuring the availability of affordable housing (see below and Chapter 4), we expect the homeless situation to worsen in the immediate future. To an extent, the number and plight of the homeless serve as a barometer of the health of the low-income housing economy in general in the United States.

SOCIAL UNREST

Severe shortages in affordable low-income housing can lead to "violent confrontations between citizens and authorities, and even revolutions" (Rosentraub and Warren 1986). This is persuasively demonstrated in Friedland's (1982) comprehensive study of black urban riots in the 1960s, during which 100,000 were arrested, 10,000 were injured, and 300 were killed. Friedland found that "local public policies played an important role in conditioning the city's level of black political violence" (162). He also found that when other factors were statistically controlled, the amount of urban renewal and the lack of available low-rent housing were significant determinants of riot severity (ibid.).

Between 1949 and 1974, urban renewal demolished a half-million low-income housing units, of which only one-fifth were replaced, primarily with middle-income units (Shipnuck, Keating, and Morgan 1974). Overcrowded and high-priced housing was also touted as a cause of the 1992 Los Angeles riots. During the late 1970s and early 1980s, riots broke out over the lack of decent, affordable housing in West Germany, Holland, Switzerland, and England (Hall 1981, 15–16). More recently, rioting in France in fall 2005 was associated with Muslims living in faceless housing super-projects that ring the outside of France's cities. The projects are known to isolate poor Muslims in housing that lacks "pride of place" because of its cold, institutionalized look (*Expatica News* 2005).

UNHEALTHY CHEMICALS IN THE HOME?

There is growing evidence that newer or renovated housing can be unhealthy. This is more problematic for the poor, who often live in housing where the building materials contain a toxic glue to hold together cheaper processed wood. Multiple chemical sensitivity (MCS) impacts millions in the industrial world with health problems such as insomnia, breathing problems, migraine, nausea, fatigue, asthma, and cancer (Chiras 2004, 53). The primary villain is formaldehyde, which is used for engineered wood such as plywood and particle board and also can be found in walls, floors, ceilings, shelves, and cabinets (Chiras 2004, 53–56). The use of formaldehyde is especially prevalent in manufactured homes, which doctors have associated with a higher incidence of asthma and other medical problems. Environmentalists are beginning to document the problems associated with MCS (http://www.louisville.edu/org/sun; http://www.mcsrr.org).

TRAILERS AS AN ALTERNATIVE TO THE STICK-BUILT HOUSE

As the cost of housing increases, many people are looking to lower-priced alternatives for housing options. One such option is manufactured housing, commonly referred to as trailers or mobile homes. Many changes have been made in the manufactured housing industry. In 1976 HUD required that all manufactured housing be built in compliance with the National Manufactured Home Construction and Safety Act of 1974. This helped to improve the quality of manufactured homes (Wubneh and Shen 2004, 56). In rural areas, manufactured housing has become the dominant form of low- and middle-income housing. In Kentucky, for instance, half of the new housing produced is manufactured housing.

Despite the downfalls of manufactured housing, there are some good points that may help to answer the growing problem of affordable housing. In Seattle a nonprofit housing group constructed seventy-five homes priced between $155,000 and $250,000, compared to the median home cost in the area of $350,000 (Watson 2002, 22). Manufactured housing is not the same concept as was previously thought; today home buyers in Malibu, California, are paying more than a million dollars for a mobile home (Krantz 2005).

Manufactured housing has its benefits and its problems, but ultimately it needs to be sustainable housing for families that use it as an affordable alternative.

There are many concerns about manufactured housing. First, some studies show that manufactured housing has a negative effect on the site-based housing near the manufactured housing. In a study based on three North Carolina counties, the closer a site-based neighborhood is located to a manufactured housing area, the lower the property values of the site-based housing neighborhood (Wubneh and Shen 2004, 71).

Manufactured housing is also not of the same quality as a stick-built home. *Consumer Reports* (1998) conducted an investigation of manufactured housing to see if it was a good investment for families. Those consumers who lease the land that their manufactured home sits on are subject to steep increases in rents on their lots. A study conducted by Gilderbloom and Friedlander (2003) noted that manufactured housing is also valued less than site-based housing but that the new style of upscale manufactured housing is evaluated at a higher level than the traditional single-wide manufactured home (204–205).

Manufactured housing is also a drain on the consumer for several reasons. Studies conducted by the Consumers Union (2002) indicated that the owners of manufactured housing are subject to predatory lending. The Consumers Union studied 127 families' loans; of those, most had interest rates of 9 percent to 13 percent, and 19 families had loan rates higher than 13 percent. Interest rates were double or triple the rates that homeowners paid for stick-built housing. The report likens manufactured housing sales to auto sales because of the high-pressure environment and lack of home inspections.

Consumer Reports (1998) found that manufactured homes had problems with leaky windows and roofs. Many manufactured homes presented installation problems that caused them to be unsafe in bad weather (30–32). Manufactured housing has no appreciation, unlike stick-built homes, further underscoring the differences that make it an affordable alternative in the short term but problematic in the longer term.

RENTING AND HOMEOWNERSHIP

Despite the widening gap between renters' and homeowners' incomes, the latter also experience considerable affordability issues. Between 1990 and 2000, the median sales price of existing single-family homes rose 45.5 percent from $95,500 to $139,000 (National Association of Realtors [NAR] 2002). As can be seen in Table 2.4, the rise in median price of existing homes varied

TABLE 2.4. *Median Sales Price of Existing Single-Family Homes by Location, 1990 and 2000*

Location	1990 ($, thousand)	2000 ($, thousand)	Percent Change
U.S. Average	95.5	139.0	46
New York City	174.9	230.2	32
Boston	174.1	314.2	81
Los Angeles	212.1	215.9	2

SOURCE: NAR 2002

widely in different parts of the country between 1990 and 2000. However, over the 1990s, interest rates on thirty-year fixed-rate mortgages fell from 10.01 percent to 8.04 percent. Houses have become even less affordable for Americans in recent years (Table 2.5). From 2002 to 2004, the hurdle of qualifying income rose 6.6 percent, while the median family income only rose 5.5 percent (NAR 2005). Clearly, the cost of becoming a homeowner is simply outpacing what families actually earn.

In 1981, first-time homebuyers constituted 13.5 percent of the sales market (U.S. League of Savings Associations 1982), compared with 40 percent in 2004 (Flandez 2004). This large number of first-time homeowners helped to carry the housing market in 2004. The near-unprecedented levels of first-time buyers are easily attributed to historically low interest rates. The National Association of Realtors found that the average first-time buyer was thirty-two years old with a household income of $54,500 (Flandez 2004). The national median family income for that same year was $54,527 (NAR 2005). These recently high numbers of first-time purchases helped to create an abundance of rental housing, but following chapters in this book illustrate that this is not the case.

Research by Henretta (1984, 131) in the early 1980s found that a caste system might have evolved in terms of attaining homeownership. However, it appears that the transition from renter to homeowner is more attractive and attainable for those located near the income median, given the historically low interest rates. It remains to be seen whether the current conditions of the housing market will stay the same. High housing costs have understandably led to higher rent levels. According to Jay M. Kaplan, former executive vice president of Consolidated Capital Mortgage Corporation, "People who can't buy houses are going to be renters and that's good for owners of apartment buildings" (Kinchen 1982, 30). Despite the historically high homeownership levels, the financial burden levied on renters has not lessened.

TABLE 2.5. *National Association of Realtors Housing Affordability Index, 2002–2004*

Year	Median Price of Existing Single-Family Home	Mortgage Rate[1]	Payment as Percent of Income	Median Family Income	Qualifying Income[2]
2002	$158,100	6.55	18.7	$51,680	$38,592
2003	$170,000	5.74	18.1	$52,682	$38,064
2004	$184,100	5.72	18.9	$54,527	$41,136

SOURCES: Federal Housing Finance Board; NAR 2005
NOTES:
[1]Effective annual interest rate on loans closed on existing homes, from the Federal Housing Finance Board
[2]Based on a 25 percent qualifying ratio for monthly housing expense to gross monthly income with a 20 percent down payment

Today, homeownership rates are at their highest levels in U.S. history. From 1996 to 2004, homeownership rates increased 5.5 percent, from 65.4 percent to 69 percent (U.S. Census Bureau 2005). It must be noted that homeownership rates have risen every year since World War II with the exception of the period from 1980 to 1990. Historically, homeownership has been disproportionately concentrated among those who are white and have incomes above the median. However, recent data show that minorities constitute a larger percentage of those who can call themselves homeowners.

From 1996 to 2004, the percentage of white homeowners rose 5.5 percent, while the percentage among African-Americans rose 11.3 percent and among Hispanics 12.4 percent (U.S. Census Bureau 2005). The recent change in the disparity of homeownership by ethnicity is due to the increasing number of mortgage loans to low-income, minority households. A 2002 report from the Brookings Institution found that mortgage lending increased by 98 percent for African-American homebuyers and by 125 percent for Hispanic homebuyers during the 1990s (Retsinas and Belsky 2002). However, if current economic conditions (high unemployment and high foreclosures) persist, the gains made by homeowners in recent years will be overshadowed by the new struggle for homeownership.

Despite the unprecedented levels of homeownership in the United States today, there are areas around the country where the impediments to homeownership remain extremely high. California is a state plagued by extremely high financial prerequisites to homeownership. San Francisco and a number of coastal California areas from Santa Cruz to Orange County have exorbitantly high median home prices. The National Housing Conference found that in 2005 a median-priced home in San Francisco cost $705,000, compared to $567,000 two years earlier, an increase of 24.3 percent. It also found that an income of $223,576 was needed to enter the ranks of homeowners (Zito 2005). The median household income in California in 2003 was $49,300, a shortfall of $174,276 (U.S. Census Bureau 2004). Consequently, only 13 percent of California households have the necessary income to buy an average-priced home. Twenty years ago, the average price for a home in San Francisco was $147,000 (Gilderbloom and Appelbaum 1988).

In Los Angeles, home prices have hit the stratosphere—only 12 percent of households in Los Angeles County could afford a median-priced home in 2006, compared to 38 percent in 2000 (Wedner 2006). According to experts, the situation probably will not change anytime soon, although some speculate this might cause an exodus of the middle class to the Midwest. Bob Toll, one of the nation's largest housing developers, estimates that the cost of buying a home will steadily increase (cited in Gertner 2005). He notes that Americans currently pay three and one-half times their annual salary on a house. This could increase to five times their annual salary or possibly as high as seven times, as is the case in Great Britain. Ironically, the British pay twice as much on housing as the Americans but get half the space:

> The British get 330 square feet, per person, in their homes; in the U.S., we get 750 square feet. Not only does Toll say he believes the next generation of buyers will be paying twice as much of their annual incomes; in terms of space, he also seems to think they're going to get only half as much. And the average, million dollar insane home in the burbs? It's going to be $4 million. (Gertner 2005, 5)

Some have predicted that housing prices might take a dip in certain regions such as New York and Boston, Florida, and the West Coast, from San Diego to Seattle, beginning in 2006. Foreclosures are at record highs in early 2007, and housing prices are beginning to rise again in certain regions where they were down. Homeowners with variable interest rates or interest-only payments are in for a tough ride. This may cause an increase in foreclosures and a reduction in housing prices. These home prices will eventually recover, as they did in San Francisco in early 2000 and Los Angeles after the urban riots of 1992.

In Louisville, which is far more typical of your average city, median home prices over the past thirty-five years have increased at an average rate of 6 percent a year, and the average home prices fell in only one year. Housing markets that have experienced lower appreciation levels for the past ten years will start to catch up with inflated markets. The long-term picture is that home prices will continue to rise.

Homeownership has become part of the American Dream. Owning a home provides a sense of accomplishment and provides most middle-class families with their largest investment. The American dream of home-ownership is rewarded by the federal government. Americans are allowed to deduct their mortgage interest and local property taxes from their taxable income. There are many misconceptions about the overall benefits of the homeownership tax credit. For example, many people argue that the homeownership tax credit benefits lower-income families at the expense of middle-income families, but research shows that the wealthiest are paying for the upper middle class to have the benefit. Many also believe that home-ownership has increased over several decades due to the tax credits, but according to one research study, there is no evidence of this result (Bourassa and Grigsby 2000, 526). Some also argue that the tax breaks for homeowner-ship can cause an over-investment in the real estate market that diverts investment from opportunities such as manufacturing (Bourassa and Grigsby 2000, 527). People invest in real estate because there is no tax on rental income, as opposed to other investments in which capital gains would be taxed (ibid.).

In some instances non-taxation of capital gains on property does create a great loss because inflation soaks up much of the gains that are made (Gilderbloom and Appelbaum 1988). Also, some argue that if gains are taxed, then the losses should be deducted, which would decrease revenues. This is another place where taxing the capital gains would make the tax system difficult to administer. The disadvantage of this type of non-taxation is that it promotes investment in real estate over other types of investments. Overall, the profits investors gain from this non-taxation do not create the need to further complicate the federal income tax system (Bourassa and Grigsby 2000, 526).

The mortgage interest deduction has pros and cons. This deduction helps to increase homeownership rates in the United States as well as maintain housing construction, which thereby prevents a housing shortage and keeps the value of existing homes at equilibrium. There are several negatives to the non-taxation of mortgage interest as well. There have been no significant benefits to homeownership; capital values of homes could be protected by introducing tax reform; it is not likely to have a strong impact on new construction; high-income households receive the greatest share of benefits; renters are not given the full benefits; it adds another level of complexity to the tax system; and as it encourages new construction, it contributes to urban sprawl (Gilderbloom and Appelbaum 1988). Bourassa and Grigsby (2000, 526) argue that the benefits of the mortgage tax deduction are not great enough to continue it.

Finally, the tax concession is the real estate tax deduction. There are several pros for the real estate tax deduction to remain: it operates like a high sales tax, which begs for the federal government to offset the tax. It is not related to one's ability to pay, because the assessment of it is not done equally across the board; the tax is regressive based on income. There are several cons for tax concession. Housing deductions themselves are regressive, and a federal tax credit cannot offset it, so the real estate tax deduction would become more regressive if the mortgage interest deduction was eliminated. Bourassa and Grigsby (2000, 526) contend that the real estate tax deduction should be eliminated because of its regressive nature and because the intended results have not been realized.

As mentioned above, one common misconception about the home-ownership tax credit is that it overwhelmingly benefits the poor as compared to the wealthy, but according to research conducted by Bourassa and Grigsby (2000), this assertion is not true. Congress intended for low- to moderate-income families to benefit the most from the homeownership tax incentives, but 90 percent of the tax benefit goes to homeowners who have incomes over $50,000 annually (531). The researchers argue that low- to moderate-income families find it more advantageous to take the standard deduction as opposed to itemizing. Through mortgage interest tax concessions, those earning more than $200,000 annually receive less tax incentive than those earning between $100,000 and $199,999 (532). In many cases the low- to moderate-income family is not receiving the greatest benefit of the homeownership tax incentives.

Bourassa and Grigsby (2000, 531) also argue that non-taxation has not had the overall impact on homeownership that some claim for it, even though the increase in homeownership was its primary purpose. In order to take a closer look at the impact on housing, Bourassa and Grigsby (2000, 531) compare the United States to Australia and Canada. Both of these countries are similar to the United States economically, but they do not provide the same homeownership incentives that the U.S. government does, and their homeownership rates are close to those of the United States. But in these other nations, it is difficult to determine which groups would be locked out of homeownership and forced to rent permanently without the homeownership tax credit (ibid.).

MARXIST VIEW OF TENANTS

One school of thought that has explicitly addressed tenant movements has been the Marxist view formed by Friedrich Engels (1970), who collaborated with Marx on several key theories. Engels was one of the first social theorists to write about the movement for decent and affordable housing within a political economy perspective. Even though he wrote about housing struggles more than one hundred years ago, his analysis has been lauded by later theorists (Angotti 1977). Engels' perspective has served as the framework for many housing activists who have refused to support homeownership because it could thwart a socialist revolution. In *The Housing Question*, Engels (1970, 19) called the housing crisis "one of the innumerable, smaller, secondary evils, which result from the present day capitalist mode of production." While sympathetic to the plight of renters, he generally frowned on housing rights movements as a distraction from the "primary struggle" of the proletariat seizing power and transforming the state from a capitalist economy to a socialist system. Only under socialism, he argued, would the "housing problem" be resolved. Struggles demanding more affordable housing by *themselves* were seen as futile attempts to change historically prescribed circumstances under which people live.

Engels' opposition to the workers movement seeking more affordable housing was both economic and political. He opposed programs that allowed tenants to purchase homes, even if these meant a substantial reduction in the amount of wages going into shelter (1970, 18, 48). He argued that the net gain tenants received through homeownership was negated by a corresponding reduction in wages, calling this one of the "iron laws of the doctrine of the national economy" (48). Citing Germany, Engels wrote that Germany's ability to produce goods with "extraordinary cheapness" was due to inexpensive worker-owned housing, which allowed capitalists to pay the workers "infamously low wages" (14).

Engels opposed homeownership opportunities for tenants not only on economic grounds; he also criticized them as having a poor political strategy. Housing struggles, he argued, do not materially contribute to the building of class-consciousness, a necessity for challenging the capitalist system. In fact, movements for better housing could result in a more conservative workforce. This is because the housing crisis hurts not only the proletariat but also the "petty bourgeoisie." As a result, when tenants organize for better housing, the class-consciousness of workers becomes blurred. Workers may organize *with* the petty bourgeoisie rather than *against* it, viewing it as a class that shares a similar exploitation (70–80). How are workers to see themselves as a distinct class if other classes, including the petty bourgeoisie, share the same socially defined problem? While some contemporary theorists see cross-class alliances as powerful challenges to entrenched elites, Engels considered them a mistaken strategy.

From the point of view of "class consciousness," housing struggles contained some other pitfalls. Engels argued that "the worker who owns a little house to the value of a thousand tales is, true enough, no longer a proletarian" (48). Homeownership makes it more difficult for workers to be organized to resist exploitation by capitalists since they are less mobile than their counterpart workers/tenants. Workers/tenants are more apt to resist exploitation by moving to places with higher wages. Workers/homeowners, on the other hand, are forced to remain in the area with low wages because of debt payments owed. Property ownership also could have a conservatizing effect on workers; they become a part of the capitalist private property relations system and have a stake in its continuance. Engels concluded that worker/homeownership "is reactionary, and the reintroduction of the individual ownership of his dwelling by each individual would be a step backward" (96). The contradictory nature of the worker/homeowner meant that his or her class allegiance fell with neither the worker class nor the capitalist class. Far from being confined to Engels' time, this argument, grounded in the Marxist tradition, has resurfaced as a bone of contention for modern-day tenant organizers and academic theorists.

TENANTS: POLITICAL BEHAVIOR AND TENANT CONSCIOUSNESS

It is important to understand that housing space is not the only space that tenants occupy in a fragile and tentative way. Tenants' civic and political space is also weakened. Historically, tenants have been outside the political process, especially in terms of participating in electoral politics. When the first settlers came to America, those who did not own property were not permitted to vote or seek elected office (Heskin 1981b, 95). Tenants did not have the right to vote in federal elections until 1860 (Martin 1976). Even after tenants became eligible to cast a ballot, landlords in certain parts of the eastern United States were able to control large blocs of tenant votes (Flanigan and Zingale 1979, 12). Today, tenants are still barred from voting in certain property bond, tax, and special district elections (Heskin 1981b,c).

In a study done by the U.S. Census Bureau (1979), homeowners voted twice as often as renters. In the November 1978 election, only 46 percent of the eligible voters turned out. Of those who turned out, 59 percent of the homeowners voted, compared to only 28 percent of the renters. In the study, of all the variables related to voting (age, income, region, sex, and race), housing status "appeared to have the strongest relationship with voting" (1). Interviews conducted by the Census Bureau found that 39 percent of renters did not vote because they were "not interested, they did not care" (84).

Although political citizenship is no longer as dependent as it once was on landownership, the inferior status of tenants persists through both formal and informal norms. Public areas technically open to all citizens are defined in practice by those who ordinarily use them (Lyman and Scott 1967). In the United States, private property ownership has consistently been a ticket to political participation, and this relationship continues even after formal property requirements have been abolished. City councils have typically been dominated by homeowners and investors (Domhoff 1978; Logan and Molotch 1987; Molotch 1976; Nader 1973), while tenants have been viewed as transients and non-citizens in their own communities. Thus, through a mixture of their own views of themselves and definitions imposed upon them by others (Capek 1985), tenants have not traditionally seen public forums as their "home territories."

Another political relationship that should be examined is the widespread belief in the conservatizing impact of homeownership, which has had a strong influence on both national housing policy and progressive movements for social change. The view that housing ownership leads to conservative social and political behavior has been widely held by theorists on both the left and right of the academic and political spectrum (Ball 1976; Castells 1977; Harvey 1976; Kemeny 1977, 1980; Saunders 1978; Sternlieb 1966). The belief that homeownership will cause individuals to rethink their politics and move to the right has become conventional wisdom. Herbert Hoover advocated homeownership as early as 1923:

> Maintaining a high percentage of individual homeowners is one of the searching tests that now challenge the people of the United States. The present large proportion of families that own their own homes is both the foundation of a sound economic and social system and a guarantee that our society will continue to develop rationally as changing conditions demand.

Leadership in the housing rights movement and progressive elected officials in the United States have declined to place homeownership on the political agenda, citing fears that their constituents' political sentiments will shift to the right. As a result, the modern housing movement channels its energies into winning greater tenant rights and better public housing. While some important gains have been made in this direction, this approach ignores the fact that most renters do not want to be tenants but dream of someday becoming homeowners (Heskin 1983; Hohm 1984; Morris, Winter, and Sward 1984). The political right, on the other hand, has traditionally pushed for greater homeownership opportunities, hoping this will translate into greater political gains for their respective political parties. This is an attempt to appeal politically to the desires of the working class and to build a more unified conservative base.

A substantial body of empirical literature has investigated this connection between housing status and political behavior. Research has shown that homeowners are more likely than tenants to be involved in community political activities (Alford and Scoble 1968; Steinberger 1981), to be members of church and community organizations (Homenuck 1977), to make greater claims on government services (Guterbock 1980), to be less residentially mobile (Cox 1982), and to be more aware of local affairs (Sykes 1951). They are also more neighborly (Fischer 1982). However, Blum and Kingston (1984, 162) note that "their [homeowners'] substantive orientations are not directly considered" in terms of a political ideology. Contrary to conventional wisdom, support for the tax revolt cannot be distinguished by housing tenure in a majority of the studies conducted (Lowry and Sigelman 1981). Moreover, national survey data show that support for tax-slashing initiatives does not substantively vary by housing status (Lowry and Sigelman 1981).

Kevin Cox (1982) has found that neighborhood activism in the United States varies according to whether an individual is an owner or a renter. Research by Terry Blum and Paul Kingston (1984, 159) has found that homeownership plays a role in measuring attitudinal support for the status quo, participation in voluntary organizations, and informal interaction with neighbors. Although only a negligible impact on political attitudes was found, this issue was pursued more fully by Kelley, McAllister, and Mughan (1984) using a different data set. They found that housing status had no measurable effect on party identification, ideological views, or socioeconomic policy. However, they found that homeowners tended to vote more in national elections and that their votes tended to favor conservatives.

In 1992, the Fannie Mae National Housing Survey reported that in national elections 73 percent of homeowners voted, while only 47 percent of renters participated. The percentages for local elections were similar, with 61 percent of homeowners and 33 percent of renters voting. The issue then is whether the mode of tenure was responsible for the dichotomous voting behavior or whether it was caused by other factors. Unfortunately, the survey did not control for crucial variables such as income and education that actually may have been more significant in determining voting behavior than housing status. To assume that the differing rates of political participation were solely caused by housing tenure is reductionist and potentially damaging to the formation of public policy.

As noted above, both the left and right claim that important political differences exist between renters and homeowners within the working class. Why are homeowners more active in local politics than tenants? The traditional explanation rests on the concern for the home as an investment. A major inference drawn from this finding is that local political participation is conservative in orientation, signaling an attempt to preserve and enhance positive neighborhood externalities and, concurrently, to reduce or abolish negative neighborhood externalities (Agnew 1978; Harvey 1973, 57–60, 1978). This argument implies that local political activity is a proxy for homeowners, developers, landlords, and commercial enterprises hoping to increase their property values. These interests tend to lean toward the conservative side. Tenants, on the other hand, lack any investment stake to involve them in local political affairs.

Kevin Cox (1982, 107) rejects this strictly "economist" explanation by testing the argument empirically in a detailed survey of 400 Columbus, Ohio, owners and renters. He compares those homeowners who bought their houses "primarily so they could sell it for profit in the future" versus those homeowners who indicated that this was not a primary consideration in their decision to buy. Cox finds that the presence or absence of this economic concern has virtually no effect on neighborhood political involvement. He points out that a more realistic approach for homeowners with a strong investment orientation is simply to move rather than lobby city hall (or fight, as the case may be) (see also Orbell and Uno 1972; Williams 1971; Wingo 1973). Cox finds that homeowners facing strong "transaction cost barriers to relocation" are the ones most likely to be active on the local political front over other homeowners. Homeowners are also, as a group, less mobile than tenants, enabling them to be more politically active.

Major exceptions are the work of Allan Heskin (1983), who specifically explores "tenant consciousness" and its relationship to social movements, and our own collaboration on housing status and progressive political beliefs. As we noted above, there is a paucity of research on the impact of housing status on political attitudes. I base these conclusions on a regression analysis of various factors measuring political opinions on two data sets. In studying a Midwestern industrial city (Capek and Gilderbloom 1992; Gilderbloom and Markham 1995), we found that politically active individuals do not hold a conservative ideology in regard to environmentalism, political ideology, distribution of wealth, or trade union consciousness.

Pursuing these questions further using the National Opinion Research Center 1988–1989 survey, we developed eight dependent variables through factor analysis. We found that housing status had no measurable impact on seven of the dependent variables: equal rights for women, spending on city problems, domestic spending, support for socialist countries, sexual tolerance, civil rights, and support for President George W. Bush. The results are consistent, however, with previous work showing homeownership status as positively correlated with local political participation (Baum and Kingston 1984; Cox 1982). Our findings indicate that homeowners are more likely to vote, but when this variable is run as a dependent variable in the regression analysis, no correlation is found with the other seven dependent variables, meaning that homeownership does not affect opinions about those seven variables. Given these results, the traditional theoretical proposition of the relationship between homeownership and a conservative political ideology needs to be reexamined.

CONCLUSION

In this chapter we have attempted to show that high rents play an important role in the lives of tenants. For low- to moderate-income households (the vast majority of renters), housing has become a significant problem over the past decade. During the late 1970s and early 1980s, rents increased more rapidly than tenants' incomes, resulting in shelter poverty, overcrowding, displacement, psychological problems, and (for some) homelessness.

High rents may also make it harder for renters to buy a home because they make it difficult for tenants to save enough money for a down payment and because rising rents have been associated with even more rapidly rising home prices and interest rates. Even middle-class renters have come to feel that homeownership, under present economic conditions, is no longer a realistic possibility. For such renters, this spells serious short- and long-term economic loss. Homeownership affords considerable income tax savings as well as substantial equity appreciation and thus has traditionally served as the principal long-term form of investment for retirement. Moreover, security of tenure is more tenuous for a renter than a homeowner.

Earlier, we reviewed much of the sociological literature showing how housing impacts patterns of behavior. Housing affects economic, social, and political relationships. It is a deep aspect of social status, and it is a symbol of self. The economic literature, on the other hand, has generally concerned itself with treating housing as a dependent variable, for example, predicting rents through hedonic price equations. If sociologists have ignored the economic factors in housing market operation, economists have ignored the institutional factors. It is this imbalance that we seek to address in the chapters that follow.

CHAPTER 3

WHY RENTS RISE

WITH ZHENFENG PAN, TOM LEHMAN, STEPHEN A. ROOSA, AND RICHARD P. APPELBAUM

In this chapter we will explore the factors that help to determine rents across U.S. cities, an issue that has long been a topic of controversy. A comprehensive theory of urban rent that integrates the insights of sociology with economics has not been developed. In a previous study, my colleague Richard Appelbaum and I attempted to formulate a more dynamic, nuanced, sociological theory that moves beyond the rudimentary supply-and-demand theory, which fails to explain contemporary rental housing rates. The key theoretical arguments were: first, exogenous supply factors play little role in the determination of rents; and second, institutional factors such as the level of professionalization and the market concentration of landlords in urban rental markets play a larger role in determining rents than previously thought (Gilderbloom and Appelbaum 1988). We build and revise on that study in the section of this chapter called "Challenging Mainstream Economic Rental Market Theory."

The limitation of our theory is that it was based on 1970 and 1980 data. In this chapter we update and elaborate on that earlier work by doing an analysis of 1990 and 2000 data with an expanded sample size. While the methodology used previously was sound, two questions are unclear: Does the theory remain valid in the period from the 1980s to the year 2000? If it does hold, how might the theory manifest itself in the broader U.S. rental housing market? In this chapter, we intend to fulfill three goals: (1) produce a modified replication of our 1988 study using 1990 and 2000 U.S. Census data with an expanded sample of cities; (2) include additional variables that might improve the explanatory power of the original model; and (3) test to determine if the theory still holds in the larger rental housing market using recent data.

LITERATURE REVIEW: WHY RENTS VARY AMONG CITIES

Conventional housing theory stresses that rental vacancy rates are the best single predictor of overall rent levels. This dominant paradigm has its roots in traditional economic theory (Belsky and Goodman 1996; Beyer 1966; Blank and Winnick 1953; Ferguson and Maurice 1974; Gabriel and Nothaft 1988; Grigsby 1973; Igarashi 1991; Malpezzi 1996; Olsen 1973; Pennance 1969; Rosen 1996; Rosen and Smith 1983; Smith 1973).

The economic theory of supply and demand suggests that there is a relationship between the price of housing and construction costs. Prices in the local market are a direct reflection of the relationship between supply and demand. If the supply is large relative to demand, the price of dwelling units (including rents) tends to be lower. Conversely, if the demand is large relative to supply, house prices tend to be higher. For older houses, current price levels are more important than cost of construction. The most common measures of the degree of balance between supply and demand, both quantitatively and qualitatively, are the number and type of dwelling units that are vacant and available.

Wherever the vacancy rate is below 5 percent, housing shortages exist. Low vacancy may be a result of demand exceeding supply, causing rents to be "excessively" high (Belsky 1992; Capek and Gilderbloom 1992; Lett 1976). On the other hand, when the vacancy rate is above 5 percent, the market is assumed to be competitive. Courts have generally ruled that a "housing emergency" allowing for rent controls can exist only when a municipality's vacancy rate falls below 5 percent. John Weicher (1990), who at the time was assistant secretary for policy development and research at HUD, argued that a 7 percent rental vacancy rate provided an ample amount of competition.

A more elaborate explanation of the central role of vacancy rates in impacting rental housing markets can be found in "filtering" theory. This theory argues that rental housing costs fall if new housing is added at the "high end of the spectrum" (Mandelker and Montgomery 1973, 225). This causes the supply of rental housing to increase, thereby lowering costs (Gordon 1977, 465) as high-income renters vacate their old housing for newer residences, in turn easing supply and demand on the lower rental market units (Beyer 1958, 45). According to filtering theory, new rental construction benefits everyone, even if it is directed at the wealthy. The end result is a larger supply of rental housing, higher vacancy rates, and consequently lower rent levels (Olsen 1973).

Historically, there has been little research concerning the impact of supply on rents. In an exhaustive review of empirical work on the determinants of rent prices, Michael Ball (1973, 231) concluded that "researchers have ignored supply factors (the principal problems being a total absence of data and the difficulty of fitting meaningful supply equations) . . . [and consequently this] can generate serious biases in the coefficients, and differences in supply between cities make inter-city comparison very difficult."

For more than twenty years, new waves of studies have been produced to better understand inter-city rent variations. These include studies by both economists (Belsky and Goodman 1996; Gabriel and Nothaft 1988; Igarashi 1991; Malpezzi 1996; Rosen 1996; Rosen and Smith 1983) and sociologists (Appelbaum and Gilderbloom 1983; Dreier et al. 1991; Gilderbloom 1985, 1989; Gilderbloom and Appelbaum 1987, 1988; Gilderbloom et al. 1992).

Rosen and Smith (1983, 783) found that on average a "natural" vacancy rate of 9.8 percent is the rate when the supply and demand for rental housing is in equilibrium, causing no upward or downward pressure on rent prices. They argued in a cross-sectional analysis that the natural vacancy rate ranges from 5.5 percent in Cleveland to 16.7 percent in Dallas. They reported that an analysis of vacancy rates must consider variables such as population, housing growth, mobility, and rent variations. The chief problem with this analysis was that only fourteen cities were examined and only four variables were used as controls, resulting in an adjusted R square of 0.55 (only a modest explanation of variance). Several refinements have been made in exploring the "natural vacancy rates," yet these studies also use a small sample of cities and a limited number of control variables (Belsky 1992; Gabriel and Nothaft 1988).

Sociologists such as Richard Appelbaum and I have attempted to build a model that empirically explains variations in rent across cities. In our book *Rethinking Rental Housing* (1988), statistical regression techniques were used on a sample of 144 U.S. metropolitan housing markets where vacancy rates were statistically significant when above 10 percent. Moreover, we found that a number of other variables can better predict why rents vary across cities, such as city size, new rental construction, homeownership costs, income, and population growth. Unfortunately, economists, with one exception (Igarashi 1991), have ignored this work.

CHALLENGING MAINSTREAM ECONOMIC RENTAL MARKET THEORY

Economic assumptions of the rental housing market that were rarely challenged in the past have come under attack on both theoretical and empirical grounds in recent years (Appelbaum and Glasser 1982; Cherry and Ford 1975;

Cronin 1983; Feagin 1983; Gilderbloom and Appelbaum 1988; Linson 1978; Mollenkopf and Pynoos 1973; Vaughan 1972). Squires (1981, 756) argued that conventional supply-and-demand models omit sociological factors that could interfere with the workings of the idealized market. In other words, social organizing of landlords, banks, developers, and government creates a persuasive interference in the modern rental housing market.

Olsen's (1973) work has been widely cited by other theorists for laying out the basic assumptions of the competitive housing market (for example, Lett 1976, 31; Solomon and Vandell 1982; Stegman and Sumka 1976, 117). Olsen (1973, 228–229) lists the following conditions as necessary for perfect competition to occur:

- Both buyers and sellers of housing service are numerous.
- Neither buyers nor sellers collude.
- Entry into and exit from the market are free for both producers and consumers.
- Both producers and consumers possess perfect knowledge about the prevailing price and current bids, and they take advantage of every opportunity to increase profits and utility respectively.
- No artificial restrictions are placed on demands for, supplies of, and prices of housing service and the resources used to produce housing service.
- Housing service is a homogeneous commodity.
- The sales or purchases of each individual unit are small in relation to the aggregate volume of transactions.

As Olsen himself points out, these conditions are seldom fully realized in most housing markets (229). In Gilderbloom and Appelbaum (1988, 57–66) we provide a detailed critique of these assumptions, countering each with research from case studies. For example, we show a growing concentration of ownership in rental housing and show that a growing proportion of rental housing is controlled by management companies that determine rent levels in a quasi-monopolistic fashion. Moreover, housing is an essential need that most persons cannot do without, and paying rent that can be beyond a person's means causes shelter poverty. Finally, zoning, historic preservation, environmental protections, and planning and architectural rules can limit the amount of housing built in a city. These real-world departures are likely to cause rents to increase. This raises questions: Is the rental housing market free? Can a supply-based strategy work in the imperfect world of rental housing markets? The rest of this chapter empirically explores these critical questions.

DATA AND METHODOLOGY

The data used for the present study were obtained from the 1990 and 2000 U.S. Census Bureau national file. The sample of cities used for this study contains all urban places with a population of at least 50,000. The 1990 data set has 555 locales in the United States that met this criterion. The 2000 data set has 672 locales that met this criterion, compared to the 110 to 112 cities used in our earlier analysis (Gilderbloom and Appelbaum 1988).

Table 3.1 lists the variables included in the eight regression models developed for this chapter. Median rent (listed in the first row of each model) is the dependent variable (DV). Additionally, the independent variables are listed along with their mean values and standard deviations for both the 1990 and 2000 data sets. Finally, the last column indicates the expected direction of impact (+/–) between each of the independent variables and median rent levels across the cities included in the sample. The expected direction of impact is based upon theoretical assumptions about the causal relationships among rental housing market variables, as well as findings in the research previously cited.[1]

Dependent Variable

Median rent: This variable measures the monthly median rent price per city. We are looking for the effect of the remaining independent variables in predicting median rent.

Independent Variables

Median house value (cost): This variable is the actual median house cost within each city. The values range from a low of $29,300 to a high of $350,800, with a standard deviation of $40,131. This variable is thought to be a significant indicator of the demand for rental housing. The price of homeownership reflected in median house cost should theoretically shift the demand for rental housing and exhibit a positive relationship with rent prices. As the price of homeownership rises, as reflected in median house cost, the demand for rental housing should rise, pushing up rental prices in the process, all else held constant. Likewise, as the cost of homeownership reflected in median house cost falls, the demand for renting should fall, pushing rent prices down, *ceteris paribus.* As expected, this variable was found to have a strong statistically significant positive correlation to rent prices in the previous study using 1980 data.

TABLE 3.1. *Factors Affecting Median Monthly Rent Across a Sample of Cities, 1990 and 2000*

Variables	1990 Data	2000 Data	Expected Correlation
Median rent (DV) (in dollars)	508.29 (149.56)	673.92 (189.37)	—
Median house cost (in dollars)	115,738 (78,144)	117,632 (71,677)	+
Vacancy rate (%)	7.05 (3.54)	6.76 (3.72)	–
Region in U.S. (South)	0.36 (0.37)	0.37 (0.48)	–
% units lacking plumbing	0.55 (0.55)	0.81 (0.71)	–
% housing rental	14.68 (10.5)	6.51 (4.16)	?
Total urban population	159,396 (392,065)	157,262 (389,731)	+
% rentals created previous five years	11.78 (10.24)	6.71 (6.74)	?
% nonwhite	23.64 (17.92)	30.6 (18.7)	?
Professionalization I (% 10 or more rentals at a single address)	35.14 (13.36)	36.04 (13.61)	+
Professionalization II (% 50 or more rentals at a single address)	10.89 (7.96)	15.19 (8.41)	+
Median family income (in dollars)	31,971 (10,329)	44,534 (14,589)	+
% rentals built before 1950 and 1960	23.55 (18.71)	29.85 (19.72)	+
% medium-old rentals built 1950–1970 and 1960–1980	33.79 (12.84)	15.63 (6.33)	–
% unemployment rate	6.51 (7.91)	6.41 (2.95)	–
% rents that include utilities	12.86 (8.95)	13.80 (7.9)	+
% unmarried same-sex adults residing in homes		7.57 (8.97)	?

NOTE: The mean for each variable is listed first in each cell, followed by the standard deviation in parentheses.

Percentage vacancy rate: This variable is defined as the percentage of rental units in each city that were vacant in the previous year. The rental vacancy rate for the 164 cities ranged from 0 percent to 7.4 percent, with a mean of approximately 0.09 percent and a standard deviation of 0.59 percent. Vacancy rate is thought to predict both supply and demand conditions in rental housing markets. When the vacancy rate is low, rents are expected to be high, and higher vacancy rates should predict lower rents. However, this variable was not found to be significantly related to rent prices in the previous study, and the sign of the coefficient was in the positive direction, opposite the expected direction. Thus, rental vacancy rates may be a poor indicator of supply and demand conditions in rental markets when other factors are held constant.

Region in United States (South): This is a regional dummy variable with the reference category coded for the South census region of the United States. Regional differences were found to affect rent prices in the 1980 data, with southern cities exhibiting lower rents than other regions. This variable is included here to test for the continuation of this pattern in the 1990 data, and we would expect a negative sign on the coefficient for this dummy variable.

Percentage housing rental: This variable is defined as the percentage of total housing stock within the city that is classified as rental housing at the time the data were collected.

Total urban population: This variable measures the total population of the urban area. This variable is traditionally thought to be a good indicator of demand. Cities with a relatively large population, all else constant, should theoretically exhibit higher rental prices resulting from a larger number of buyers. Cities with a relatively small population, all else constant, should theoretically exhibit lower rental prices resulting from fewer buyers. Larger places may offer more amenities or advantages than smaller places, resulting in a greater demand for the former and, consequently, higher rents. We would anticipate a positive correlation between population level and rent prices. However, our prior study using 1980 data revealed that urban population levels are not significantly correlated with rent prices when controlling for other supply and demand variables. The average population of the cities included in the present study was 183,828, with a standard deviation of 204,045.

Percentage rentals created in previous five years: This variable is defined as the percentage of new rental housing stock created during the five years immediately prior to the collection of the census data (i.e., the 1990 data reflects the percentage of rental stock created from 1985 to 1990).

Percentage of nonwhites: This variable measures the percentage of non-white residents in the urban area. Two conflicting theories regarding this variable make it difficult to predict the direction of the expected relationship to rent prices. If nonwhites tend to have lower incomes than whites, all else held constant, then the effective demand for rental housing could be expected to be lower in cities with a higher proportion of nonwhites.

Also, if nonwhites tend to dominate a given area, the demand for housing among whites may fall as a result of fear of and discrimination against nonwhites, also leading to lower rent prices in cities with a higher proportion of nonwhites. Both of these factors could lead to a negative correlation between the proportion of nonwhites and median rent prices. On the other hand, discrimination by whites may cause nonwhites to pay higher rents for equivalent housing if white landlords selectively charge nonwhite tenants more for equal accommodations. Further, nonwhites may have a higher propensity to rent if they, as a group, are more mobile and less prone to homeownership or if discrimination in homeownership against nonwhites forces them to rent rather than own. This would drive up the demand for renting among nonwhites. Either of these factors could drive rents higher in cities with a higher proportion of nonwhites, leading to a positive correlation between these variables. The cities in the current study ranged from a low of 1 percent to a high of 74 percent nonwhite population, with a mean of 25 percent and a standard deviation of 16 percent.

Landlord professionalization: As our previous study argued, the level of professionalization of landlords may be an institutional factor having a strong influence on median rents across cities if professional landlords exhibit pricing strategies that are fundamentally different than amateur landlords. Subsequently, if landlord professionalization measures are a proxy for the market concentration and market power of landlords in urban areas, then we would expect cities with a higher proportion of professionalized landlords to exhibit higher median rents, all else held constant. Richard Appelbaum and I operationalized this concept using two separate variables: (1) the percentage of ten or more rental units at a single address and (2) the percentage of fifty or more rental units at a single address as a proportion of all rental properties located in the city. These variables are an attempt to measure the degree to which cities are dominated by professional large-scale landlords as opposed to amateur small-scale landlords, ultimately serving as a proxy for market concentration and market power of landlords in driving up rent prices. In our previous study using the 1980 data, we found a statistically significant positive relationship between these measures of landlord professionalization and median rent prices, confirming our argument that professional landlords pursue pricing strategies that are different from those of their amateur counterparts. Landlord professionalization is an institutional factor that provides market power to large-scale landlords in controlling rent levels in urban areas. These same two variables are included in the present study using the 1990 data in order to be consistent with the replication of our previous work.

Median family income: Income is a critical determinant of housing demand, and the expected relationship between income and median rent is positive. As median family income rises across cities, we expect increasing demand for rental housing to be reflected in higher median rents, all else held constant. Our previous study suggests that rental housing, in general, cannot be classified as an inferior good. Our study also found a statistically significant positive relationship between median family income and median rent, indicating that cities with higher median family income have higher median rents, all else held constant. In the cities included in the 1990 data, median family income ranged from a low of $15,315 to a high of $75,221, with a mean of approximately $25,864.

Decennial population growth rate: This variable measures the percentage of growth in city population over the decade prior to the collection of census data (i.e., the growth rate in the city population from 1980 to 1990 for data taken in 1990).[2]

Percentage of old rentals: This variable is defined as the percentage of rental units that were constructed forty or more years prior to the year of the study. The percentage of older units is rising despite new construction because of trends toward rehab, gentrification, and historic districts.

Percentage units lacking plumbing: The percentage of rental units lacking plumbing in each city is presented.

Quality of rental stock: The quality of rental stock is measured by the two previous variables: (1) the percentage of rental housing built forty years prior to the year of investigation in each city and (2) the percentage of rental units lacking plumbing in each city. If older and lower-quality rental units rent for lower prices, we would expect cities with a higher proportion of older and lower-quality rental units to exhibit lower median rents, suggesting an expected negative correlation between these variables. This was in fact the observed relationship revealed in our previous study using the 1980 data. In that study, the proportion of rentals built forty years prior (before 1940) was negatively correlated with median rent prices. However, a surprising finding was that the proportion of rental units lacking plumbing was positively and statistically significantly related to rent prices. Thus, the expected direction of the coefficients for these variables in the 1990 data was indeterminate. If older and lower-quality housing tends to have lower rent levels due to obsolescence and deterioration, all else constant, then we would expect a negative correlation. However, if older units are remodeled and refinished, the remodeling costs and added appeal of the refinished rental units could drive rents up, suggesting a positive correlation. The percentage of rental units lacking plumbing in the 1990 data ranges from 0 percent–4 percent, with a mean of roughly 0.6 percent and a standard deviation of 0.4 percent. The percentage of rental units built before 1950 in the 1990 data ranges from a low of 4 percent to a high of 74 percent, with a mean of 29 percent and a standard deviation of roughly 17 percent.

New Variables

In our recent study, we have added four new variables to the original model we used in 1988. These new variables are: (1) percentage of medium-old rentals; (2) unemployment rate of the select city; (3) percent of tenants who do not have to pay extra for the utilities of the rented unit; and (4) percent of unmarried same-sex adults residing in homes. The reason for the addition of the percentage of medium-old rental housing variable is that a regression analysis revealed a curvilinear relationship between rent price and age of rental housing. Unemployment rate has an impact on rental rates and is also an indicator of the regional economy. Understandably, those who have utilities included in rent may have different total housing costs than those who do not have utilities included in their rent costs.[3] The percentage of unmarried same-sex adults residing in homes will, we believe, have a positive correlation with rent price because both members will likely be employed, and they will be able to afford higher rent.

Percentage of medium-old housing (1950 to 1979): This variable is defined as the percentage of rental housing stock built between 1950 and 1979 in the city. This variable is created on the premise that housing built prior to 1950 could go through renovations forty years after it was built. As years go by, the number of old housing units increases, and they begin to be remodeled and renovated. Renovation and remodeling of rental units could drive up the price of rent in two ways. First, the costs of renovation could be passed on to new tenants in the form of higher rent prices. After all, landlords must expect to recover their costs as an inducement to remodel and renovate units. Second, a renovated and refinished unit is likely to be much more attractive to potential tenants, thereby driving up the demand and thus the price of rent for a remodeled unit. Based upon these assumptions, we would expect to see a positive correlation between the percentage of older housing (built before 1950) and median rent, due to remodeling. This is a finding opposite of what we found in our previous research using the 1980 data. The inclusion of the medium-old housing (built between 1950 and 1979) variable is designed to show that older rental housing commands lower rents, provided it has not been renovated. Including the percentage of rental housing built between 1950 and 1979, in addition to the percentage of rental housing built before 1950, is an attempt to capture older housing that has not been renovated. Based upon these assumptions, we would expect a negative correlation between the percentage of medium-old rental housing and median rent. The percentage of medium-old rental housing across the cities in our study ranges from a low of 22 percent to a high of 75 percent, with a mean of roughly 51 percent and a standard deviation of 10 percent.

Unemployment rate: This variable is a measure of the rate of unemployment in each urban area.

Percentage of renters paying utilities in monthly rent payment: This variable is included to test the assumption that renters who pay utility bills separately from their rent payments will tend to pay lower rents than renters who pay a rent payment that includes all their utilities. The assumption is that renters who pay one or more of their utility bills are likely to pay lower rents than those who pay no utility bills, since renters in the latter category are likely to pay a higher rent to cover the costs of utilities to their landlords. We would therefore expect a positive correlation between this variable and median rent: cities with a larger percentage of renters paying a monthly rent that includes utilities should, all else held constant, pay higher rent prices, and vice versa. The mean for this variable across all the cities in the study is 14 percent, with a standard deviation of approximately 8 percent.

Percentage same-sex unmarried adults: This variable is included due to the importance attached to alternative lifestyles and the popularity of research emphasizing the need for a diverse workforce (Florida 2002, 255–258). First available in the 2000 U.S. Census data, the percentage of unmarried same-sex adults residing in a home allows testing of an alternative theory: as it is likely that both of the partners in gay couples are employed, their combined earnings may be greater, resulting in the ability to afford higher rents. As a result, they may influence area rents upward. However, the proportion of unmarried same-sex adults sharing homes who are actually gay is unknown.

FINDINGS

Complete regression results for all eight of the models are listed in Tables 3.2 and 3.3. Because of collinearity problems between the two key landlord professionalization variables, we chose to enter these variables into the models separately in Tables 3.2 and 3.3.[4] In this study, we first tested our original models and then retested the models with the addition of several new variables.

Comparing Tables 3.2 and 3.3 to our 1988 findings, there are similarities

TABLE 3.2. *Factors Affecting 1990 Median Monthly Rent Across All Cities of Population 50,000 or More*

Variables	Model 1	Model 2	Model 3	Model 4
Median house value (1990 dollars)	0.66*** (0.0013)	—	0.65*** (0.0012)	—
Vacancy rate (1990)	-0.02 (-1.04)	-0.03 (-1.16)	-0.03 (-1.27)	-0.03 (-1.16)
Region in U.S. (South)	-0.03 (-10.35)	-0.10*** (-38.80)	-0.02 (-8.92)	0.10*** (-38.80)
% units lacking plumbing (1990)	-0.01 (-0.29)	0.03 (9.21)	0.04 (10.10)	0.03 (9.21)
% housing rental (1990)	-0.07*** (-0.90)	0.11** (1.56)	-0.08*** (-0.99)	0.11*** (1.56)
Total urban population (1990)	-0.01 (-0.0000)	-0.03 (-0.0000)	-0.02 (-0.0000)	-0.03 (-0.0000)
% rental created 1985–1990	0.13*** (1.90)	0.16 (2.36)	0.13*** (1.96)	0.16*** (2.36)
% nonwhite (1990)	0.05*** (0.46)	0.12*** (1.00)	0.06*** (0.49)	0.12*** (1.00)
Professionalization I (% 10 or more rentals at a single address 1990)	-0.02 (-0.20)	0.12*** (2.25)	—	—
Professionalization II (% 50 or more rentals at a single address 1990)	—	—	0.02 (0.33)	0.12*** (2.25)
Median household income (1989 dollars)	0.26*** (0.0000)	0.65*** (0.01)	0.25*** (0.0037)	0.65*** (0.0092)
% rentals built before 1950	-0.08*** (-0.63)	—	-0.07*** (-0.56)	—
% medium–aged rentals, built 1950–1970	—	0.11*** (1.25)	—	0.11*** (1.25)
% unemployment rate	—	-0.004 (-0.08)	—	-0.004 (-0.08)
% renters paying utilities in monthly rent payment	—	-0.10*** (-1.63)	—	-0.12*** (-1.63)
Adjusted R Square	0.84	0.61	0.84	0.62
F	259.35	70.689	259.473	75.699
N	555	555	555	555

* Sig. ≤ .10   ** Sig. ≤ .05   *** Sig. ≤ .01

NOTE: Standardized regression coefficients are presented first; unstandardized regression coefficients follow in parentheses.

TABLE 3.3. *Factors Affecting 2000 Median Monthly Rent Across All Cities of Population 50,000 or More*

Variables	Model 1	Model 2	Model 3	Model 4
Median house value (2000 dollars)	0.42*** (.0011)	0.69*** (.0018)	0.41*** (0.0013)	0.67*** (0.0018)
Vacancy rate (2000)	−0.17*** (−8.89)	−0.13*** (−7.76)	−0.19*** (11.02)	−0.14*** (−8.09)
Region in U.S. (South)	−0.05*** (−18.95)	−0.06*** (−23.83)	−0.05*** (−21.00)	−0.08*** (−29.62)
% units lacking plumbing (2000)	−0.04*** (−11.00)	−0.05** (−12.47)	−0.04*** (−11.95)	−0.05*** (−13.33)
% housing rental (2000)	0.11*** (5.12)	0.01 (0.27)	0.11*** (5.07)	0.002 (0.09)
Total urban population (2000)	0.00 (0.0000)	−0.02 (−0.0000)	−0.01 (−0.0000)	−0.03** (−0.00002)
% rental created 1995–2000	0.05*** (1.43)	0.11*** (3.04)	0.06*** (1.75)	0.12*** (3.23)
% nonwhite (2000)	0.16*** (1.57)	0.22*** (2.20)	0.15*** (1.55)	0.20*** (2.05)
Professionalization I (% 10 or more rentals at a single address 2000)	0.01 (0.09)	0.04** (0.54)	—	—
Professionalization II (% 50 or more rentals at a single address 2000)	—	—	0.05*** (1.18)	0.12*** (2.76)
Median household income (1999 dollars)	0.52*** (0.01)	—	0.50*** (0.0065)	—
% rentals built before 1960	−0.10 (−0.95)	—	−0.09*** (−0.87)	—
% medium–aged rentals built 1960–1970	—	−0.11*** (−3.303)	—	−0.10*** (−3.12)
% unemployment rate	—	−0.22*** (−0.14)	—	−0.20*** (−0.13)
% renters paying utilities in monthly rent payment	—	−0.07*** (−1.77)	—	−0.09*** (−2.08)
% same–sex unmarried partners	—	0.03* (0.63)	—	0.03** (0.68)
Adjusted R Square	0.89	0.81	0.89	0.83
F	475.098	226.555	486.071	245.706
N	672	672	672	672

* Sig. ≤ .10   ** Sig. ≤ .05   *** Sig. ≤ .01
NOTE: Standardized regression coefficients are presented first; non–standardized regression coefficients are in parentheses.

and important differences. Among the similarities, our analysis not only re-confirms the predicting power of most of the variables in the larger housing market but also provides support for their theoretical argument; despite conventional supply/demand economic theory, rental vacancy rates rarely matter in lowering rent prices in the rental market, older and lower-quality rental housing stock dampens rental prices, and rental landlord profession-alization tends to increase inter-city rent prices due to the landlords' ability to stay profitable while keeping a reasonable vacancy rate.

However, our analyses in the larger rental housing market (based on the new data in 1990 and 2000) suggest important differences from our initial theory. First, variables such as median house value and median household income became the dominant factors affecting rental prices in the 1990s and 2000 (based on the unusually large Beta coefficients). Second, landlord professionalization, which was significant in the 1970 and 1980 models, is statistically significant only after the dominating effects of either median house value or median household income is removed from the model. Third, the percentage of old housing as we had originally defined it needs refine-ment. As shown in the models, the percentage of median-age old housing is statistically significant in lowering the rent. Combined with our analyses of isolated markets (results not shown in this study), the findings suggest that the relationship between rent price and age of rental housing is curvilinear. Very old rental housing stock actually increases the rent prices. This may be due to renovation, which may command a higher price as a result of the need to recapture the renovation costs. Similarly, the increased supply of newer rental units actually increases the price of rents, due to the pressure to re-capture the cost of construction. Fourth, rental vacancy became significant in 2000, although the impact is relatively small. It was possible to conjec-ture that in the year 2000 in the larger housing market, the rental housing market reached equilibrium and rental vacancy rates became a factor in af-fecting rent price.

Consider the newly added variables in our analyses. Unemployment rates are a negative predictor of inter-city rent prices. The increase in the percent-age of those who pay extra for utilities tends to lower contract rents, since renters' utilities are not included in the rent price. Interestingly, our analy-sis empirically confirmed (using the percent of unmarried same-sex adults residing in home variable) Florida's (2002) argument that since gay and les-bian couples tend to earn more household income, they can afford higher rent prices. The percentage of unmarried same-sex adults residing in rental units, as a proxy indicator of gay couples, tends to increase inter-city rent prices.

HOUSING VOUCHERS: GOOD OR BAD FOR TENANTS?

The strong positive relationship between income and rent also signals trouble for the one remaining federal housing policy program aimed at the poor: vouchers. Do vouchers really help tenants? For those who get them, the answer is yes, but it also hurts the majority of the renters who qualify for them but cannot get them. Research by economists and sociologists shows it to be a wash. On the surface, it seems to help renters, but in reality it might be hurting tenants, and it might be one of those pork-barrel subsidies to landlords who do not need it. Current estimates indicate that one out of every four persons who qualifies for vouchers gets them. Two million people currently receive vouchers for subsidized housing. The Bush administration's budget cuts this number by 40 percent starting in 2007, directly affecting 800,000 people (Lake 2005). Proposed regulatory changes will further erode shelter support for the lowest-income segment of the population. These changes reflect the Bush administration's continuing policy to eliminate federal spending for the only remaining federal housing affordability program.

The question is whether vouchers as a subsidy for landlords can help or hurt tenants. Hartman (2002, 260) says, "What is known of the housing market and how suppliers operate under the profit system, it is hard to maintain that a substantial amount of this federal housing subsidy would not, absent government controls on the market (anathema to housing allowance advocates), wind up lining landlords' pockets." My interviews with the biggest and richest landlords in Louisville and southern Indiana confirmed this as fact—vouchers turn poor landlords into rich ones and rich landlords into millionaires. As we showed earlier in this chapter, there is a direct relationship between income and rents, with landlords capturing a significant percentage of the additional income when income rises in a city.

What is astonishing is how very few solid empirical studies have been conducted examining a housing program that is a key federal initiative and costs taxpayers billions of dollars. Chester Hartman's exhaustive review of vouchers in the United States concludes that "in short, there is no reason to believe that housing allowances will work" (Hartman 2002, 261). The one major study on vouchers was carried out more than twenty-five years ago in Green Bay, Wisconsin, and South Bend, Indiana (Stegman 1981; Struyk and Bendick 1981). These small Midwestern cities with frigid winters are hardly typical of robust housing markets and were not then representative of typical housing markets—both were going through deindustrialization at the time, which might have caused rents not to increase as much as in other places.

These cities, for many people, are not desirable places to live—especially Green Bay, with a climate that is colder than that of Anchorage, Alaska. This experiment of housing vouchers, done over a three-year period, showed only a small benefit to tenants in the program (Hartman 2003). On a more massive scale, economists see vouchers as creating "large rent increases."

> Both the Urban Institute and National Bureau of Economic Research simulations indicated that a full-scale ear-marked allowance program might cause significant rent increases for both recipients and non-recipients, and the bureau simulations pointed out that such a program might trigger large price declines and extensive abandonment in the worst neighborhoods. (Bradbury and Downs 1981, 358–359)

This finding is given further support by our research in this chapter on rents and income looking at 1990 and 2000 data on more than 500 cities.

The most powerful predictor of high rents is high incomes. Earlier we showed that landlords set rents based on income. The correlation is powerful and explains the significant inter-city rent differentials between Los Angeles and Louisville. Thus if incomes are inflated, landlords can charge higher rent, and rents are raised for most who do not get the subsidy. For every one tenant who is helped, an equal number or more will face higher rents as a result. If subsidies were completely eliminated, landlords would respond by stabilizing rents for all tenants. That is how incomes impact rents around the nation.

Vouchers are also used as a carrot to get tenants groups away from thinking about other ways to address the housing crisis, such as the rent regulation or social housing programs of Netherlands, Sweden, and Finland (Gilderbloom and Appelbaum 1988). The voucher paradigm unconditionally accepts the housing market as it is, and this is why so many landlord and real estate groups support vouchers along with the affordable housing community. It is never a sacrifice for landlords, just a big fat subsidy. Imagine that Bush cut off all subsidies tomorrow. Town meetings across this country would be talking about how best to meet the housing crisis and coming up with programs far more progressive and efficient than the voucher program. How ironic that affordable housing groups focus on a program that does so little for so very few.

In an era when taxpayers want greater accountability for how their money is spent, we need to sift out the good programs from the bad ones. The evidence is shaky over whether housing vouchers are good for tenants as a whole: Do they help tenants? Are they wasteful? Are there better programs that cost taxpayers less money? What about accountability? Do vouchers cause landlords to raise rents on tenants without them? How much do landlords profit from vouchers? Do landlords need this kind of subsidy? Who gets the subsidy and for how long? Does the program give a hand up from the participants' circumstances or a handout without any conditions?

Another issue is that with deficits at record levels, Congress appears to be cutting vouchers rather than increasing them. Currently, we have 2 million renters who are getting vouchers, and a proposal in Congress would cut the number to 1.2 million. Yet current estimates say that we need at least 8 million vouchers, if not more. So how politically feasible is this strategy? My guess is that vouchers will never happen on a large scale because Congress cannot afford them, and their proven worth as a professional housing alternative is questionable.

Given the discussion here and elsewhere, nobody has shown that vouchers work well or that they are the best kind of housing strategy for the United States to embrace. In the real world, it helps a little for a small fraction of needy tenants. Vouchers are based on supply-and-demand assumptions. Sociological analysis of rental housing markets dates from the work of Louis Wirth (1947), who called for greater investigation of housing markets. The conventional assumptions of housing supply and demand could not be proven on an empirical basis. Supply solutions like building new housing meant higher rents because older, more affordable housing was removed—new housing cannot be built for the price of old housing. Vacancy rate levels had no impact on rent levels. Similarly, on the demand side, incomes were shown to be positively correlated with rents.

There are other problems with the subsidy that are not being addressed. Presently, the only requirement to maintain a voucher is staying poor. Perhaps if greater work and educational requirements were made, elected leaders might find this program more appealing. Moreover, vouchers might be more attractive if they were aimed at the people who need short-term assistance immediately, such as those suffering from a recent injury or the loss of a job.

Vouchers are simply a handout instead of a hand up when they ask recipients to do nothing. Yet affordable housing advocates lack the political savvy to attach educational and job requirements. In today's climate, it is politically unrealistic not to demand some kind of educational or work training as part of the voucher program. Our elected leaders might be more sympathetic and supportive if this was done.

Affordable housing advocates are irresponsible when they oppose educational and job requirements. We require children to go to school. Are we against that as well? People getting vouchers are required to keep their premises drug- and gun-free, take out the garbage, and keep the porch areas neat. Are we against these rules as well? Two of the greatest joys in life are learning and working; hence, two of the most depressing situations are not having an education and not having a job. Should the government try to make incentives for folks to get out of voucher land and into the real world? For the past fifteen years, we have been at ground zero in terms of welfare reform (conducting research and social programs in public housing) and have seen with our own eyes how work and educational incentives brought folks from a funk to a fuller life (Gilderbloom and Mullins 2005). The people who take the first step by receiving job training or going back to school make their neighborhoods better places and serve as role models to others so many can follow in their footsteps. If people are given assistance, they must understand that the help does not last forever and that there are plenty of others waiting for help. For those who are fit enough to go to work or go back to school, why isn't there an action plan to lift them out of their situations so that the others who need help can be assisted?

Conventional housing theory is impoverished. We promote programs like housing vouchers on the mistaken belief that supply-and-demand forces are at work in the rental market. The housing industry loves vouchers. It does not challenge private interests but instead enriches them. Vouchers are undergoing a slow death. We need to come up with ideas, programs that work for tenants first that are efficient, responsible, and reasonable. Vouchers don't do it as housing policy.

POLICY IMPLICATIONS

Creating and maintaining affordable housing in any U.S. city is a perplexing and challenging problem. In order to accomplish this, it is essential that we know which factors create or discourage affordable housing. This study strongly reinforces our previous propositions (1988) and finds that they are generally true for all urban areas in the United States.

Most U.S. urban housing policies are structured on the common myth that a "housing crisis" is due to an inadequate number of housing units. If enough additional housing is created and brought to market, vacancy rates will increase, the price of rent will drop, and ample affordable housing will be available. The greater the housing supply, the lower the rents, the larger the market of available housing, and the more competitive the urban area will be in attracting new growth. In addition, newer housing stock is always preferable to older housing stock. It is believed that by eliminating older housing stock and replacing it with newer housing stock (even if for high income earners), housing will cease to be problematic.

Our research suggests that this approach fails the test of empirical evaluation. Despite well-meaning intentions, policies resulting from such views are often themselves problematic. In addition to consistent failure to resolve the most critical housing issues, these policies often waste public and private resources and cause public funding to be misdirected and only belatedly focused on the problems they helped create.

Our analysis suggests that vacancy rates are significant in the 2000 data (Table 3.3) and influence rental prices. Given the fact that vacancies exist, it can be postulated that housing supplies are in fact adequate and that other forces are preventing housing from being used. One such factor is the affordability of existing housing stock. Newer housing stock tends to greatly exacerbate the affordability problem by pushing rental prices even higher.

What can planners and policy makers do to create more affordable housing? Since utility costs are a significant and growing component of total housing costs, planners might find ways to creatively increase the energy efficiency of new and existing housing stock. This might include incentives for energy-efficient design, installation of more efficient heating and cooling systems, and building envelope modifications. Planners can encourage the preservation and rehabilitation of older rental stock, improve existing housing affordability by moderating median home values, and avoid landlord professionalization. Older rental stock tends to be available at lower rental rates and tends to preserve existing neighborhoods and their amenities.

Policies can be implemented that encourage scattered-site housing, placing rental housing and condominiums in existing neighborhoods where utility infrastructure is available. Decentralizing ownership (by making smaller apartments and condominiums) is one approach that can help to combat the problem that professional landlords can afford to keep vacancy rates higher while maintaining higher rental prices. However, decentralizing ownership may be consistent with low-density development, thus exacerbating sprawl. Encouraging supply-side subsidies with the goal of producing a mixture of housing options for all income groups needs further study. Demand-side subsidies have been found to possibly benefit landlords more than tenants.

A sociological view of housing sheds new light on some of the simplistic assumptions of traditional economic analysis. Housing markets simply do not work according to traditional economic theory. Conventional housing analysis is incomplete because it ignores a number of critical variables that help explain variations in rental prices across cities. More importantly, housing policy prescriptions are flawed because they are based on a traditional economic theory that does not correspond to the reality of today's rental housing markets. An approach that combines sociological and economic explanations is more effective when trying to understand the sources of inter-city rent variations. If housing policies can be created utilizing sociological and economic views, they will improve dramatically. The next chapter looks at rent control, a popular tenant strategy to reduce rents.

CHAPTER 4

PROS AND CONS OF RENT CONTROL

WITH LIN YE

This chapter presents an overview of the impacts of modern rent control laws in the United States on landlords and tenants and on the supply, condition, and value of rental units. We will make clear that passage of a rent control law is not enough to ensure success. Renters need to have a strong grassroots organization in order to assure themselves of long-term success. Without a strong grassroots organization, rent control becomes only a symbolic response to the crisis, lacking any kind of substance. Most cities that have enacted rent control laws have been unsuccessful in lowering overall rents, due to the moderate nature of the regulations. The success of Santa Monica's strong rent control laws is the exception and not the rule.

Another major theme in this chapter is how public policy is manufactured and disseminated by organizations that have a major financial stake in a particular outcome. Urban policy analysis is not a neutral field of study carried out by dispassionate academics. It is dominated by hack researchers whose conclusions are determined by the client paying for the study. As we will show in this chapter, real estate–sponsored studies of urban housing policy are often riddled with questionable methodologies, inaccurate data analyses, and conclusions that are based more on ideology than fact. Some studies reviewed in this chapter are shown to be patently fraudulent. The dominance of real estate–sponsored studies in the urban arena is shocking and demonstrates the role that ideas have in determining public-policy outcomes. Even more surprising is how influential these studies are in compelling the media, politicians, and even academics to take positions on urban policy questions based on their biased and unmerited conclusions.

Most studies on rent control utilize economic models based on computer simulations or case studies. Literature that utilizes economic modeling has concluded that rent control lowers rents (Albon and Stafford 1990; Hubert 1993; Lewis and Muller 1992; Marks 1991). Other studies that have used economic modeling have found reductions in maintenance (Ho 1992) and increases in the rate of undesirable tenants (Miron 1990) under rent control ordinances.

A number of studies have examined the empirical results of rent control, but only in one city each. These studies examined the impact of rent control on cities in Canada (Fallis and Smith 1985; Marks 1984; Santerre 1986), as well as Santa Monica (Booher 1990; Capek and Gilderbloom 1992; Levine, Grigsby, and Heskin 1990), Los Angeles (Murray et al. 1991), San Francisco (Lima 1990), New York (Rapaport 1992), and Cambridge, Massachusetts (Navarro 1985). Other studies have examined the empirical effects of rent control, but with a small number of cases. These studies range from five cities in New York State (Vitaliano 1985) to twenty-six cities in New Jersey (Appelbaum and Gilderbloom 1990; Gilderbloom 1983, 1986). Still other literature critiques existing studies (Gilderbloom 1981; Gyourko 1990; Wolkoff 1990) or examines the impact of rent control on homelessness (Appelbaum et al. 1991; Gilderbloom et al. 1992; Lowry 1992; Quigley 1990; Tucker 1991). Finally, some literature has examined the impact of rent control on mobility (Strassman 1991), the arguments in support of rent control (Barnes 1989), and the quantitative importance of different aspects of rent control (Gupta and Rea 1984).

The battle over rent control is often over which study is right and which is wrong. Accurate information is difficult to come by because of the lack of support in both academic and government circles. Academic social science tends not to reward applied academic research. In an age of austerity, government prefers to get by cheaply and obtain its studies from industries. This is a conflict of interest that supports the interests of real estate profits and goes against the interests of the disadvantaged. If real estate organizations are allowed to frame, analyze, and define urban issues from their perspective, government will not be properly equipped to deal with the problems of homelessness, slum formation, unaffordable rents, abandonment, and arson for profit. Power is the ability to identify, frame, and define issues of social concern, and currently real estate organizations are in power. Government abandons its responsibility to the public when it depends almost exclusively on the work of industry analysts.

CONVENTIONAL ECONOMIC THEORY

The conventional wisdom on rent control suggests that rent regulation has an extremely adverse effect on local housing. Opponents argue that rent control interferes with landlords' ability to respond to market signals, thus reducing the profitability of rental investment, discouraging new construction, and encouraging under-maintenance, all of which eventually produce a deteriorated housing stock. If this were not bad enough, opponents also contend, apartments will increasingly be abandoned or converted to condominiums if rent control is imposed. Ironically, the short-term benefits to tenants will lead to a shrinking property tax base while pressuring landlords to disinvest. These benefits will lead to poorer-quality rental housing or conversion of units into condominiums, removing them from the rental market altogether.

Economists are well known for their opposition to rent control (see Alston, Kearl, and Vaughan 1992; Arnott 1995; Epple 1998; Kearl et al. 1979; Moon and Stotsky 1993). In their surveys of economists, Alston, Kearl, and Vaughan (1992, 204) found a consensus (over 93.5 percent) of agreement that "a ceiling on rents reduces the quantity and quality of housing available." In an earlier survey, Kearl et al. (1979) also found a similar consensus toward rent control. One economist (Fisch 1983, 18) even went so far as to declare that rent control "can be the same as a nuclear blast in very slow motion."

The majority of the literature opposes rent control on the grounds that it creates major inefficiencies that are unnecessary to achieve the desired goals. Economists contend that, among the other damaging effects mentioned above, limiting rents could lead to under-maintenance, maintenance abandonment, and no new construction, resulting in deterioration of the housing stock (Keating, Teitz, and Skaburskis 1998; Moon and Stotsky 1993). Rent control is considered not only a highly inefficient but also an extremely inequitable redistributive device. The evidence suggests that housing markets are rather competitive and there is no justification for financing benefits to tenants by any implicit regulations (Arnott 1995; Olsen 1998). Opponents are afraid that a disproportionate share of the burden of assisting low- and moderate-income households is shifted onto landlords. Some argue that rent control discourages residential mobility because rent increases for continuing tenants are generally smaller than for new residents (Strassman 1991).

Professional real estate organizations on the federal, state, and local levels have been both eager and successful in disseminating this knowledge to the media and their members. I have shown how major media organizations, including the *Wall Street Journal, San Francisco Chronicle, Los Ange-*

les Times, and *Forbes Magazine,* have editorialized against all forms of rent control, referring to them as "a disaster" and "unworkable" (Gilderbloom 1983, 137–138).

In 1983, the U.S. President's Commission on Housing called for federal legislation banning local rent controls, which the commission straight-facedly characterized as "so dangerous and addicting a narcotic that it cannot be withdrawn cold turkey" (xxviii; see also Downs 1983). The widely held belief that any form of rent control spells disaster for a city reflects the power of the real estate industry to influence the media, politics, and academia. Through the expenditure of millions of dollars on lobbyists, print and electronic advertising, film documentaries, and sponsorship of supportive research, the real estate industry has successfully demonized rent control. Politicians at the state and local levels receive generous campaign contributions for supporting and sponsoring anti-rent-control legislation.

In California, where most of the rental housing in the Los Angeles and San Francisco Bay areas is subject to some form of rent regulation, the state legislature routinely considers legislation that would inhibit the ability of localities to enact rent control. In 1986, one measure that passed required all local rent control ordinances to provide for the decontrol of vacated units. This law significantly weakened more restrictive voter-adopted measures in Berkeley, Santa Monica, and West Hollywood. For the most part, tenant groups lack the money to effectively combat the anti-rent-control propaganda. Any debate on the pros and cons of rent control must take into account the wide diversity of laws regulating rent. Yet many of the debaters have invoked New York City's original restrictive rent control law as somehow typical of all rent control. The U.S. President's Commission on Housing (1982, xxviii), for example, erroneously asserted that "abandonment has swept bare large sections of the city."

Curiously, until the 1990s, little research had been done that systematically examined the differences between restrictive, moderate, and strong rent controls in cities across the United States (Marcuse 1981a,b; Gilderbloom and Appelbaum 1988; Gilderbloom et al. 1992; Gilderbloom and Markham 1993). Thus, a comprehensive review of studies directed by economists, political scientists, planners, and sociologists was needed. Neither moderate nor strong forms of rent control caused a decline in either the quality or supply of the rental housing stock.

Although such findings did not prove that rent controls were without deleterious effect, they likewise provided no warrant for drawing conventional conclusions. In fact, the very lack of restrictiveness that characterizes moderate rent control in particular may also account for its failure to provide across-the-board general rent relief for tenants. While moderate rent controls serve to limit extreme or erratic rent increases ("rent gouging"), they often intentionally had little effect on tenants whose landlords were merely earning a fair and reasonable return on their investment.

Much of the criticism of rent control has been misdirected. Our comprehensive review of numerous studies on the effects of rent control indicates that criticism was based almost exclusively on the experience of extremely restrictive forms of rent control. Extreme forms of rent control were rarely encountered among the approximately 200 localities that had some form of rent regulation in the United States. Our systematic review of studies that evaluated the impact of modern, non-restrictive rent control revealed a very different pattern of effects. We found that such controls had not caused a decline in construction, maintenance, or value of controlled units relative to uncontrolled units. However, in attempting to avoid the problems traditionally associated with more restrictive measures, most moderate rent controls worked mainly to control extreme or erratic rent increases. In effect, research on modern rent control had revealed that while most owners had little to fear, most renters gained very little, in purely economic terms. Modern, non-restrictive rent controls may have provided protection against rent gouging, but they did not reduce rents for the majority of tenants whose landlords were merely earning a reasonable rate of return. The exception to this general rule lay in strong rent control, which can cause a significant reduction in rent paid over time. Yet only three cities in the United States had these kinds of laws at the time of our study.

HOUSING AFFORDABILITY AND RENT CONTROL

An abundance of cities and counties around the United States have enacted some form of rent regulation over the past thirty years. More than 100 communities in New Jersey as well as Washington, D.C., and cities and counties in Massachusetts, New York, Virginia, and California have enacted rent control laws and ordinances, most of them in the early 1970s. In 1983 it was estimated that approximately 10 percent of the nation's rental housing stock was covered by some form of rent control (Baar 1983). By 2000, cities in Massachusetts, Virginia, and Florida dropped rent control programs, while cities in California had court rulings and state legislation softening the bite of rent control. Even New York saw its restrictive laws loosened as well.

THE VARIETIES OF RENT CONTROL

Although rent regulation was the principal objective of the tenants' movement in numerous cities across the United States, the actual forms of rent control ordinances diverged widely. All rent control laws are intended to provide protection against extreme rent increases, unjust evictions, and poor maintenance. One of the communists' first acts when they got into power was to implement rent control, whether in Cuba, the Soviet Union, or China. Even Caesar enacted rent control in Rome during his rule. Beyond these common attributes, however, it is possible to categorize rent control measures into three general classes: restrictive, moderate, and strong. In the following list we summarize the characteristics of the various types of rent control, along with those studies concerning their effects that we discuss in this and the subsequent section.

PROVISIONS AND EFFECTS OF RENT CONTROL LAWS

1. Restrictive Rent Control
    a. Vacancy decontrol-recontrol provisions: none
    b. Administration: appointed rent board
    c. Effects of rent freezes
de Jouvenel 1948; Friedman and Stigler 1946; Hayek 1972; Keating 1976; Paish 1950; Pennance 1972; Rydenfelt 1949; Samuelson 1967; Seldon 1972; Willis 1950 (New York City)
    d. Effect on abandonment and demolitions: none
Bartlet and Lawson 1982; Marcuse 1979; Roistacher 1972 (New York City)
2. Moderate Rent Control
    a. Vacancy decontrol-recontrol provisions
    Effect on rent: large increases upon decontrol
Clark, Heskin, and Manuel 1980 (Los Angeles); Gilderbloom 1986; Gilderbloom and Keating 1982 (New Jersey)
    b. Administration
        1) appointed boards: tenants in minority
Baar and Keating 1981 (New Jersey); Mollenkopf and Pynoos 1973 (Cambridge, MA)
        2) minimal cost of administering
Baar 1983; Gilderbloom and Keating 1982 (New Jersey)
    c. Rent increase formulas: effect on rents
        1) full CPI formulas
Gilderbloom 1984 (New Jersey)
        2) hardship appeals
Baar and Keating 1981; Gilderbloom and Keating 1982 (New Jersey)
    d. Effect on new construction: none
Gilderbloom 1983; Gruen and Gruen 1977 (New Jersey); Vitaliano 1983

(New York State); Clark, Heskin, and Manuel 1980; Los Angeles Community Development Department 1979; Los Angeles RSD 1985 (Los Angeles); Sorenson 1983 (Alaska)

 e. Effect on maintenance and capital improvements: none

Gilderbloom 1978; Sternlieb 1975 (Fort Lee, NJ); Sternlieb 1974 (Boston); Vitaliano 1983 (New York State); Wolfe 1983 (Berkeley, Oakland, and Hayward, CA); Eckert 1977 (Brookline, MA); Apartment and Office Building Association 1977 (Montgomery County, MD); Urban Planning Aid 1975 (Boston area); Clark, Heskin, and Manuel 1980; Los Angeles RSD 1985; Rydell 1981 (Los Angeles)

 f. Effect on abandonment and demolitions: none

Gilderbloom 1983 (New Jersey); Marcuse 1981a,b; U.S. General Accounting Office 1978 (various cities)

 g. Valuation of rental housing and the city's tax base

Massachusetts Department of Corporations and Taxation 1974 (Cambridge, MA); Gilderbloom 1981 (Fort Lee, NJ); Los Angeles RSD 1985; Clark, Heskin, and Manuel 1980, 105; Appelbaum 1986 (Los Angeles); Gilderbloom 1978, 1983 (New Jersey); Eckert 1977; Revenue and Rent Study Committee 1974 (Brookline, MA)

 h. Affordability: little impact

Gilderbloom 1986; Heffley and Santerre 1985 (New Jersey); Gilderbloom and Keating 1982 (Springfield, NJ); Hartman 1984 (San Francisco); Clark and Heskin 1982; Los Angeles RSD 1985; Rydell 1981 (Los Angeles); Mollenkopf and Pynoos 1973 (Cambridge, MA); Daugherbaugh 1975 (Anchorage and Fairbanks, AK); Vitaliano 1983 (New York State)

 3. Strong Rent Control

  a. Vacancy decontrol-recontrol provisions: none

  b. Administration elected boards: tenants control

  c. Rent increase formulas: partial CPI or net operating income (NOI)

  Formulas and landlords' costs

Santa Monica Rent Control Board 1979 (Santa Monica); Los Angeles RSD 1985 (Los Angeles)

  d. Effect on new construction: none

Appelbaum 1986 (Santa Monica)

  e. Valuation of rental housing and the city's tax base

Appelbaum 1986 (Santa Monica)

  f. Affordability: substantial impact

Shulman 1980 (Santa Monica); Appelbaum 1986 (Berkeley, West Hollywood, and Santa Monica); Sorenson 1983 (Alaska); Vitaliano 1983 (New Jersey)

RESTRICTIVE RENT CONTROL

Prior to the 1960s, most rent control programs in the United States were restrictive in that they set absolute ceilings on rents without considering for the landlord's rate of return. Such controls were typically enacted as general wage and price controls during World War II and rescinded after the war. Among major cities, only New York maintained restrictive rent controls well into the postwar period; as a consequence, the very term "rent control" came to be widely associated with the New York City rent freeze. Most studies claim that such controls contributed to disinvestments in rental housing and a decline in construction maintenance and overall rental property value (see, for example, de Jouvenel 1948; Friedman and Stigler 1946; Hayek 1972; Keating 1976; Paish 1950; Pennance 1972; Rydenfelt 1949; Samuelson 1967; Seldon 1972; Willis 1950). Rent freezes, however, were atypical of the ordinances widely adopted around the nation. Keating, Teitz, and Skaburskis' (1998, 168) review of forty-five years of rent control in New York calls it a "protracted saga" in which "it is difficult to give any definitive answer as to whether New York City's rent controls have worked," especially given the numerous changes in the law, politicized studies, and varying rent control systems for different kinds of rental units.

MODERATE RENT CONTROL

Attempts to avoid the problems associated with restrictive rent control resulted in the introduction of moderate controls in the early 1970s. Moderate controls were the only form of rent controls enacted in the United States during the early 1970s, with more than twenty New Jersey cities and five Massachusetts cities enacting regulations. No efforts were made to enact restrictive forms of rent control. Moderate rent controls are diverse in scope but have in common the intent of balancing the interests of both landlord and tenant. This is achieved by guaranteeing a "fair and reasonable return" to landlords while eliminating the possibility of "excessive" rent increases ("rent gouging").

"Fair return" formulas varied from locale to locale. Hoboken, New Jersey, for example, defined this as 6 percent above the maximum local passbook savings account interest rate. In 1985, Los Angeles determined that a 4 percent annual rate of rent increase was equitable to both landlords and tenants, in light of the rate of inflation at that time. Prior to that, maximum rent increases were pegged at 7 percent. Santa Monica sought to limit annual rent increases to an amount sufficient to guarantee a constant net operating income adjusted for inflation. The formula governing annual rent adjustments can be established in the original ordinance or may be periodically determined by local authority. Rather than holding rent levels relatively constant, moderate rent controls are intended to regulate the increase on a year-to-year basis.

The rents charged under these rules are supposed to represent what would naturally occur in a "competitive" housing market. In order to meet this criterion of guaranteeing a "fair return," most moderate rent control ordinances share the following features: exemption of new construction, adequate maintenance requirements as a condition for rent increases, guaranteed annual increases sufficient to cover increases in operating costs, and provisions for "passing through" major capital costs (generally on an amortized basis). If the allowable rent fails to provide for a reasonable return on investment or is inadequate to cover costs of major capital improvements, the landlord may apply for a "hardship increase" in the rents charged.

On the other hand, should maintenance or services decline or code violations exist in the building, the rent control board can either reduce the amount of rent collected or prohibit future rent increases until the problems are corrected. Additionally, moderate ordinances are typically coupled with "vacancy decontrol recontrol," which is the provision stating that a unit is temporarily exempted from rent control when it becomes vacant and then is recontrolled once it is occupied again. Under this provision, the rent on vacated units may increase considerably faster than that on controlled units. Clark, Heskin, and Manuel (1980, 6, 34) reported that rents on "decontrolled" units in the City of Los Angeles increased two to three times the rate of rents on controlled units.

Moderate rent control ordinances were usually administered by non-elected local rent control boards. Tenants rarely constituted a majority on these boards, since board members were typically appointed by the city government, which ordinarily took care to ensure a balance of landlord, homeowner, and tenant interests (Baar and Keating 1981; Mollenkopf and Pynoos 1973). The typical New Jersey rent control board consists of five members: two tenants, two landlords, and one homeowner. Baar and Keating (1981, 60) found in their study of forty-six rent-controlled cities in New Jersey that twenty-seven out of sixty-five rent control board members surveyed in these cities (42 percent) identified themselves as either a "landlord or realtor." No board members identified themselves as "tenant organizers." In an early case study of Cambridge, Mollenkopf and Pynoos (1973) also found that real estate interests dominated the rent control board and its administration.

Depending on the city, the annual cost of administering moderate rent controls in the 1980s ranged from $1 to $72 per unit (Baar 1983, 763; see also Baar and Keating 1981). In New Jersey, where approximately 110 cities had moderate rent control, the annual cost of administration was estimated to be less than $3 per unit (Baar 1983). Most rent-controlled New Jersey municipalities employed only a part-time secretary and legal counsel, with the rent control board working on a volunteer basis (Gilderbloom and Keating 1982). Funds for administering New Jersey's rent control laws came out of the municipality's general budget. In municipalities elsewhere, a fee was charged either to the landlord or tenant. Rent control boards, without adequate funding and professional staff, favored landlord interests over those of tenants (Gilderbloom and Keating 1982). Strong rent controls, which have high administrative costs (Berkeley, Santa Monica), tended to be more beneficial to renters, permitting smaller annual allowable rent increases and imposing more stringent hardship requirements.

In general, cities that had enacted moderate rent control have set allowable percentage rent increases according to changes in the full Consumer Price Index (CPI). Data I collected (1984) examined allowable rent increases in eighty-nine rent-controlled New Jersey cities between 1975 and 1976. The data showed that a majority of rent-controlled cities allowed rent increases similar to those in non-rent-controlled areas. Only 35 percent of the rent-controlled cities had allowable rent increases that were below the national CPI rent index. This figure, however, is almost identical to the percentage of non-rent-controlled cities surveyed by the Bureau of Labor Statistics. Furthermore, all but two of the rent-controlled cities were only one or two percentage points below the national CPI rent index. Those New Jersey cities that were found to be well below the national rent index had also had their rent control laws ruled unconstitutional as confiscatory (Atlas 1981; Baar and Keating 1981).

The non-restrictive nature of moderate rent control laws can also be demonstrated in terms of landlord requests for hardship appeals. These appeals are requests by landlords for additional rent increases above the allowable rent ceilings to guarantee "a fair and reasonable return on investment." In a survey of forty-six rent-controlled cities in New Jersey, Baar and Keating (1981) found that, on average, a city's rent control board received only three or four requests annually for hardship increases from landlords. Of the 616 requests sampled in the forty-six cities, more than 70 percent of the hardship appeals were granted either full or partial approval by the rent control board. Because a landlord has the money to hire expert lawyers and accountants, the rent control board could usually be persuaded to support a landlord's request for a hardship appeal in spite of tenant protests (Gilderbloom and Keating 1982).

STRONG RENT CONTROL

A third form of rent regulation, strong rent control, arose in the highly inflationary California rental housing markets of the 1980s, where moderate controls were perceived as inadequate to mitigate excessive rent. Strong rent controls were enacted in three California cities: Berkeley, Santa Monica, and West Hollywood. These ordinances typically called for rent increases that were substantially lower than the CPI, prohibited vacated units from being even temporarily decontrolled, and provided for well-funded administration. Rent control boards were made up of elected members who reflected their overwhelmingly tenant constituencies and frequently gave preference to tenant needs over landlord interests. This, in turn, permitted smaller allowable annual rent increases and more stringent hardship requirements. Strong rent controls grew out of (and contributed to) broad-based tenant movements focused on acquiring overall municipal power (Capek and Gilderbloom 1992).

The restriction of rent increases from one-third to one-half of the CPI was intended to keep rent adjustments in line with increases in the landlord's actual costs. "Net operating income" (NOI) formulas peg increases in rent to increases in landlord costs and net capital costs, assuming the latter consist of fixed mortgage payments that do not fluctuate from year to year. On average, one-third to one-half of landlords' costs were found to be unaffected by inflation (Gilderbloom 1978; Jacob 1977, 2; Los Angeles RSD 1985; Santa Monica Rent Control Board 1979, 14; Sternlieb 1974, 33; Sternlieb 1975, III-4). Sternlieb (1974, 33) examined the operating expenses of 3,893 non-rent-controlled units in the greater Boston area. Total operating costs, including mortgage payments, rose 6.85 percent between 1971 and 1973; at the same time, the CPI for all items rose 12.9 percent. These findings were replicated in another study by Sternlieb (1975, III-4) examining rent-controlled apartments in Fort Lee, New Jersey.

In the 1975 study, Sternlieb examined the operating expenses of 2,769 apartment units between 1972 and 1974. Total operating expenses, including mortgage payments, increased 10.9 percent over the two-year period, compared to a 23.3 percent rise in the CPI. Using figures supplied by the Institute of Real Estate Management, the Santa Monica Rent Control Board (1979) estimated that landlords' costs in 1978 went up 4.7 percent, in contrast to the 10.5 percent increase in the CPI for that year. In Los Angeles, operating and maintenance expenses in rent-controlled units increased 36 percent between 1977 and 1983, while the CPI rose 64 percent over the same period (Los Angeles RSD 1985, exhibit 3-12 and p. 75). Operating and maintenance costs were especially likely to increase more slowly than the CPI in California.

Under California Proposition 13, annual property taxes increases are limited to 2 percent until the property is sold. By pegging rent increases to the full CPI, moderate rent controls can therefore result in increased income over time, while strong rent controls are intended instead to maintain the same level of profitability.

THE EFFECTS OF RENT CONTROL ON RENTAL HOUSING MARKETS

New Construction of Multi-Family Housing

As we have previously noted, rent control discourages rental housing construction. To the extent that profits are artificially lowered, builders will seek other investment outlets such as single-family home construction or commercial buildings. Even moderate rent control, which typically exempts new construction, is believed to have a dampening effect, because it creates a climate of bureaucratic regulation that, in many builders' minds, could easily be extended to new construction at the whim of tenants. In fact, most studies found that moderate rent controls had no impact on the rate of rental housing construction.

Several studies have argued that moderate rent control leads to a decline in conventional multi-family construction (Brenner and Franklin 1977; Coalition for Housing 1977; Gruen and Gruen 1977; Lett 1976; Phillips 1974; Sternlieb 1974, 1975; Urban Land Institute 1976). These studies have relied almost exclusively on the empirical evidence of the Sternlieb and Urban Land Institute reports to support their claims. However, certain deficiencies in Sternlieb's and the Urban Land Institute's data gathering and analysis put into question the validity of other studies that have used their work.

In Sternlieb's (1974, 1975) Boston and Fort Lee studies, he conducted a survey of banks to determine if rent controls affect bankers' lending practices for both construction and long-term financing. Sternlieb (1974, 1975) reported that 74 percent of the bankers interviewed in Boston and 68 percent of those interviewed in Fort Lee indicated that rent controls "influenced" loan activity:

The majority of mortgagors in the sample presently lending on multi-family structures regard rent control as an influential factor in their lending decisions. Many believe that rent restrictions coupled with continually rising costs of construction and operation produce a high level of mortgage risk. Indeed, so prohibitive to investor return is the combination of spiraling costs and controlled income that a number of commercial bankers are shying away from rent controlled areas. (Sternlieb 1975, VIII-12)

However, there were a number of methodological problems with Sternlieb's approach. First, the sample was too small. Only twenty-two lending institutions in Fort Lee and fifteen in Boston that were financing multifamily structures responded to Sternlieb's questionnaire. This made statistical inference problematic (Sternlieb 1974, 94; Sternlieb 1975). Second, the reliability of the questionnaire is debatable. The questions were ambiguous, for example, whether rent control "influences" lending practices may mean different things to different lenders (Sternlieb 1974, 97; Sternlieb 1975).

To determine whether lenders were giving preference to non-controlled areas, we can examine permits issued for new multi-family construction. Building permit data, as an indication of construction, was used in previous rent control research (California Housing Council 1977; Coalition for Housing 1977; Selesnick 1976; Urban Land Institute 1976). Though these data indicated planned rather than actual construction, the New Jersey Department of Labor and Industry (1975) and Selesnick (1976) found that 95 percent of all structures that received permits were built.

The Urban Land Institute used this approach in its 1976 study of Washington, D.C., but its analysis lacked the proper controls to make it meaningful. After enactment of controls, it reported that multi-family residential construction dropped 92.4 percent, from 10,667 units in 1970 to only 814 units in 1974 (Urban Land Institute 1976). The researchers failed to control for other important independent variables that could have influenced construction (e.g., availability of land, inflation, interest rate, and socioeconomic factors). They also failed to match construction activity in Washington, D.C., with other non-controlled cities during the same period.

For example, could the Urban Land Institute explain the significant 90 to 100 percent drop in construction from 1970 to 1974 in such non-controlled cities in New Jersey as Trenton, Camden, and Vineland or in such California cities as Anaheim, Torrance, Emeryville, San Bruno, San Mateo, and Palo Alto (New Jersey Department of Treasury 1970, 1974; U.S. Bureau of the Census 1970a,b, 1974)? What about the doubling of construction in the rent-controlled cities of Jersey City, Bayonne City, Edison Township, Dumont Borough, Linden City, and Springfield during the same period (New Jersey Department of the Treasury 1970–1977)?

Gruen and Gruen's (1977) assertion that permits for apartment construction declined in rent-controlled areas is unsupported by their data. In the seven New Jersey counties with 25 percent or more of their municipalities under rent control, no discernible pattern emerged on whether builders were choosing to build more in non-controlled municipalities. Overall, the totals for the seven counties indicated that no significant shift (-0.5 percent) occurred: three counties showed declines in percentage of apartment construction in rent-controlled cities; three counties showed increases; and one county indicated no significant difference (-1.7 percent). Beyond these data, Gruen and Gruen's statistics failed to sufficiently isolate the relative impact of rent control compared to other factors. Comparisons between counties classified as either "rent controlled" (25 percent or more of the municipalities have ordinances) or "non-rent controlled" (one non-rent-controlled county, Mercer, had 23 percent of its municipalities under rent control) might have reflected many factors other than rent control. Apartment construction as a percentage of state construction, before and after imposition of rent controls, remained about the same in five "rent-controlled" counties, while in two rent-controlled counties (Essex and Middlesex), apartment construction actually increased (Gruen and Gruen 1977).

Overall, the total apartment construction in rent-controlled counties as a percentage of state construction increased slightly, from an average of 5.92 percent in 1972 to 9 percent in 1976. On the other hand, the percentage decline of apartments constructed between 1972 and 1976, as compared to total units built, revealed that apartment construction increased more than the statewide average in three out of seven "rent-controlled" counties, while four counties fell slightly below it. Again, these statistics revealed no strong relationship between permits issued for multi-family construction and moderate rent control ordinances.

My earlier studies (Gilderbloom 1983; Gilderbloom et al. 1992; Gilderbloom and Markham 1996) showed no statistically significant differences in the rate of multi-family housing construction between twenty-six rent-controlled and thirty-seven non-rent-controlled New Jersey cities in the mid-1970s, once other factors were statistically controlled. Multiple regression analysis showed no statistically significant differences in the rate of multi-family housing creation between seventy-five rent-controlled and fifty non-rent-controlled New Jersey cities, after statistically controlling for a variety of intervening variables. We found that the number of rental units created from 1975 to 1980 and from 1970 to 1980 was unrelated to the presence of rent control. The studies found that new construction "has declined over time to the point where it is undetectable." Other less rigorous studies produced similar findings, including studies of New Jersey (Gruen and Gruen 1977), Alaska (Sorenson 1983), Massachusetts (Achtenberg 1975), and Los Angeles (Clark, Heskin, and Manuel 1980; see also Los Angeles Community Development Department 1979).

Builders continue to build in rent-controlled communities with both moderate and strong regulations because the laws either permanently exempt new construction or allow builders to freely set initial rent levels. Even where rent control covers new units, it still guarantees a "fair and reasonable" return on investment. However much they might complain about the actual or potential adverse consequences of rent control, most builders would likely prefer to remain in communities with which they are already familiar. An understanding of local demographic trends, awareness of general business plans and government projects, an intimate familiarity with local building codes and planning, and project review bureaucracies are critical to a builder's success. Such an understanding can only occur through a long and intimate involvement in municipal affairs. Neither moderate nor strong rent controls pose a serious enough economic threat for most builders to move to new markets.

Maintenance and Capital Improvement

Critics of rent control argue that by restricting revenues, rent control ordinances force landlords to reduce their expenditures on maintaining and improving rental units. To the extent that landlords find their profits reduced, they will be forced to cut corners, resulting in a badly deteriorated rental housing stock.

Rising Rent Versus Rising Costs

Some opponents of rent control have cited Sternlieb as proof that the maintenance of properties declines under moderate rent control ordinances (Kain 1975; Lett 1976). If allowable rent increases lagged behind rising costs, then maintenance expenditures would be reduced. In his Boston study, Sternlieb found that operating expenses increased 15.2 percent, while rents increased only 6.7 percent. Similarly, in his Fort Lee study, he found that rents rose only 5.5 percent, while expenses jumped 22 percent (Sternlieb 1974, 1975).

Upon investigation, Sternlieb's estimates of percentage increase in rents and costs prove to be erroneous and deceptive. The major problem is his failure to include mortgage payments in expenses, payments that comprise from one-third to one-half of the landlord's total costs. With the exception of refinancing costs, mortgage payments generally are unaffected by inflation, and fixed by the terms of the initial loan. Inclusion of mortgage payments in total costs significantly reduces the alleged percentage increase in "total expenses." This is particularly important since landlords were required by rent control boards in New Jersey to include mortgage costs when applying for a hardship increase. If Sternlieb had included mortgage payments in computing total increases in expenses, he would have found that expenses in Boston went up only an estimated 9.5 percent—a marked contrast to Sternlieb's 15.2 percent figure (1974). Similarly, if Sternlieb had included mortgage payments in Fort Lee, he would have found an estimated 11 percent increase in expenses as contrasted to his calculated 22 percent figure (1975).

Even if mortgage payments were included, a gap remains between allowable rent increases and costs. In rent-controlled Boston, rents went up 6.7 percent, and recomputed costs rose 9.5 percent; in Fort Lee, rents went up 5.5 percent, and costs increased 11 percent. However, even these remaining differences are questionable because Sternlieb obtained most of his data from real estate organizations that had a direct stake in attaining and disseminating biased results. Sternlieb did not utilize the audited landlord operating statements from Massachusetts rent control boards (Achtenberg 1975). Instead he relied on landlords' own claims about expenses. In Sternlieb's (1974) Boston study, increases in taxes in non-controlled properties (11 percent) were lower than those in controlled housing (14.4 percent).

In addition, other operating expenses (e.g., administrative insurance) rose 10.4 percent in the controlled properties but only 6.2 percent in the non-controlled ones (Sternlieb 1974). Overall expenses for the non-controlled properties went up 6.8 percent—a figure comparable to allowable rent increases in controlled areas—while expenses in the controlled units increased 9.5 percent. It seems plausible that if Sternlieb had had the landlords' operating statements audited by certified public accountants, the gap between rising costs and allowable rent increases would probably have been greatly reduced (Katz, Biber, and Lawrence Inc. 1977). Unfortunately, landlords are willing to open their books only to those sympathetic to their interests. Indeed, Boston's Rental Housing Association denied Selesnick (1976) permission to examine the same statements made available to Sternlieb.

Sternlieb's study was further weakened by an unrepresentative sample of the housing stock, consisting mostly of apartment buildings with twenty or more units. Furthermore, the Boston study utilized only fourteen management firms or individual owners, and his Fort Lee study examined only eleven high-rise luxury units. In the Boston, Cambridge, and Brookline areas, 83 percent of the registered rent-controlled buildings had fewer than twenty units, yet only 17 percent of the apartments in Sternlieb's sample fell into this category (Achtenberg 1975). In the non-controlled sample, no building had fewer than twenty-five units (Achtenberg 1975). In the Fort Lee study, Sternlieb looked at no apartments under six stories, and his analysis of net income based only on cash flow is understated. Both tax shelter and appreciation benefits also give strong incentives for investment and provide clues to understanding an owner's behavior.

Maintenance and Service

Even if we assume that Sternlieb's data were accurate, there is still no evidence that maintenance and services were reduced. Sternlieb first differentiates two costs in rental housing: (1) "ironclad" costs involving taxes and mortgage payments and (2) "discretionary" costs encompassing maintenance and fuel expenditures. He states that if rent increases could not keep up with growing expenses, then maintenance would be reduced and eventually the housing could "degenerate into slums" (Sternlieb 1974).

According to his Boston data, however, a consistently higher percentage of total rents went into building maintenance, services, and fuel in the rent-controlled sample than in the non-controlled sample. In the controlled sample, 16.6 percent of the rent dollar went into maintenance, compared to 15.0 percent in the non-controlled sample; and 5.4 percent of the rent dollar went into fuel in the non-controlled sample, compared to 6.5 percent in the rent-controlled housing (Sternlieb 1974). It could be argued that the percentage of the rent dollar going into maintenance of rent-controlled buildings was inflated by holding down rents and that the data must be analyzed in absolute rather than relative terms. But Sternlieb's Boston data for 1971–1973 showed that maintenance expenditures increased almost as fast in controlled (19.7 percent) as non-controlled (21.4 percent) apartments. His Fort Lee study did not compare controlled and non-controlled housing. Yet the data indicate an increase in the proportion of the rent dollar going into maintenance of rent-controlled housing. In 1972 only 21.67 percent of the rent dollar went into maintenance; by 1974 this percentage had jumped to 24.9 percent.

Sternlieb's data also revealed that rents in the non-controlled sample were far outstripping actual cost increases. Re-computing Sternlieb's (1974) data, rents increased 13.5 percent, while total expenses (including mortgage payments) went up 6.8 percent. Moreover, the amount of money going into the category of depreciation and profits rose 13.4 percent.

Abandonment and Demolition

In extreme cases, rent control reduces profitability to the point that it becomes economically irrational for landlords to continue to operate their rental properties. This purportedly occurs when the rate of return falls below similar alternative investments of comparable risk, at which point the landlord has deferred maintenance and capital expenditures. Once the unit is seriously deteriorated and the landlord has "milked" the property for its tax advantages, he or she is forced to default on taxes and/or mortgage payments as well, resulting in the threat of foreclosure. At this point the building is simply abandoned, contributing to the image of blocks of boarded-up apartment units—the results of rent control in New York City. Ultimately, apartment owners and public authorities are forced to raze the abandoned units in the interest of health and safety. Rent control is thus seen as contributing to a significant decline in both the quantity and quality of the rental housing stock in the long run.

Several studies have argued that rent control leads to abandonment and demolition (Apartment and Office Building Association 1977; Phillips 1974; Sternlieb 1974). However, no empirical evidence is offered to support the claimed correlation. In fact, if abandonment were occurring, the first sign would be declining maintenance; yet all available data suggest this was not the case. Even studies examining the restrictive controls of New York were unable to prove a causal relationship between controls and abandonment.

For example, a nationwide study of abandonment ranked New York fifth, behind four non-rent-controlled cities (St. Louis, Cleveland, Chicago, and Hoboken), in rates of abandonment (National Urban League and the Center for Community Change 1971). A study by the Women's City Club of New York (1977) concluded that no significant relationship existed between abandonment and rent control. Instead, the report contends that abandonment resulted from redlining, vandalism, and failure of tenants to pay rents. Marcuse (1979), in an extensive study on New York City rental housing undertaken for the city's Division of Rent Control, drew similar conclusions. Based on data analysis from the 1978 Special Census of Housing and Vacancy, Marcuse concluded that losses from the housing inventory were a function of the age of the structures and general neighborhood deterioration rather than rent control. It seems clear that abandonment had less to do with rent control than with other causes such as redlining, vandalism, arson for insurance purposes, neighborhood decline, and the exhaustion of accelerated depreciation and other tax benefits (New York Temporary State Commission on Living Costs and the Economy 1974).

There is no evidence that any form of rent control, moderate or restrictive, actually leads to abandonment. In 1978 the General Accounting Office conducted a major study of abandonment by mailing out questionnaires to the chief executive officers of 201 of the largest cities in the United States.

Of the 149 who responded to the survey, 113 declared that abandonment was a problem in their respective cities; at that time only six of these cities had rent control. Of the eight city officers who stated that abandonment was a "major problem," only one place, New York City, had rent control. Of the eighteen officers that declared abandonment was a "substantial problem," only two cities (Jersey City and Trenton) had rent control.

Marcuse (1981a, 5–6), using Annual Housing Survey Data, listed the twenty cities sampled with the highest rates of abandonment and found that only four of the cities had rent control. Marcuse then used both the Annual Housing Survey Data and the General Accounting Office study (1978) to study whether cities with rent control had problems of abandonment. Marcuse could identify only 8 out of 101 cities with moderate to major problems of abandonment. Marcuse (1979) went against conventional wisdom of the real estate industry. He found that the levels of abandonment tended to be highest in neighborhoods with the fewest number of units subject to the city's rent stabilization ordinance, while levels of abandonment tended to be lowest in neighborhoods with a relatively high proportion of apartment units regulated.

Demolitions do not appear to be a likely consequence of modest rent control. The inference made by rent control critics that one can measure abandonment by counting the number of demolished units is wrong. While it is true that the end result of the abandonment process is usually demolition, it is also true that many buildings are demolished simply to make way for new construction. It is difficult to interpret the meaning of an increase in the number of demolitions in a particular community without investigating them case by case. Does it mean rent control is forcing more units off the market, or does it mean new construction is occurring, or is it both if new units are exempt? Gilderbloom (1980) collected data on the number of units demolished in twenty-six rent-controlled cities and thirty-seven non-rent-controlled cities in New Jersey between 1970 and 1977. The study found that total demolition of residential housing units decreased 13 percent in rent-controlled cities and increased 25 percent in non-rent-controlled cities. In rent-controlled urban center cities, demolitions fell 11 percent while increasing 72 percent in comparable non-rent-controlled cities.

Demolitions in controlled urban-suburban cities rose 20 percent during the rent control period; in non-controlled urban-suburban cities, they decreased 56 percent. In suburban cities, demolitions of residential units decreased 59 percent in rent-controlled cities; in non-controlled cities, demolitions fell 15 percent. A regression analysis controlling for multi-family construction, median rent, percentage African-American, percentage tenant, municipal population growth, city type, and city size found that the variable of rent control had no net effect on demolitions of housing units (Gilderbloom 1980).

Analysis in Gilderbloom and Markham (1996) of rent-controlled and non-rent-controlled New Jersey communities found no statistically significant relations between demolitions and rent control, once other variables were considered. In fact, in simply comparing the numbers of demolitions between 1970–1972 and 1975–1977 for the two categories of communities, I found a decrease of 13 percent for rent-controlled areas and an increase of 25 percent for non-rent-controlled communities.

Valuation of Rental Housing and the City's Tax Base

The final result of rent control, according to its critics, is that rent controls significantly reduce city property tax revenues that are derived from this source. This conclusion follows from the presumed effects we have previously detailed: a decline in new construction, maintenance and capital improvements, abetted by abandonments and demolitions in extreme instances, which reduces the total value of rental housing. This decline in tax revenues places a severe fiscal burden on cities with rent control, forcing them to recoup such losses by increasing the tax burden on homeowners and businesses. Many claim that rent control causes the local tax base to decline. Both the construction of new rental housing and the condition of the existing stock determine the size and health of a city's rental property tax base.

The notion of an eroding tax base is plausible only to the extent that the alleged adverse effects of rent control upon new construction and maintenance are accepted. Sternlieb (1975) and others have argued that declining construction and maintenance in cities make the erosion of the tax base "imminent." However, the foregoing sections demonstrate that moderate rent control has not adversely affected new construction and maintenance. Therefore, in the absence of any other generally accepted correlation between controls and ill effects, the claim that rent control erodes the tax base should be re-examined.

Furthermore, the practice of drawing a correlation between rent control and the total tax base is subject to question (Gilderbloom 1976). Rent-controlled properties are not sufficiently isolated from other types of non-controlled properties (industrial, commercial, single family, vacant, etc.) to establish the claimed negative correlation. For example, apartments in New Jersey made up only a small proportion (6 percent) of the total property tax base in 1977 (Gruen and Gruen 1977).

Assuming a correlation between rent control and the total tax base, I compared (1978) the tax base of twenty-six rent-controlled and thirty-seven non-rent-controlled cities in New Jersey. The data offered no evidence to suggest that rent control caused a decline in a city's tax base. In fact, controlled cities experienced a parallel increase in total assessed value compared to non-controlled cities.

APPRECIATION OF PROPERTY

Contrary to Sternlieb's claim that the value of apartment buildings in Fort Lee, New Jersey, would fall in value, the assessed valuation of these properties rose sharply. Sternlieb forecast that the assessed valuation of the eleven Fort Lee apartments he examined would drop in value by 1980. This forecast was based on his analysis of landlord income operating statements, data I have shown to be questionable. Given the problem with Sternlieb's data, his reliance on the income capitalization approach as a method for determining value is of dubious worth. Sternlieb (1975) "arbitrarily" assumed that rent boards would allow only a 2.5 percent yearly increase in rents, while expenses would rise 8 percent annually for the next six years. Such assumptions had no real justification. Sternlieb failed to consider that moderate rent control provided for a hardship increase in rent for any landlord who could not meet expenses.

In addition, the courts repeatedly ruled that landlords must be granted a rent increase sufficient to guarantee a "fair and reasonable return on investment" (Atlas 1981; Blumberg, Robbins, and Baar 1974; Marcuse 1981a). In Pentifallo (1977), tax assessor records in Fort Lee, New Jersey, stated: "Eleven high rise owners applied to our rent leveling board for hardship increases; three were denied, three were granted, four were preempted from controls by HUD and one case is pending." Sternlieb's remaining arguments were based not on data but on predictions for the future. He predicted in his 1975 study of Fort Lee that the assessed valuation of eleven buildings would fall 50 percent from 1974 to 1980. Contrary to the decline in value Sternlieb predicted, tax records show that the assessed value of the eleven buildings continued to increase an average of 35 percent and as much as 193 percent between 1974 and 1980.

Since we have previously shown that moderate rent control does not adversely affect construction, maintenance, capital improvements, or in general the quality or quantity of the housing stock, it should come as no surprise that the valuation of rental property (and hence a city's tax revenues from this source) is similarly unaffected. Increases in value for rent-controlled units were reported for Cambridge, Massachusetts (Massachusetts Department of Corporations and Taxation 1974), Fort Lee, New Jersey (Gilderbloom 1981), Los Angeles (Clark, Heskin, and Manuel 1980, 105; Los Angeles RSD 1985), and Brookline, Massachusetts (Revenue and Rent Study Committee 1974).

Numerous studies have found that few changes actually occurred in the relative value of rent-controlled and non-rent-controlled units. This is true whether the studies were concerned with changes in gross rent multipliers (Eckert 1977, in Brookline, Massachusetts), market values (Appelbaum 1986, 14, in Santa Monica; Clark, Heskin, and Manuel 1980, 105, in Los Angeles), or assessed valuation (Gilderbloom 1978, 28; 1983, 31, in New Jersey municipalities). While rent controls are obviously intended to hold down increases in the value of rental property from what they might reach in inflationary markets, they do not depress values below what would otherwise exist under competitive market conditions. Although rental property tax revenues may not be as high as they would in the absence of rent controls, they do not erode relative to their present levels; nor do they suffer a decline relative to homes, businesses, or other property tax sources.

RENT CONTROL AND HOMELESSNESS

The assault on rent control has taken many forms, one of which is rent control's responsibility for the nation's growing homeless problem. William Tucker, a journalist for the conservative *American Spectator*, conducted research on the sources of homelessness for the Manhattan and Cato Institutes, two neo-conservative think tanks. The results, published in a variety of conservative and mainstream outlets, received enormous public attention. Tucker's findings were cited in such diverse mass circulation periodicals as the *New York Times*, the *Village Voice*, and *Parade Magazine*, as well as by Reagan and George H. W. Bush administration officials. Tucker's argument drew on the familiar themes we have previously questioned: rent control is alleged to cause disinvestment in housing, leading in the long run to scarcity in rental housing; lower rental housing vacancy will presumably force people onto the streets, causing increased homelessness in cities that have enacted rent control. To test this hypothesis, Tucker drew upon HUD's (1984) study of homelessness. This study used a stratified random sample of sixty cities across the country, composed of twenty cities in each of three size categories. For these places, HUD researchers contacted homelessness "experts" such as shelter operators, service providers, and police officers. The homeless estimates from these sources were then averaged to produce a single figure for each city. Tucker modified HUD's data set, "omitting five small mid-western cities with traits similar to several that were retained and adding fifteen others to include some notable HUD omissions" (Tucker 1987, 1). This adjustment yielded fifty cities for his analysis. For these places he added "seven conceivably relevant factors" to HUD's homeless estimates (2): poverty and unemployment rates, the incidence of public housing, city size, temperature, rental vacancy rates, and the presence or absence of rent control.

Tucker found that a 1 percent decline in rental vacancy was associated with a 10 percent increase in homelessness. In his view, when rent control was included in the regression equation, the vacancy effect disappeared. Rent control then accounted for 27 percent of the variation in homelessness across cities. He noted, "The nine cities with rent control had the nine lowest vacancy rates" (3).

There were glaring problems with both Tucker's revised data set and his subsequent analysis. HUD's homeless estimates have long been discredited and are no longer even cited as authoritative by the federal government. Tucker provided no justification for his addition of fifteen non-randomly selected cities, his deletion of five cities that HUD had selected using randomizing procedures, or that he inflated median rents in certain cities and declared one city with a high homeless rate as rent-controlled when it was clearly not rent controlled. Nowhere did Tucker entertain the seemingly obvious possibility that low vacancies, high rates of homelessness, and the presence of rent control might all result from the same single cause: high rents. In fact, this is the most plausible explanation for his findings: rent control is typically a response to extremely high rent levels.

We corrected the model for variables we believed to be of theoretical importance (such as rent) and readjusted his data set to include HUD's original cities. We also conducted a regression analysis that allowed us to parcel out the impact of each variable. Tucker only controlled one or two variables at the most. Our preliminary analysis indicated that when the data set is restricted to HUD's actual random sample of forty large and medium-sized places, rent control cannot predict homelessness (Gilderbloom 1988). The same result occurred when rent control was included as a variable. These results were hardly surprising; what is surprising is the degree of attention that the Tucker study received among housing experts, policy makers, and the popular press. Other studies confirm our results (Appelbaum et al. 1991; Early and Olsen 1998; Gilderbloom et al. 1992). We are concerned that the misplaced effort to link rent control with homelessness will be effectively used by federal or state officials to prevent localities from enacting or enforcing rent control ordinances.

RENT CONTROL AND AFFORDABILITY

The success or failure of rent control in providing across-the-board rent relief to tenants depends on the kind of rent control enacted. Moderate rent control in New Jersey resulted in moderately lower rent levels relative to non-rent-controlled cities. In 1986 I examined the mean rents in 1970 and 1980 for the twenty-six rent-controlled and thirty-seven non-rent-controlled cities from my original studies (Gilderbloom 1978, 1983), using 1980 Census data to update the impact of moderate rent control on the rent levels of rental housing in New Jersey. The average percentage rent increase between 1970 and 1980 was almost identical for the rent-controlled and non-rent-controlled cities (105 percent versus 106 percent).

Similar results were found by Heffley and Santerre (1985) in their study of New Jersey rent controls. They examined 101 rent-controlled cities in New Jersey and found that the average price per room was 8 percent higher in rent-controlled cities, a difference that was not statistically significant. Studies on the impact of rent control on rent levels in other parts of the country reached similar conclusions. In their early study of Cambridge, Massachusetts, Mollenkopf and Pynoos (1973, 71) asserted that rent control had failed to reduce rents but in some cases had also resulted in "increasing rates of returns to landlords." Daugherbaugh (1975, 2) found that Alaska's rent control programs in Anchorage and Fairbanks were ineffective in holding down rents because of the structure and administration of the law. Vitaliano's (1983, 15–23) study of eleven rent-controlled and twenty-three non-rent-controlled cities in New York between 1960 and 1970 offers additional evidence. Constructing nine different multiple regression models to test the impact of rent control on gross room rent, Vitaliano found no statistically significant relationship between regulated cities and gross room rents. In fact, the correlation coefficient showed the sign to be positive between rent controls and rents.

The vacancy decontrol characteristic of moderate rent control results in significantly higher average rents than those that would occur in the absence of such provisions (for example, under strong controls). A study conducted by myself and Keating (1982) found that in Springfield, New Jersey, rents in decontrolled apartments increased an average of 56 percent, with increases ranging from a low of 21 percent to a high of 89 percent. A similar finding was noted in San Francisco, where rents in decontrolled units went up an average of 30 percent per year over a two-year period (Hartman 1984, 241). Clark and Heskin (1982) found that rent levels for "decontrolled" units were substantially higher than for controlled units in all six rent-controlled districts in Los Angeles. Depending on the part of the city, rents in decontrolled apartments ranged from 22 percent to 39 percent higher than controlled units, with an overall average of rents being 29 percent higher in non-controlled units.

Given the vacancy decontrol provision in the law, minorities appeared to get the greatest amount of protection from rent controls because their mobility rate was lower than that of whites in Los Angeles (Clark and Heskin 1982, 112). Rydell (1981) estimated that if Los Angeles had maintained the 7 percent annual maximum rent increase that existed under rent control in 1980, rents in decontrolled units would have risen an average of 16.7 percent. He estimated that if allowable rent increases were limited to 5.6 percent, rents in decontrolled units would have risen an average of 18.6 percent. The Los Angeles RSD study (1985) found that under the city's vacancy decontrol provision, a significant proportion of the average monthly rent savings resulted from an income transfer from tenants who moved frequently to those who did not, since the vacancy decontrol provision resulted in landlords "marking up" vacated units to compensate for below-market rents on occupied units. Contrary to the widely held belief that rent control was primarily a middle-class subsidy (see, e.g., Devine 1986), the principal beneficiaries of rent control have been the least mobile tenants, which include low-income families, senior citizens, and single-person households.

A SURVEY OF 161 NEW JERSEY CITIES

The studies reviewed were deficient due to their failure to control for suppressor effects or confounding variables. One way to overcome this problem is through regression analysis. Appelbaum (1986, 16–17), conducting a time-series analysis that allowed for other influences to be controlled, found that rent control was unrelated to either increases or decreases in multi-family construction levels in Santa Monica. Vitaliano (1983, 27–31) examined eleven rent-controlled cities. Through regression analysis, Vitaliano compared them to twenty-three non-rent-controlled cities in the state of New York. He found that rent control did not predict a decline in the number of rental units available between 1960 and 1970. In fact, there was a slight positive correlation between rent control and increases in rental housing construction.

One of the most exhaustive studies of rent control in a single housing market (Los Angeles RSD 1985, 1–2) concluded that the low vacancy levels in Los Angeles were "more attributable to broad market forces than rent stabilization." The study found that new construction declined more in

TABLE 4.1. *Rent-Controlled and Non-Rent-Controlled Cities, 2000*

Variables	Non-Rent-Controlled Cities (N=85)		Rent-Controlled Cities (N=76)		T-Test (2-tailed)
	Mean	Std. Dev.	Mean	Std. Dev.	
Dependent Variables					
Median monthly contract rent	$780	$183	$744	$129	1.43
Median rooms	4.1	0.56	3.7	0.31	5.74***
Rent per room	$190	$42	$202	$40	−1.79
% units built 1990–2000	6.81	7.73	5.43	4.02	1.40
% plumbing deficiency	0.45	0.45	0.86	1.16	−2.98***
Control Variables					
Vacancy rate (%)	3.91	3.58	3.21	1.96	1.52
% units renter occupied	28.13	15.87	44.20	18.47	−5.96***
Median household income	$62,904	$22,230	$53,027	$15,450	3.23**
Population	17,803	8,696	39,511	44,820	−4.38***
Population change 1990–2000 (%)	5.97	17.59	15.08	19.69	−0.22
% black	9.09	13.81	15.09	19.69	−2.26*
% units built before 1940	20.70	14.80	26.11	12.94	−2.45*

* Sig. < .05   ** Sig. < .01   ***Sig. < .001

adjacent non-rent-controlled cities than in Los Angeles during the period 1978–1982.

For the present study, we updated earlier studies (Gilderbloom 1983; Gilderbloom et al. 1992; Gilderbloom and Markham 1996) by doing an analysis of the impacts of moderate and strong rent control for 2000. The data in this study were collected by the New Jersey Tenants Organization (NJTO) in its 2003 rent control survey.

Cities with populations over 10,000 were chosen. Out of the 104 cities that had rent control in 2000, 76 had populations over 10,000. There were 85 other cities in New Jersey that did not have rent control and had a population over 10,000 in 2000. A between-group bivariate analysis of the data was conducted for cities that had and did not have rent control policies; results are summarized in Table 4.1.

There were no significant differences between rent-controlled and non-rent-controlled cities regarding different housing measures. Monthly median contract rents were $36 lower in rent-controlled cities, but the difference was not significant. Rent per room was also higher in rent-controlled cities, but the difference was not significant.

STRONG RENT CONTROL LAWS

On the other hand, there is evidence that strong rent control ordinances adopted by Berkeley, Santa Monica, and West Hollywood resulted in some income redistribution between landlords and tenants. In several housing market simulations, Appelbaum (1986) directly compared the effects of strong and moderate rent controls. Using Berkeley, West Hollywood, and Santa Monica as case studies, Appelbaum compared a ten-year forecast of rents and affordability under those cities' strong rent control laws, with the probable results of more moderate ordinances that would have permitted vacated units to be temporarily decontrolled. The results for Berkeley, California, are illustrative of the three cities.

Under Berkeley's strong rent control law, Appelbaum and I found the proportion of income going into rents declined from an average of 23 percent to just below 16 percent. On the other hand, under a vacancy decontrol provision, average rents rose to about 30 percent of tenants' incomes as landlords took advantage of tenant turnover to raise vacated units to market levels. Under this simulation, we predicted that average decontrolled rents in 1997 would reach about $843 in comparison with $436 under the ordinance at that time. In 1986 there were approximately 10,900 "unaffordable" (by the 30 percent of income standard) rental units in Berkeley. Under the city's strong rent control law, this number was projected to decline to 7,700 by 1997. Under moderate rent control with a vacancy decontrol provision, on the other hand, the number of unaffordable units would increase to 13,100.

Over the entire ten-year period, landlords realized an additional $729 million in rents under the more moderate ordinance. Strong rent control, in other words, produced a substantial redistribution of wealth from landlords to tenants in comparison with more moderate ordinances. Similar results were obtained for Santa Monica and West Hollywood. However, it is worth noting that even under Berkeley's strong rent control measures, two-thirds of the city's landlords surveyed by Wolfe (1983) reported believing that "ownership is profitable."

The success or failure of rent control in providing across-the-board rent relief to tenants depends on the kind of rent control enacted. Moderate rent control, at least in New Jersey, resulted in rents on average being only $13 less a month relative to non-rent-controlled cities. Average monthly rents in 1980 were significantly lower under strong rent control laws and vacancy decontrol prohibition. An alternative specification of the dependent variable, the amount of rent increase between 1970 and 1980, found that stronger rent control laws caused rents to be significantly lower.

These data suggested that, at a minimum, the impact of moderate rent control resulted in the elimination of rent gouging, keeping rents in line with non-rent-controlled jurisdictions. Such rent controls likely had minimal impact on reducing landlords' incomes or tenants' expenditures. At the same time, it seems likely that rent controls were initially adopted in housing markets that were experiencing the greatest rent pressures. Where this was true, to the extent that rent controls resulted in rent levels comparable with less inflationary markets, they did in fact produce some rent relief relative to increases that might have occurred in the absence of controls altogether.

The preceding review of studies on the effect of moderate rent control shows that only limited economic gains were achieved. It should also be kept in mind, however, that rent control is a relatively recent phenomenon in the United States. In 1969 very few American cities had rent control or tenant unions. In 2007, the tenants' movement is a potent political force in many cities and several states, and rent control is widespread.

In purely economic terms, most rent control ordinances serve to avert very large rent increases, bringing highly inflationary housing markets more into line with other ones. Rent control also provides protection against arbitrary evictions, incentives for maintaining units, and predictable rent increases. From the tenant's perspective, these are tangible improvements. Most rent control ordinances do not bring average rents down to affordable levels. Recognizing this problem and playing on the willingness of many tenants to accept government intervention in the marketplace, tenant groups pushed harder for strong rent control.

The future of rent control as a housing policy is unsure. The benefits are often small, and the effort required to enact and defend regulations is enormous. Many tenant organizers came to question the efficacy of rent control as the chief objective of the tenants' movement, and many pressed for additional innovative housing programs in addition to rent control. Large-scale cooperative housing programs for low- and moderate-income persons became one of the main organizing themes of many tenant rights groups (Gilderbloom 1982, 212–260; Gilderbloom 1987; Lawson 1984). Rent control advocacy groups appeared to be waging a defensive campaign to preserve the existence of rent control rather than an offensive campaign of spreading the law to other cities. Real estate groups launched a well-financed attack on rent control, lobbying and passing legislation that undermined the potency of rent control laws.

Since the early 1970s, more than 100 cities in the United States have enacted rent control. A considerable number of the nation's renters are covered by some form of rent regulation, yet very little is known about the economic consequences of rent control. Most evidence suggests that modern rent controls have little or no impact on the amount of construction, maintenance, or taxable valuation of rental properties.

In their book, Keating, Teitz, and Skaburskis (1998) revealed the small amount of rent relief tenants could expect from moderate rent control programs. Turner (1988) noted that the best estimate of monthly rent savings then in Washington, D.C., was approximately $100 a month. Teitz (1998) writes that in Los Angeles rents in controlled areas increased at about the same rate as in uncontrolled areas outside of Los Angeles. Nash and Skaburskis' (1998) study showed that Toronto's rent control saved tenants $32.11 in 1986, but in 1991 rents in Toronto were $15.51 higher than those for comparable unregulated housing in the city of Vancouver. This was based on the assumption "that depreciation rates and tenure discounts in Vancouver would have been similar to those in Toronto were it not for rent control" (Keating, Teitz, and Skaburskis 1998, 189).

In analyzing rent control in Los Angeles, Teitz agreed that "rent stabilization is probably best described as a marginal factor. Its greatest effect appears to have been in smoothing the impacts of housing market fluctuations on tenants in time of inflation without destroying owners' incentives to stay in business" (Teitz 1998, 140).

Such a finding is due primarily to the non-restrictive nature of most rent control ordinances, which typically exempt newly constructed housing, guarantee a fair and reasonable return on investment, and allow annual rent adjustments to cover increases in operating costs. This relatively mild type of rent control succeeds in limiting extreme rent increases. It does not, however, result in significant relief from escalating rents in most regulated cities. Only with strong rent control ordinances will rents be significantly affected.

In a study of Santa Monica, for example, Shulman (1980) estimated that under rent controls, rents increased from $281 to $320 in 1980—a rise of 14 percent. If no controls had existed during that same time period, he estimated that rents would have risen to an average of $446 a month—an increase of almost 59 percent in two years. Shulman (1980, 13) calculated that as a result of rent control, the amount of rent lost by landlords and the amount of income gained by tenants was roughly $108 million over a twenty-four-month period. In several housing market simulations, Appelbaum (1986) directly compared the effects of strong and moderate rent controls. Using Berkeley, West Hollywood, and Santa Monica as case studies, Appelbaum compared a ten-year forecast of rents and affordability under those cities' current strong rent control laws, with the probable results of more moderate ordinances that would have permitted vacated units to be temporarily decontrolled. The results for Santa Monica are illustrative of the three cities.

Under Santa Monica's strong rent control law, the proportion of income going into rents declined from an average of 23 percent to just below 17 percent. Under a vacancy decontrol provision, average rents rose to about 30 percent of tenants' incomes, as landlords took advantage of tenant turnover to raise vacated units to market levels. Under this simulation, average decontrolled rents in 1997 would have reached about $1,125, in comparison with $630 under the ordinance at the time. In 1986 there were 15,400 "unaffordable" (by the 30 percent of income standard) rental units in Santa Monica—some 48 percent of the city's approximately 32,000 rental units.

However, as the city's rent control law was strengthened, that number was projected to decline to 9,400 by 1997. Under moderate rent control with a vacancy decontrol provision, on the other hand, the number of unaffordable units would increase to 17,000. Over the entire ten-year period, landlords would realize an additional $1.1 billion in rents under the more moderate ordinance. Strong rent control, in other words, would produce a substantial redistribution of wealth from landlords to tenants in comparison with more moderate ordinances.

Rent relief in Santa Monica was only temporary. Because the laws faced prolonged and vicious counterattacks that landlords usually won, the strong rent control law was gutted by court rulings and legislation. Rents then rose to a rate that was near market rates. Similar court and legislative rulings also turned the strong rent control ordinances of Berkeley and West Hollywood into moderate forms.

Barton's (1998) study of rent control in Berkeley showed how one of the nation's strongest rent control laws could result in some momentary rent relief. Nonetheless, the study cautioned, "it is still important to recognize that rent control alone was not a sufficient means of assisting poor tenants" (96). I have argued (Gilderbloom 2000) that based on the numbers provided, approximately 70 percent of very-low-income, non-student tenants were paying more than 30 percent of their incomes into rent, and 36 percent were paying 50 percent or more of their incomes into rent. Even the strongest modern rent control law in the country has not stopped three-fourths of the low-income tenants from paying unaffordable rents (Gilderbloom 2000). In comparison, under Berkeley's system of controls, rents were at market rates. Keating, Teitz, and Skaburskis (1998, 140) note that perhaps the benefit of moderate rent control regulations is not necessarily a substantial reduction in rents.

Barton (1998) notes that rent control programs might divert the energy of housing activists away from other innovative affordable housing programs. By 1996, local nonprofit housing organizations had acquired only 100 units in Berkeley, while surrounding cities without rent control, such as Hayward, "had far larger nonprofit housing sectors" (107). Unfortunately, many rent control leaders minimize homeownership strategies for renters, fearing they will lose some of their political base. The question is what kind of housing policy activists seeking greater fairness and equality should address in the new millennium. Rent control is the past, not the future.

CONCLUSION

Political Ramifications of Rent Controls

Santa Monica provides an interesting case study of the kinds of political and economic gains tenants can make by organizing themselves as a collective force. Up until 1978, Santa Monica was run like most other American cities. A local growth machine made up of the local newspaper, banks, real estate interests, and commercial interests had the final say on most political matters—especially development issues (Molotch 1976). Political analysts could safely label the town as "conservative" (Capek 1985; Capek and Gilderbloom 1992).

When rising rents became an issue, tenants organized to put rent control on the ballot. Initially, rent control proponents lost by a narrow margin. Aside from the fact that the tenants' pro-rent-control campaign was poorly funded and organized, landlords were able to successfully argue that rent control was not the answer to tenant woes. Instead, the answer was Proposition 13, passed in 1978, which cut landlord taxes by at least half. When Proposition 13 failed to deliver the promised reduction in rents, rent control was again put on the ballot, and victory for the renters' coalition soon followed, in 1980. After the rent control ordinance was put on the books, a slate of pro-rent-control candidates was elected to the city's Rent Control Board and City Council. The central theme of these campaigns was the defense of the rent control law from landlord court challenges.

The renters who wrested control of the City Council from the city's conservative pro-business faction won not only rent control but also a progressive political program that provided tangible benefits for the city's tenants, who made up 70 percent of the population. This progressive political program spoke to the needs of tenants and inspired them to vote, as Derek Shearer, campaign coordinator for the victorious Renters' Rights Coalition, assessed the win in 1980:

> I think it shows that the vote for Reagan was not a conservative vote. It was a vote against inflation and wishy-washy, middle of the road, Carter-type Democrats. When Democrats and local activists ran on a progressive program very clearly spelled out, there was a lot of support for it. (In Cockburn and Ridgeway 1981)

The Renters' Rights Coalition, presenting a politically progressive platform at the local level, campaigned for rent controls, cooperative housing, limited commercial expansion, inclusionary zoning programs, farmers markets, food cooperatives, neighborhood anti-crime efforts, and controls on toxic wastes. The group attempted to democratize City Hall by urging funding for numerous neighborhood organizations, appointing citizen task forces and commissions, and making extensive use of public hearings (see Capek and Gilderbloom 1992).

Tenants have also been instrumental in electing progressive candidates in other parts of the country. In March 1981, the voters of Vermont's largest city, Burlington, voted out of the mayor's office a five-term conservative Democrat and elected Bernard Sanders, a self-proclaimed "socialist." Sanders focused on the basic issues confronting Burlington's heavy blue-collar population: high rents, unchecked development, property taxes, and neighborhood preservation. Sanders' victory was largely attributed to his pro-tenant stance, which drew together a coalition of tenants, senior citizens, municipal unions, and liberal homeowners. During the election Sanders appealed to their votes by proclaiming:

> We have a city that is trying to help a developer build $200,000 luxury waterfront condominiums with pools and health clubs and boutiques and all sorts of upper middle class junk blocks away from an area where people are literally not eating in order to pay their rent and fuel bills . . . The issue here is that people have been exploited, thrown out of houses. In Burlington, a tenant has no rights at all. Hundreds of people have been forced to move from apartments in Burlington because of rent increases. It's about time tenants have legal protection. (In McKee 1981, 8)

Sanders went on to become a congressman and the only proclaimed socialist in the Congress; in 2007 he became a self-described socialist U.S. senator representing Vermont.

Tenants have also played a role in effecting reforms in archaic landlord/tenant laws. This was especially true in New Jersey, which had one of the most progressive landlord/tenant laws in the United States. Through the efforts of the NJTO, in 1981 more than 100 cities had rent control (Atlas and Dreier 1981, 34). The NJTO passed numerous pro-tenant laws that affected security deposits, eviction for just cause, receivership, state income tax credits, and landlord disclosure of ownership. Victories in passing pro-tenant legislation contributed to the continual growth of the NJTO. The laws that were passed by the NJTO were copied by other tenant groups and successfully passed in cities and states around the nation.

Coalition Formation

Rent control can lead not only to protection against arbitrary rent increases but also to election of pro-tenant officials, reform of landlord/tenant laws, and the building of a broad-based tenant coalition (Capek 1985; Lawson 1983). Generally, this coalition consists of seniors, blue-collar workers, and minorities (Jacob 1979; Kirschman 1980; Leight et al. 1980). These coalitions cut across age, race, and sex lines. Women often play a prominent leadership role in tenant movements. Over the past twenty years, women have been elected president of statewide tenant associations in New Jersey and California, where many citywide organizations have also been headed by women.

The uniting of working and non-working people in the struggle for better housing is significant because conservative politicians have historically used the non-working poor as scapegoats for the working person's problems (O'Connor 1981, 54–55). People learn that better housing conditions are accomplished through collective action, not individual feats.

The debate over whether a city should adopt a rent control ordinance is centered on the rights of landlords versus the rights of tenants. When people affirm the need for rent control—either through referendum or their elected officials—they state that landlords' private property rights are not absolute and that the needs of the landlord must be balanced with the needs of the tenant. The traditional sanctity of private property rights falls under public scrutiny (Harvey 1979). In other words, landlords no longer have the right to raise rents to unlimited amounts. Instead, rents must be linked to rates that are reasonable for both tenant and landlord.

Once rent control is enacted, the parameters of the discussion are changed even further. John Atlas and Peter Dreier (1980, 11) found that in areas where people have fought for rent control, it is always attacked as being anti-free enterprise and anti-business. After victory the debate shifts to what level of profit the landlord deserves. For example, at one time most New Jersey tenants accepted that landlords could charge as much as they wanted, just like any business (That's the way it has been, and that's the way it is). Now many contend that a landlord's need for profit must be balanced against the tenant's needs for an affordable and decent place to live. These are important changes in people's consciousness.

Assessment of Future Trends

Analysis of the tenants' movement in the United States shows how certain economic and political gains can be made. While it is certainly true that the economic gains made by the tenants' movement have been modest, it seems likely that more radical affordable housing programs will appear on future government agendas. It should also be kept in mind that the tenants' movement in the United States is relatively new. In 1969 there was very little tenant activity in the United States; only a few cities had rent control or tenants' unions. Today the tenants' movement is a force that politicians must not ignore.

Provisions for decent and affordable housing are only beginning to be made. The struggle for decent housing links various disenfranchised groups into an organized body, demanding greater economic and political change in all spheres of life. Unlike most housing reforms that are sponsored by real estate groups to accommodate their interests, programs pushed by the tenants' movement directly challenge the status quo.

The debate over rent control has had an important political impact. It has taught tenants that in order for housing conditions to improve, they must get involved in the political system. They must vote for referendums and elect political candidates who represent their interests. Traditionally, tenants have been apathetic toward the political system, but when confronted with an issue that directly affects them, they respond. Participation of tenants in politics can also affect other political matters.

Rent control and the need for decent and affordable housing make housing a public issue. The issue of rent control raises important political and economic questions of how housing is to be produced and distributed. The central theme of this debate is one of "property rights versus human rights."

The evidence in this chapter suggests that the movement for rent control in the United States has had more of an impact politically than economically. In terms of rent control's distributional impact, it appears that most rent control ordinances have succeeded in preventing only excessive rent increases. They have, however, provided protection against arbitrary evictions incentives for maintenance of rentals and have allowed the tenant to know what kind of rent increases to expect in the future.

Certainly, this is an improvement for tenants who have had none of these protections in the unfettered market. But rent control has not reduced rents to a level that is affordable by the majority of tenants. Moreover, rent control does not cure the problem. Recognizing this problem—and the public's acceptance of government intervention in the marketplace—numerous tenant groups are pushing for even tougher rent restrictions and an array of other "non-market" housing programs. How successful these attempts will be is contingent on the continued growth of the tenants' movement.

CHAPTER 5

INVISIBLE JAIL

Providing Housing and Transportation for the Elderly and Disabled

WITH MARK S. ROSENTRAUB

In this chapter we look at how barrier-free and affordable housing and transportation services for elderly and disabled persons have generally not been developed.[1] As we show later, very few books on housing address the considerable and important housing and transportation needs of the disabled and elderly. Here we will attempt to make this an important issue for progressive planning and housing. The elderly and disabled are often prevented from participating in employment, health care, shopping, social, and recreational activities, as well as exercising their freedom to live independently. Historically, our society has placed great emphasis on the institutionalization of elderly and disabled people who need assistance. This has relegated these people to environments that inhibit the development of self-sufficiency and community integration (Rosen, Clark, and Kivitz 1977). In many instances, terms or phrases used to describe these populations were developed to justify their exclusion from the larger society. For people with mental retardation, the words "moron," "imbecile," and "retarded" have been used. Each term creates its own stigma, which actually encourages people's isolation from society by its non-disabled and non-elderly members (Sarason and Doris 1979).

There have always been calls for more progressive policies with regard to the habilitation of elderly people and those with disabling conditions. However, in most instances, these demands were made by a limited number of academics and social reformers. In the 1970s, however, the pressure for programs and policies that were intended to integrate handicapped and elderly people into society reached a new pinnacle. Political and economic factors, together with research findings suggesting the possibilities that exist for people with handicaps, have created a demand for more community-based and socially integrated programs and policies. At the political level, court decisions that ruled institutions unfit required public action to develop community-based programs for many disabled people (see, for example, *Lelsz v. Kavanagh*, U.S. Court of Appeals, 5th Circuit, 85-2485 and 86-1166, reported January 21, 1987). The monetary costs of institutionalized programs, even in the face of lawsuits arguing the existence of inferior care, continued to rise and created another pressure for the development of alternative programs.

In addition to these factors, older people and the disabled are more vocal in their support for independent living arrangements that take advantage of technology and innovative support systems. Their goal of being free in urban environments is actually made attainable as a result of a combination of housing and transportation design modifications and creative housing programs.

In 1990, President George H. W. Bush signed into law the Americans with Disabilities Act (ADA), which was seen as a civil rights victory for the disabled, many of whom are elderly. Disability is defined in the law as "a physical or mental impairment that substantially limits a major life activity."

As the population grows older, there is an ever-expanding need for more available slots in nursing homes for those people who are either unable to take care of themselves or have families who are unable or unwilling to take care of them. As it currently stands, there is a nursing home crisis in this country due to bed shortages and deplorable conditions that will continue to worsen in the years to come. In spite of this situation, legislatures around the country have turned their backs on this segment of the population, truly making them invisible.

To a very real extent, the issue of a physical disability has always been a function of the state of technology. For example, without the advent of eyeglasses and hearing aids, many productive workers and family members would have to be considered disabled. Technological advances in transportation have also made it possible for individuals with limited physical strength to maneuver extremely large vehicles and aircraft. In a similar fashion, advances in wheelchair design, computers, and the construction of homes and buildings create the potential to make many people who were once disabled and dependent able and independent. The entire question of disability and dependency for the majority of people considered handicapped can be related to the application of existing technology.

In recognition of the possibilities that exist, several groups have called for the development of accurate databases to describe existing housing and transportation problems that can thwart independent living for the elderly and disabled people (Harlow and Rosentraub 1984).

A group of concerned citizens and public officials in Houston created a multi-institutional task force in 1985 to examine the state of housing and transportation for the elderly and the handicapped. The task force would develop plans and programs for improved social integration and access for all Houston citizens. This task force included members from the Area Agency on Aging, Harris County Community Development Agency, Houston Center for Independent Living, Housing Authority of the City of Houston, Sheltering Arms, City of Houston Planning and Development Department, Houston Metropolitan Transit Authority, Houston City Council, University of Houston, Texas Southern University, and the University of Texas at Arlington. This task force initiated a research project to assess the needs of disabled and elderly persons. The study involved interviews with more than 1,640 Houston/Harris County area residents who had special housing and transportation needs. This comprehensive study revealed certain facts with the potential of having a major impact on housing and transportation policy in the years ahead. The research also was passed along to Congress and the first President Bush in their debate concerning passage of the ADA.

ARCHITECTURAL AND LOCATION NEEDS

A substantial number of elderly and disabled persons require architectural modifications in their homes. At the time of the study (Gilderbloom 1987), one-third of Houston's seniors and more than one-half of the disabled needed grab bars in their homes (Table 5.1). At least 20 percent of the elderly and disabled wanted ramps placed in their homes. Not surprisingly, the desire for ramps and rails increased with age and severity of disability. The desire for ramps and rails doubled as elders move between the sixty to sixty-five age group and the seventy-five years and older category. Our research found that for seniors over the age of seventy-five, almost one out of three desired ramps and more than one-half wanted rails. For persons with severe disabling conditions, one-third needed rails and two-fifths required ramps.

The problem of architectural barriers within the household is further amplified by inaccessible cabinets and closets. Even with the provision of stools, one out of three disabled and one out of seven elderly were unable to use cabinets and closets within their homes (Table 5.2). Approximately one out of every seven persons in Houston was over sixty years old. One out of every twenty residents had a disabling condition. One out of every ten Houstonians required special architectural modifications in their homes to *sing and Neighborhood Features Deemed Important, by Household Type*

	Household Type								
	Low-Income			Disabled			Elderly		
	UNIM	UNSUR	IMP	UNIM	UNSUR	IMP	UNIM	UNSUR	IMP
	38	3	59	44	5	51	52	3	44
	16	2	82	15	2	83	21	3	76
	16	1	82	19	1	50	18	2	80
	59	5	36	55	3	42	60	4	36
	57	4	39	54	4	42	63	3	34
	18	4	78	18	2	79	23	3	75
	20	4	74	24	3	73	21	3	76
	68	27	27	61	6	24	76	5	19
	51	15	46	43	3	54	60	4	36
	20	5	76	15	5	77	62	4	74
	49	8	43	50	1	43	62	6	33
	46	6	48	52	8	42	44	6	41
	6	2	92	5	4	92	4	2	94
	15	0	85	12	2	85	13	2	85
	28	21	61	26	56	24	13	62	25

portant; UNSUR = Unsure; IMP = Important
osentraub, and Bullard 1987

TABLE 5.2. *Unable to Use Cabinets and Closets, by Household Type*

Response	Household Type			
	Low-Income	Disabled	Elderly	All
NO	75%	68%	85%	83%
YES	25%	32%	15%	17%
N=	253	275	634	768

Gilderbloom, Rosentraub, and Bullard 1987

enable them to have complete access to all parts of their homes. Close to one-third of the disabled and 15 percent of the elderly could not use cabinets and closets in their own homes. Outside of the home, substantial transportation and environmental barriers often prevented the disabled and elderly from participating in the economic and social life of Houston. Less than 10 percent of the disabled and elderly used public transportation.

When away from their residences, the elderly and disabled desire certain amenities that foster greater mobility. More than three-fourths of the elderly and disabled indicated that the presence of sidewalks and first-floor location were important. Persons with severe disabilities strongly desired a first-floor location. Location is a major concern of elderly and disabled persons when considering a residential move. In general, our research indicated that a significant number of disabled and elderly persons wanted the amenities found in the city. Close to one-half wanted to be located near Metro bus stops, and more than three-fourths wanted to be near medical services. The desire to be close to medical facilities increased with age and severity of disability. Eighty percent wanted to be near shopping areas. Two-fifths of the disabled and one-third of the elderly indicated that being close to work and near a public park were important in their decision to choose a residence.

Another important factor for more than eight out of every ten persons interviewed was proximity to family. Finally, slightly more than half of our respondents mentioned "zoning and rigid deed restrictions" to be important. The desire for strict zoning and deed restrictions was particularly strong among the moderate- and high-income persons with disabling conditions.

SOCIAL SERVICES

Low-income households, the elderly, and people with disabling conditions are sometimes concerned with their access to social service centers. Ap-

TABLE 5.3. *Desire to Move from Existing Home, by Household Type*

Response	Household Type			
Plan to move	Low-Income	Disabled	Elderly	All
No	67%	70%	75%	72%
Unsure	7%	7%	5%	6%
Yes	26%	23%	20%	22%
N=	262	283	647	744
Reason				
Home too small	13%	20%	9%	12%
Better home	12%	7%	11%	12%
Closer to family	29%	22%	26%	26%
Better location	13%	13%	9%	8%
Retire/change job	3%	3%	6%	4%
N=	42	28	75	117

Gilderbloom, Rosentraub, and Bullard 1987

proximately one-third of our sample wanted access to meals programs, and two-fifths wanted to be near senior citizen centers. The desire for these services increased with age and severity of disability. Low-income disabled persons tended to have a higher demand for meals programs and senior centers than higher-income disabled persons. Surprisingly, just the opposite is true for low-income elders. Moderate- and high-income seniors tended to want these services more than low-income elders. Approximately three-fourths of all respondents believed that patrol guards, burglar alarms, and window bars were critical. The desire for security was greatest in Houston's Community Development Block Target Areas. Elders and disabled persons in Harris County were the least concerned with this issue.

Given the responses to questions about what is important in residences, it is not surprising that approximately 25 percent of the disabled and elderly population wanted to move from their residences in the next year (Table 5.3). Of those who would like to move, one out of every four persons desired to find a better location. One out of every five disabled persons believed their "home is too small," while one out of every seven disabled persons wanted to live closer to family. It is important to recognize that low- and moderate-income housing can be designed in such a way as to create a community feeling and inhibit crime. Oscar Newman (1980) demonstrated that multi-family housing that fulfills certain minimal leasing requirements can be as livable as conventional homes.

Newman calls for low-rise units with a clear demarcation between private, semi-private, and public space. Child care and playground facilities should be incorporated whenever appropriate into the design that should complement prevailing community standards. Many people oppose public housing because of its drab and jail-like atmosphere. Housing should incorporate a "human feel" of uniqueness and individuality that makes residents and neighborhoods proud; examples include Pilgrim Terrace in Santa Barbara and Savo Island in Berkeley.

Amazingly enough, while close to 50 percent of the elderly and disabled lived within two blocks of a bus stop, the lack of sidewalks, curb cuts, and bus shelters actually made the use of the transportation system impossible. In Houston, three out of five disabled and elderly persons did not have sidewalks between their homes and the nearest bus stops. An even greater percentage of households lacked curb cuts (71 percent) and bus shelters (76 percent) by the nearest bus stops.

In addition to these physical barriers, the fear of crime prevented close to two-thirds of the elderly and disabled from walking to the bus stops at night. While the elderly and physically handicapped may not be more victimized by crime than other segments of society, their perception of their own vulnerability creates a fear that inhibits their social and economic involvement in society. Given these numbers, it is not surprising to find that 25 percent of the disabled and elderly population wanted to move from their homes within the next year.

Independent housing arrangements for the elderly and disabled will become critical as we progress through this new century. Demographers predicted that the population of the disabled and elderly would increase dramatically from 1987 to the present as new medical techniques prolonged human life. In Houston, such growth has been augmented by senior citizens who migrate to take advantage of a hospitable topography and climate, a cost of living below that in other areas, and a concentration of medical facilities and institutions. Texas ranks fourth among Sun Belt cities that attract the elderly from other states.

While the disabled and elderly have certain design and location requirements, one out of every four persons was making housing payments that were considered unaffordable by traditional government standards. Moreover, close to one-half of low- and moderate-income families were making excessive housing payments.

POLICY RECOMMENDATIONS

Two recommendations for local government that derived from the study involved making public transportation more accessible and fostering crime watch strategies and programs. There is evidence to suggest that changes such as transportation accessibility could have a great impact on the elderly and the disabled. Tacoma, Washington, for example, made a limited number of bus lines accessible for wheelchair users by fitting the buses with lifts. As a result, wheelchair users began to use the accessible bus line, reducing their dependence on paratransit services (Pusch 1987, 5). Harris County and the City of Houston were encouraged to begin the development of neighborhood associations and civic clubs to devise anti-crime and fear-reduction strategies at the neighborhood level. Neighborhood watch programs are an especially effective measure in fighting crime.

NATIONAL NURSING HOME CRISIS

A national nursing home crisis exists and will worsen in the decades ahead.[2] We predict that more than a half-million new nursing home beds will be needed by 2020. A federal government study of nursing home conditions found significant problems with the quality of nursing home care as well (Centers for Medicare and Medicaid Services 2002). If the number of nursing home beds were increased to provide a healthy vacancy rate, greater competition among providers would be created, and the quality of nursing homes would improve.

Surprisingly little information is available to predict nursing home bed needs. Our recent examination of general housing books found only 4 out of 6,502 pages dedicated to the needs of the elderly. When we looked at books on elderly housing, only 65 of 3,320 pages were dedicated to the subject of nursing homes. Theoretically, any model for forecasting (or method for projecting) nursing home bed needs should take into consideration the following factors:

- The national average rate of people (at any age or in different age cohorts) staying in nursing homes and the possible increase or decrease of this rate
- The different rates of people needing nursing home beds across age cohorts
- Future population projections
- The existing number of nursing home beds

· The number of nursing home beds lost due to closure or other reasons based on current attrition rate
  · The number of nursing home beds that may be lost in the future
  · A healthy vacancy rate of nursing home beds

Unfortunately, available data and research do not provide numbers for several of the factors mentioned above. The need for a substantial increase in nursing home beds is demonstrated by National Center of Health Statistics (NCHS) data: there were 1,628,300 nursing home patients and 1,879,600 nursing home beds in 1999. The number of nursing home beds increased by 1.55 percent annually from 1977 to 1996 and by 1.61 percent from 1997 to 1999 (CDC/NCHS 1999).

Using the 1.61 percent increase in nursing home beds in previous decades, as of the year 2000 there were an estimated 1,909,862 nursing home beds (Gilderbloom, Pan, and Ye 2005, 2). Based on the raw numbers, we estimate that the aggregate vacancy rate nationally in 2000 was 8.9 percent. Furthermore, 4.5 percent of the population age sixty-five and older stayed in nursing homes in 2000, according to the 2000 U.S. Census (ibid.), while less than 1 in 4,000 persons under sixty-five stayed in nursing homes, if we use calculations based on the U.S. Census.

We argue that a minimum healthy nursing home bed vacancy rate should be 5 percent, but ideally it should be at 10 percent. A 5 percent vacancy rate assumes a near-zero vacancy rate is adequate in supplying the market. Some beds need to be vacant when patients sharing rooms with other patients have contagious diseases. A 10 percent vacancy rate adjusts for this reality (and other technical reasons for vacancies) and allows room for temporary fluctuations in nursing home demand.

By 2005 the United States needed between 14,115 and 46,052 additional nursing home beds, assuming a 5 percent vacancy rate was maintained, or between 121,002 to 154,714 beds, assuming an ideal 10 percent vacancy rate (Table 5.4). By 2010 the United States will need between 151,014 and 236,095 nursing home beds, assuming a 5 percent vacancy rate, or between 265,506 and 355,315 beds, assuming a 10 percent vacancy rate.

The biggest supply shortage will be between 2015 and 2020, when about a half-million nursing home beds will be needed due to the aging of baby boomers. By 2030, the demand could be 100 percent of the existing nursing home stock in 2000. U.S. Census Bureau data suggest that every seven seconds, one baby boomer turns fifty years old (Gilderbloom, Pan, and Ye 2005). Most of the baby boomers will be over sixty by 2015. The projected demand for nursing homes shows dramatic increase in Table 5.4. The Nursing Home Abuse Resource Center (2002) suggested that by 2007 the demand for nurs-

TABLE 5.4. *Projected Nursing Home Bed Needs, 2005–2030*

Year	Highest Series		Lowest Series	
	5% vacancy rate	*10% vacancy rate*	*5% vacancy rate*	*10% vacancy rate*
2005	46,052	154,714	14,115	121,002
2010	236,095	355,315	151,013	265,506
2015	595,992	735,206	436,416	566,765
2020	1,034,514	1,198,091	778,827	928,198
2025	1,540,209	1,731,879	1,160,469	1,331,043
2030	1,992,768	2,209,581	1,459,011	1,646,171

SOURCE: U.S. Census Bureau, National Population Projections
NOTE: Highest series or lowest series are projections based on highest or lowest census population projection by age.

ing home beds would exceed the supply. However, our conservative projections suggest that if a minimal 5 percent vacancy rate was maintained, demand actually surpassed supply by 2005. Finally, our projections of nursing home beds are national aggregate numbers, and local vacancy rates vary from state to state and from region to region. Transfer trauma—adverse physiologic and psychosocial effects of elderly people being uprooted from familiar surroundings—can easily occur if a healthy vacancy rate is not maintained across all regions.

The lack of nursing home beds can best be understood within the political context of state government. State governments fear skyrocketing Medicaid bills; two-thirds of nursing home patients rely on Medicaid for their nursing home expenses (Gilderbloom, Pan, and Ye 2005). Consequently, state governments have been withholding permission to increase the number of nursing home beds.

In Kentucky, despite evidence of near-zero vacancy rates for nursing homes, the state has succeeded in virtually banning new nursing home bed construction or conversion. The issue has been tied up in the courts with lawsuits because the elderly have had to move to neighboring states, which has resulted in a greater supply of beds in Kentucky. With many states experiencing budget shortfalls, other states are also freezing or considering bans on new nursing home beds.

The government should reduce barriers to the supply of nursing home beds while remaining vigilant in ensuring the quality of nursing home care. Without careful strategies implemented quickly, the future looks bleak for those who need nursing homes and who are likely to receive increasingly poor quality of service, experience transfer trauma, and lack viable long-term care options concerning quality and location.

BEYOND NURSING HOMES

Between independent living and nursing homes, there is a need for a third stream of housing options that are less expensive and provide a non-institutional living environment. Cooperatives and communal housing for the elderly are one such option discussed in the last chapter. As Ira Rosofsky (2007) correctly notes, the average cost of living in a nursing home is $75,000, and round-the-clock home care is more than double that cost at $166,000. If three elderly persons shared a three-bedroom home or apartment, the cost for twenty-four-hour care would fall to only $55,000. A nursing home is a depressing place that strips the patient completely of the home as a symbol of self. Nursing home rooms are adorned with white walls; only a curtain separates the resident from a stranger; the blaring sound of loud speakers and noisy beeping medical equipment are a constant; the patient's door is constantly opening; and a patient's valuables are removed for safekeeping from their children. Another alternative is assisted living, which costs about $35,000 a year, but Medicaid does not cover any of these costs (Rosofsky 2007).

CONCLUSION

In the 1950s and 1960s, cities displaying signs that limited the movement of blacks were condemned. Ultimately, laws were passed prohibiting discrimination in any form. These achievements notwithstanding, cities still erect implicit signs telling disabled persons not to live in certain areas and cities. When a city does not have curb cuts or sidewalks, it is a blatant sign that the disabled are not welcome in that community or city. When a mass transit system cannot be used by the elderly or the disabled or a city does not provide the leadership to produce housing for all of its citizens—those are signs to the disadvantaged and nursing home-bound that they are not wanted. As a society we have tried to remove signs that discriminate against minorities and religious groups. It is time that we apply the same effort to help people with disabling conditions. Raymond Lifchez and Barbara Winslow (1979, 68) noted:

> At the community level, one of the most important aspects of shelter is its environmental messages. A town like Berkeley, which has demon-

strated its concern for the welfare of the disabled population with visible acts such as curb cuts, timed stop lights, and ramps, sends a message to disabled inhabitants and visitors that clearly says, 'You are welcome here; this place offers shelter and concern.' The physical environment was frequently the first subject mentioned by the informants in discussing Berkeley. It induced an immediate sense of security to many upon their arrival. 'If they care enough to make things physically accessible, which was never true anywhere else I lived, then probably they will also be more accepting of me personally.'

Historically, cities ignored the planning needs of its disadvantaged residents. Legislation like the ADA that was designed to meet the needs of the disabled community was proposed as a way to reverse the unfortunate planning practices. Progressive urban planning that envisions the needs of everyone can provide the solution to these environmental problems. An important step in that direction is for political leaders to put into action the recommendations of groups such as the Housing Advisory Committee. An important goal of urban planning is to design a barrier-free urban environment that can guarantee the full participation of the disabled in public life.

American cities have the potential to become a user-friendly environment, a city in which all citizens can partake in its rich culture, education, and entertainment, a city providing business opportunities and state-of-the-art health facilities. For too long, planners and city officials have ignored the environmental needs of its disadvantaged households. The disabled deserve respect and attention. We should keep in mind that eventually every one of us, if we live long enough, will become disabled. Few of us will die of what was once called natural causes; rather we will enter an increasingly lengthy period of the terminal stages of one or more disorders, leaving us partially or totally disabled (Zola 1979, 12).

We must design an urban environment that frees the disabled so that they can participate in city life. Goodman (1956, 97) observed that "a man has only one life and if during it he has no great environment, no community, he has been irreparably robbed of a human right." In the past the disabled had to fight social injustice that rivaled the treatment of black slaves in the South.[3] Raymond Lifchez (1987, 2) found that the disabled have been singled out for harsh discriminatory treatment. At one time, numerous American cities adopted "ugly laws" that banned the disabled from public places because their presence might be "offensive" or cause "legal liabilities."[4] Beginning with the disability rights movement in the early 1970s, such legislation was removed from the statutes of most American cities. However, as we have seen in this report, physical barriers remain a major challenge for persons with disabilities.[5]

The disabled do not want sympathy. Their main goal is to live as independently as possible and to be integrated into the mainstream of society. The disabled need to have the opportunity to realize their potential in a fully supportive environment. Although our society has made great strides in its treatment of the disabled, further progress is still needed. In 1950, M. Emmett Walter of the Houston City Planning Commission declared that Houston's greatest shame was "mediocrity in planning" (McComb 1969, 158). He told the Kiwanis Club:

> We have an opportunity in Houston to develop a magnificent city; a city that will be adequate to the economic demands and also provide facilities needed to make it a satisfactory place in which to live. Such a city can be built, if a little attention is given to planning, and it will cost less in the long run than a haphazard development. Surely a program that will satisfy every man's craving for the beautiful should receive the support of all citizens.

Walter's call for a "magnificent" Houston needs to be renewed not only in Houston but also across the nation. A city is judged great not by the number of people or monumental buildings within its border, but by its ability to provide justice and civility: How well does the city address the needs of its citizens, whether they are rich or poor, black or white, old or young, able-bodied or disabled? Great cities are measured by the kind of job, housing, educational, aesthetic, and spiritual opportunities offered to their citizens. All urbanites should live with dignity and without fear. Great cities provide for all; great cities exclude no one.

CHAPTER 6

HOPE VI

A Dream or Nightmare?

WITH MICHAEL BRAZLEY AND
MICHAEL ANTHONY CAMPBELL

In this chapter we address the dramatic change in direction that housing policy has undergone since 1989, when the U.S. Congress enacted the Department of Housing and Urban Development Reform Act. The act entailed establishing the National Commission on Severely Distressed Public Housing (NCSDPH) to assess public housing stock and make recommendations for improvement. NCSDPH recommendations eventually led to establishment of the HOPE VI revitalization program.

The HOPE VI program began with five primary objectives: (1) change the physical shape of public housing; (2) reduce concentrations of poverty; (3) provide support services; (4) maintain high standards of personal responsibility; and (5) form partnerships. The overall goal was to create mixed-income communities.

We will analyze two Kentucky HOPE VI projects for best practices: the award-winning but generally failed Park DuValle project in Louisville and a less recognized but more successful counterpart in Newport, about 100 miles away. Despite the hype surrounding it, the Park DuValle project has a number of problems involving exorbitant cost of housing, lack of racial integration, isolation from basic necessary services, and a very low rate of former public housing residents who moved back to the HOPE VI homes. On the other hand, the Newport HOPE VI development did not make these mistakes and has emerged as a model program based on the scattered-site approach to public housing that research has generally favored. Instead of keeping an old public housing site like Park DuValle, Newport managers saw in HOPE VI an opportunity to provide infill housing to integrate residents into more racially and socioeconomically diverse neighborhoods. The cost of building the Newport HOPE VI units was far less than at Park Du-Valle, while the social returns are far greater.

We examine here the enormous potential costs and/or benefits of HOPE VI in terms of human capital, research and theoretical implications, public housing policy, and a local economic development tool. We also review research on resident satisfaction in scattered-site housing, the factor that most clearly distinguishes the Newport HOPE VI program from the Park DuValle program. Two central questions we address in this chapter are whether HOPE VI is achieving its stated objectives and what impact the HOPE VI environment has on resident satisfaction.

HISTORY OF HOPE VI

In the early 1990s, public attitudes toward inner-city public housing were largely negative, and even residents were unhappy with public housing. Historically, public housing has suffered from major problems that include economic isolation, residential segregation (by concentrating the very poor in economically distressed and minority neighborhoods), federal laws that discourage working families from occupancy for extended periods, and work prevention for unemployed families. Quality control standards in public housing have lacked the discipline of the open market, resulting in unhappy residents who are unable to find suitable housing elsewhere.

In 1992 NCSDPH completed its study of distressed public housing, finding 6 percent of public housing, approximately 86,000 units, uninhabitable. Congress crafted legislation intended to overhaul and "save" public housing. Senator Barbara Mikulski (D-MD), chairwoman of the Appropriations Housing and Urban Development Subcommittee, introduced $300 million in appropriations in fiscal year 1993 for funding a public housing revitalization program to demolish uninhabitable public housing, replace it with renovated and new human-scaled units, and provide social services to residents (Twohey 2000). The legislation for the Urban Revitalization Demonstration (URD) program was passed by Congress and has become known as Homeownership and Opportunity for People Everywhere, or HOPE VI. The HOPE VI program proposed to demolish 115,000 public units, replacing them with 60,000 new or rehabilitated units, resulting in a shortfall of more than 55,000 public housing units.

The program has faced tremendous hardship while George W. Bush has been president. With his reelection in 2004, Bush began his new term trying to either cut back or end the HOPE VI program—which ironically was a signature program of his father at the end of his term. In his 2004 budget, George W. Bush sought to eliminate the program. The HUD secretary at the time, Mel Martinez, went along with Bush's proposal and said new approaches needed to be taken. At this writing, potential changes to HOPE VI with a new Democratic majority in Congress remain to be elaborated.

Before discussing the particular programs at Park DuValle and Newport, we now examine the scattered-site approach to public housing that underlies HOPE VI.

SCATTERED-SITE PUBLIC HOUSING AND RESIDENT SATISFACTION

David Varady and Wolfgang Preiser use three quantifiers to define the term "scattered-site housing": the number of units at the site, which may range from two to a few hundred; structures, usually including garden apartments, duplexes, townhouses, or single-family detached houses; and deconcentration of units away from high-density, low-income minority populations (1998, 190). Varady and Preiser's definition of scattered-site housing and the HOPE VI program are one and the same.

In 1987 Francescato, Weidemann, and Anderson completed one of the largest and most sophisticated surveys to date on "resident satisfaction in HUD assisted housing." The survey covered thirty-seven HUD housing developments including ten public housing projects. As reported in Varady and Preiser (1998, 190), the survey "found no relationship between satisfaction on the one hand and project height, size, and density on the other. The implication is that residents of scattered-site housing are not necessarily more satisfied than residents of traditional family developments."

Burby and Rohe (1989) argued that the deconcentration of public housing increases resident satisfaction and reduces the fear of crime. Research on the Gautreaux program in Chicago, the first scattered-site and mobility program (Rosenbaum 1993, 1995; Rosenbaum and Popkin 1990), showed that individuals in public housing benefited from scattered-site housing through better employment for adults and better educational opportunities for children. The results of the Gautreaux program also disproved the "culture of poverty model" while providing legitimacy to the "geography of opportunity model" (Galster and Killen 1995). Fischer (1991) and Varady and Preiser (1998) contend that public housing residents who move to the suburbs in scattered-site housing are more satisfied than those who decide to remain in public housing.

Scattered-site housing is the model for the "geography of opportunity" hypothesis. Advocates argue that public housing residents who live in scattered-site housing have higher levels of resident satisfaction, greater access to better schools and jobs, lessened fear of crime, and the cultural enrichment of exposure to more diverse populations (Briggs 1997, 1998; Briggs, Darden, and Aidala 1999; Burby and Rohe 1989; Kingsley and Tatian 1997; Rosenbaum 1991, 1995; Rosenbaum and Harris 2001; Rosenbaum and Popkin 1990, 1991).

Varady and Preiser's (1998) study of housing satisfaction in public housing units found that approximately three-fourths of the individuals living in scattered-site single-family detached homes, clustered scattered-site housing, and traditional public housing were satisfied with their homes (201). Varady and Preiser argued that "home satisfaction" is influenced by maintenance of the unit, the surrounding neighborhood, crime, neighborhood social interaction, resident involvement in decision making, and the quality of the home (203). The research showed that "resident satisfaction" is based more on environmental influences than the home.

The present consensus among policy makers and scholars is that high concentrations of low-income households lead to negative behavioral and social outcomes (Popkin et al. 2000, 928). Dispersed development and mixed-income strategies now dominate federal public housing policy, a legacy of the Gautreaux program. Varady and Preiser (1998, 189) argue that since the 1970s, public housing policy has shifted away from large, more traditional projects and toward scattered-site units located away from the inner city.

Popkin et al. (2000) argue that there is a lack of research and data supporting the idea that low-income public housing residents benefit from the HOPE VI program. While counterintuitive, it is possible that HOPE VI leaves the most vulnerable and poorest families in a worse condition than when living in the public housing ghettos. The fear is that these families are losing their homes and have no other viable options.

HISTORY OF PARK DUVALLE

African-Americans first occupied the western Louisville area now known as Park DuValle in the 1880s. The area was called "Little Africa" and was considered the black section of Parkland, a Louisville suburb. In the late 1940s "Little Africa" was razed for urban renewal, and a public housing project was built in 1952 and named after educator and noted poet Joseph Cotter Sr. Another public housing project, Lang Homes, was built in the same area in 1958 (Jones 1999).

Cotter and Lang Homes established an enormous area of low-income housing for families that were both socially and physically isolated from the rest of the Park DuValle neighborhood. Cotter Homes had 620 apartments in fifty-five identically designed buildings on a thirty-four-acre site. Lang Homes comprised 496 apartments in sixty-three identically designed buildings on a forty-one-acre site. The design and size of the public housing complex made it impossible to blend with the existing neighborhood, and as a result, the complex became its own neighborhood of low-income residents.

The Cotter and Lang sites were chosen to house as many African-Americans as possible in "Little Africa" by isolating them from both the Central Business District and the suburbs. Cummings and Price (1997) have documented that Louisville's public housing reinforced residential segregation.

The implementation of HOPE VI in 1996 brought important changes to the Park DuValle area involving demolition and construction of units for more than 1,000 families, relocation of residents, mixed-income residences, homeownership along with rentals, and social components that are an essential feature of HOPE VI.

However, despite two decades of research favoring scattered-site suburban housing and supporting the "geography of opportunity" concept,[1] the HOPE VI Park DuValle revitalization entailed building the new housing community on the old, isolated public housing site, thereby reinforcing patterns of public housing residential segregation. HUD and the Housing Authority of Louisville had the opportunity to integrate public housing into the larger community but chose not to do so.

RESIDENT SATISFACTION WITH HOPE VI IN LOUISVILLE

Cotter and Lang public housing in Louisville was in a state of decline until the HOPE VI intervention in the late 1990s. The neighborhood had high crime, high density, housing stock in disrepair, and declining family incomes. The Cotter and Lang population was one of the youngest and poorest groups of families when compared to other public housing populations around the country. Before HOPE VI, the Park DuValle community was known as the most crime-ridden and dangerous neighborhood in Louisville.

The HOPE VI Park DuValle revitalization sparked a surge in middle-class African-American residents; 80 percent of the heads of households have full-time employment with a median yearly household income of about $30,000. Most of these households are headed by single African-American women. Nearly 100 percent of the heads of household have at least the equivalent of a high school education and live with two or more children.

Initial reactions to the HOPE VI revitalization of the Park DuValle area have been positive (Brazley and Gilderbloom 2007). The majority of residents surveyed (Brazley 2002) stated that they were satisfied with their Park DuValle neighborhood in terms of schools, churches, public transportation, child care, medical services, and employment. The majority of respondents were satisfied with Park DuValle housing, street lighting, sidewalks, cleanliness of area, neighborhood in general, and adult and child recreation. Some respondents were dissatisfied with shopping and entertainment in and around the neighborhood.

Brazley's (2002) survey had an open-ended question giving the residents the opportunity to express themselves in their own words. Those who responded to the open-ended question stated that they needed more shops, stores, restaurants, local employment, better public transportation, more entertainment, parks, and playgrounds, "more jobs, transportation, and community recreation" (166). One respondent stated:

> The only real complaint I have with the neighborhood is lack of commercial development. The only convenience foods available are Kentucky Fried Chicken. Cannot get a pizza delivery—no cleaners, laundry, drug store, supermarkets, etc., maintenance inspections and services starting to slow down. Management not open to scheduling of inspections for tenant convenience and safety. (Ibid.)

Another Park DuValle resident responding to the open-ended question answered:

> The only thing I can see is no grocery store close by for the kids to buy anything. They have to walk to the truck (ice cream truck); we need a store for those that don't have transportation. Otherwise, I love the peace and quiet here. I came from a house to this apartment, I love it. It's like moving to the country but better. I have the best of both worlds a few blocks away. (167)

In response to the question of how to improve the development, a resident replied, "true assistance when it's proven that you need it and management that will listen and care instead of feeding you false hopes of assistance." Another commented, "Be committed to put more money in an area where low-income African Americans live and want to improve their living conditions" (96).

HOPE VI OBJECTIVES IN PARK DUVALLE

The Park DuValle project has completed or is in the process of completing the five major objectives of the HOPE VI program. The first—"change the physical shape of public housing"—was accomplished at Park DuValle by demolishing existing public housing and building a New Urbanism community. The flat-roofed, concrete structural frame, non-load-bearing concrete block wall design of public housing was transformed into human-scale, wood-framed, brick-veneer, gable-roofed townhouses and single-family detached homes. The HOPE VI residential development is based on three architecture styles found in Louisville: Victorian, Colonial Revival, and Craftsman. New Urbanism argues that traditional architectural styles need to be part of the development for continuity. The HOPE VI development has traditional housing elements including front porches, front and rear yards, narrow streets, alleys, and walkable neighborhoods. HOPE VI has changed the shape of public housing.

The second objective of HOPE VI—"reduce concentrations of poverty"—was accomplished by reducing residential units in Park DuValle by approximately one-half. Cotter Homes averaged seventeen dwelling units per acre, and Lang Homes averaged twelve dwelling units per acre. Park DuValle's Oaks (Phase I) averages eight dwelling units per acre, and The Village (Phase II) averages seven dwelling units per acre (Housing Authority of Louisville 1998). The yearly incomes of residents in Cotter and Lang Homes averaged $5,000 in 1994. While the mean income of the HOPE VI Park DuValle residents in 2001 averaged $26,134, Brazley (2002) found that the median household income for the Park DuValle community and the value of the property had increased. These increases coincided with improved housing stock as housing units per acre were reduced and the level of serious crime and concentration of poverty dropped (ibid.).

The third objective of the HOPE VI program is to provide residents with support services in the form of self-sufficiency programs. These programs are proposed to help all public housing families achieve and sustain self-sufficiency and to encourage economic and community investment through employment, education, and human services initiatives. This objective was met at Park DuValle with ongoing programs such as job training, educational courses, neighborhood leadership, and child care, along with a new program in homeownership counseling and home repairs. University of Louisville Sustainable Urban Neighborhoods provided leadership training in environmental justice.

The fourth objective of the HOPE VI program—to maintain high standards of personal responsibility among residents—began with President Bill Clinton's "Three Strikes and You're Out" policy reinforcing efforts to keep drug dealing and other criminal activities out of public housing. To live at Park DuValle, applicants must pass the HOPE VI screening process. Park DuValle has some of the highest standards of personal responsibility requirements in the country, requiring criminal background check, credit check, rental history check, and inspections for employment, job training, family self-sufficiency, and housekeeping.

The fifth objective of HOPE VI is to establish public-private partnerships for program completion. HUD's initial $51 million grant to the Park DuValle project in 1994 was leveraged into $180 million of public-private funding. The public-private partnership includes HUD, the City of Louisville, the Housing Authority of Louisville, Community Builders Inc., the University of Louisville, the Housing Partnership Inc., Louisville Real Estate Development Co. Inc., PNC Bank, and National City Community Development Corporation.

HOPE VI IMPLEMENTATION IN PARK DUVALLE

The HOPE VI Park DuValle revitalization program in Louisville has been often cited as a model and one of the most successful HOPE VI developments in the nation. It has received national awards from HUD, the American Institute of Architects, and the Congress on New Urbanism. National and local media also have lauded this development. Our research shows that while it has had some success, the praise is not wholly deserved.

The decision makers who ultimately implemented the Park DuValle program chose to build a new housing community on an isolated site previously utilized for public housing. This choice reinforced a pattern of racial segregation that has constituted an element of continued failure at Park DuValle.

The HOPE VI program is not another "bricks-and-mortar" project. It is different because it involves physical and social planning to improve both the resident and the neighborhood. The physical planning portion of Louisville's Park DuValle HOPE VI program involved demolishing the existing public housing community of 1,116 families, building a New Urbanism community of 1,273 families, returning original public housing residents to their neighborhood as renters or homeowners, and attracting mixed-income non-public-housing residents to the neighborhood as renters and homeowners.

The social planning element provides public housing residents the opportunity to receive self-sufficiency services regardless of whether they choose HOPE VI replacement units, Section 8 housing, or traditional public housing. Services at Park DuValle include case management, employment and career training, computer training, youth activities, family health services, and health insurance for children.

Tracking Displaced Tenants

HUD hired ABT Associates Inc. to track public housing residents who were relocated by HOPE VI. On April 27, 2001, an "Interim Memo on HOPE VI Tracking (Retrospective) Study" was issued to Ron Ashford of HUD by Larry Burton, Heather Handle, and Saty Patrabansh of ABT Associates. The ABT report tracks residents in eight housing authorities across the country including the former Cotter and Lang Homes in Louisville.

ABT's study included the Family Self-Sufficiency (FSS) program. The HOPE VI self-sufficiency program for Cotter and Lang Homes residents was singled out as offering only one new service—homeownership counseling—that was not part of an existing program. Park DuValle also was noted in the study as the only HOPE VI program to require residents to work or participate in the FSS job training program. Park DuValle residents are required to travel off-site to receive their supportive services (Burton, Handle, and Patrabansh 2001, 17).

Like other applicants, former Cotter and Lang residents must pass screening criteria to live in the HOPE VI Park DuValle community. Of the eight HOPE VI sites that ABT studied, Park DuValle had the most demanding screening requirements. "Interviews with Public Housing Authority (PHA) staff confirmed that the inability to meet the screening criteria has been a reason that former residents were disqualified from moving into new units built as part of the HOPE VI revitalization" (Burton, Handle, and Patrabansh 2001, 19).

Before HOPE VI revitalization, the household characteristics of Cotter and Lang residents were as follows: the total public housing population included 1,343 households; three-fifths of the heads of household were between 25 and 44 years old, one-fifth were between 18 and 24 years old, and 96 percent were African-American. Cotter and Lang Homes had the lowest percentage of elderly heads of household and the largest percentage of the youngest heads of household. After revitalization, ABT's study revealed that the 1,343 households had dropped to 711 households by 2000, a reduction of 632 households, or 47 percent.

Every public housing authority that receives a HOPE VI grant must submit quarterly progress reports to HUD. The Housing Authority of Louisville (1998) reported that 1,273 households were relocated from Cotter and Lang Homes; among them, 611 households were relocated to public housing, 232 households moved to Section 8 housing, 198 households were evicted, and 232 households went to "Other" situations (bought homes, lived with relatives, became homeless, etc.).

A total of 1,116 public housing units were demolished. The Louisville Housing Authority quarterly report stated that of the new rental housing units, 250 families were in the Annual Contribution Contract (ACC) with HUD program; 189 families were non-ACC members, with 128 non-ACC families becoming new homeowners; and 69 families were reoccupancy residents, that is, former Cotter and Lang public housing residents. No data were available on the families that were evicted or that left the housing assistance program. The report indicated that of the 1,273 households that comprised Cotter and Lang Homes, only 150 were scheduled to live in the new HOPE VI community.

The quarterly report included worksheets on self-sufficiency caseloads. The worksheets were subdivided into the following sections: pre-revitalization residents, post-revitalization residents, crime reduction, economic development, homeownership, Section 8, employment, number of enrollments, and number of successful completions.

The section on pre-revitalization of residents gave the following numerical information: out of 1,304 original potential household cases, the caseload at the time of the report was 594 households; 95 households did not accept services, 12 households no longer needed services, 747 households moved out or their whereabouts were unknown, 144 households had cumulative additions, 284 households relocated to other public housing, 121 households relocated using Section 8 certificates and vouchers, 156 households were not assisted by HUD, and 33 households returned after revitalization. The self-sufficiency program staff was unable to locate almost 60 percent of the original caseload.

After relocation, the self-sufficiency program had cases in only three areas: homeownership (eleven homeowners in three years), job placement, and job skill training. There were no cases or activity in the following self-sufficiency programs: post-revitalization residents, crime reduction, economic development, Section 3, successful completions, employment preparation, placement, or retention, high school or equivalent education, child care, transportation, and substance abuse programs.

Residents' Relocation

Information Technology, a consultant of the Housing Authority of Louisville, provided the most complete and accurate assessment of residential relocation of the reported 1,343 families in Park DuValle prior to the HOPE VI program's inception there. The Park DuValle Information Technology assessment reported the relocation of 1,302 Cotter and Lang families as follows.

A. Households evicted
   Lease violation: 19
   Non-payment of rent: 248
   Drug involvement: 31
      Total: 298
B. Housing Authority of Louisville (HAL) relocated 351 families to other public housing projects and 185 families to Section 8 housing.
C. The remaining 468 families moved because
   Purchased homes: 17
   Moved to better housing: 73
   Moved to Section 8: 31
   Rent was late four times: 17
   Leaving city: 20
   Illness: 17
   Rent too high: 19
   Disliked regulations: 4
   Moved without notice: 92
   Other: 178

The data indicate that more than half of the Cotter and Lang residents no longer received housing assistance. The research also suggested that the majority of public housing residents relocated by the HOPE VI project failed to experience increased opportunities in homeownership.

Police Reports

Louisville Police reports of serious offenses in the Park DuValle area show a significant drop in crime from 1990 to 2001. In 1990, the Park DuValle neighborhood had 2 homicides, 8 rapes, 46 robberies, and 75 assaults with serious injuries, for a total of 131 registered serious offenses. The 2001 totals indicated no homicides or rapes, 2 robberies, and 5 assaults with serious injury. It is obvious that the razing of the slums known as Cotter and Lang Homes, construction of The Oaks and The Villages, and the "Three Strikes" policy helped to reduce serious crime in the Park DuValle neighborhood.

THE ECONOMICS OF HOPE VI

The HOPE VI Park DuValle revitalization program reinforces historical patterns of public housing segregation and economic isolation. The neighborhood lacks commercial development, has poor access to public transportation, fails to provide community employment, and offers few entertainment opportunities. Park DuValle is an environment of limited opportunity for the poor. Public housing residents do not participate in the self-sufficiency programs. Most residents enlist in Section 8 rather than participate in the mandatory HOPE VI family self-sufficiency program. The support services and FSS programs are not being utilized by a large number of tenants.

One also must question the cost of producing "affordable housing" in the HOPE VI project when compared to other nonprofit urban housing efforts (Capek and Gilderbloom 1992; Gilderbloom and Appelbaum 1988; Gilderbloom and Mullins 2005). Comparisons show that the cost of producing one housing unit is two to three times higher for the HOPE VI developments than for comparable community-controlled nonprofits. During the same period as the HOPE VI project, 1994 to 2004, the nonprofit Louisville Central Development Corporation built three-bedroom units for as low as $49,500 (Gilderbloom and Mullins 2005). These units were attractive and were within walking distance of downtown, high-wage jobs, shopping, entertainment, and recreational activities. They were constructed on sites adjacent to middle-income homeowners. Altogether, nonprofit organizations provided approximately 100 of these units at a very low cost compared to the $54,232,667 spent on Park DuValle by 2006 to produce 320 residential units at a cost of $169,000 per unit.

HOPE VI officials note that the cost of a single unit will fall to $139,000 when all 1,273 units are built, for an expected overall cost of $177,940,000. In 2003, 18,000 new homes were sold in the Louisville market, 70 percent of them for less than $150,000. What would have happened if the same amount of money invested in HOPE VI were directed to nonprofit housing developers?

Scattered-site housing in middle-class residential areas would substantially reduce economic isolation and residential segregation, a problem that the HOPE VI program has not adequately addressed. Moreover, funding community-based nonprofits appears to be significantly more cost-effective and pragmatic, since they are building within existing communities. Louisville's HOPE VI program has won national awards and is often declared the best in the nation. Yet Louisville's HOPE VI program has significant flaws.

LESSONS FROM NEWPORT

Policy makers need to focus on Newport, Kentucky, across the Ohio River from Cincinnati (Gilderbloom 2004). Unlike the HOPE VI program in Louisville's Park DuValle, which was built in an isolated part of the city, Newport has not built any low-income housing on old, isolated sites. All new low-income housing—a combination of single-family dwellings, townhomes, and renovated older buildings—is being scattered throughout the city. To help integrate instead of isolate the poor, Newport HOPE VI offers residents counseling as well as job and educational opportunities as a hand up and not a handout (Gilderbloom and Mullins 2005). HOPE VI also has been an important part of Newport's revival of the downtown and surrounding middle-class neighborhoods.

Newport shows how the mistakes of Louisville's Park DuValle HOPE VI program can be avoided. Let's look at the demographic information on Newport HOPE VI. Statistical data were collected from HUD, the Newport Housing Authority (NHA), Brighton Center, and Newport Independent School District. Census data were collected for Kentucky Census Tract 501, the City of Newport, and Campbell County, and data were provided by the Northern Kentucky Chamber of Commerce and the City of Newport.

Demographic Profile of Public Housing Residents

Brighton Center, a Newport nonprofit organization begun in 1966 (http://www.brightoncenter.com), maintains records concerning local public housing residents. Table 6.1 provides a demographic sketch of public housing residents that is fairly typical, with one major exception—the racial composition of residents: in Newport, nearly three-fourths of the public housing residents are white.

Brighton Center is providing excellent benefits and services and has become a model for similar programs in other cities around the nation. Table 6.2 shows how many of the programs have met or exceeded their goals of helping people out of public housing. Brighton Center sponsors various community projects in hopes of improving both community and individual awareness in areas such as education, employment, youth activities, and homeownership. Brighton Center Inc. Community and Supportive Services (CSS) HOPE VI Project was instituted in March 2001 in collaboration with NHA. The data displayed in Table 6.2 are from the first half of year 5, July 1–December 31, 2005.

TABLE 6.1. *Demographics of Newport Housing Authority Residents*

Factor	Group	Number	Percent
Race	African American	32	22.4
(head of household)	Asian	1	0.7
	Hispanic	1	0.7
	Caucasian	106	74.1
	Native American	1	0.7
	Other	2	1.4
Gender	Male	17	11.9
(head of household)	Female	126	88.1
Age (residents)	0–3	106	29.2
	4–12	53	14.6
	13–17	36	9.9
	18–59	155	42.7
	60+	13	3.6
Education	Less than HS	94	56.0
	GED	30	17.9
	HS diploma	40	23.8
	Other/no response	4	2.4
Employment status	Employed	54	32.1
and disability	Unemployed (ssi)	68	40.5
	Unemployed (no ssi)	46	27.4
Average monthly	TANF	$237	20
income per	Child support	$220	10
household	Employed	$916	32
	Self-employed	$175	19
	Social Security	$500	29
Average family	Employed	$840	49
income	Unemployed	$336	51

Gilderbloom and Hanka 2006

Support Services

NHA has contracted with Brighton Center to provide and coordinate social services for NHA residents throughout the term of the HOPE VI project. The NHA contract with Brighton Center includes a clause that allows for annual revisions of goals as necessary to reflect NHA population changes.

Overall Project Effectiveness

A total of 25 of the 34 (73.5 percent) support service participation goals have been completed or exceeded. All but 2 of the current support service

TABLE 6.2. *Newport Community and Supportive Services Work Plan Goals, July 1–December 31, 2005*

Program/Activity	Participation Goal (Persons)	Participation to Date (Persons)
Job center/one-stop job training development	25	54 Goal exceeded
Assist families with entering post-secondary degree program/training	7	22 Goal exceeded
Enroll residents in a certificate or degree program @ NK Vo-Tech or NKU	7	7 Goal completed
Residents will enroll in the Bureau of Vocational Rehabilitation program	7	6
Career training through CET	35	29
Residents completing CET will obtain full-time employment	16	9
Residents completing CET will obtain full-time employment for 9 months	12	6
Residents completing CET will be offered health insurance	12	6
Residents will complete CET	20	9
Individuals use of the YMCA computer lab	10	17 Goal exceeded
Individuals will attend Newport Adult or Community Learning Center	25	42 Goal exceeded
Residents will obtain GED or increase TABE by 4 grade levels	12	Increase TABE: 18; Received GED: 10; Goal exceeded
Youth will participate in the YLD/Summer Youth program	10	18 Goal exceeded
Youth participation in YMCA activities (per year)	30	55 Goal exceeded
Form a Girl Scout troop	10 Girls	21 Goal exceeded
Youth participation in Boys and Girls Club activities (per year)	15	42 Goal exceeded
Participation in w/a youth programs	8	8 Goal completed
Participants' awareness of child care availability and funding	45	52 Goal exceeded
Health Point will provide services to families on a sliding scale fee	60	95 Goal exceeded
Families will purchase a new residence	10	8
First-time moms will receive home visits from Every Child Succeeds	10	13 Goal exceeded

TABLE 6.2. *Continued*

Program/Activity	Participation Goal (Persons)	Participation to Date (Persons)
Families will receive health insurance for kids through K-Chip	10	22 Goal exceeded
Moms and babies will visit the Healthy Moms and Babies van	15	17 Goal exceeded
Newport school-based health center will provide families with monthly care	10	28 Goal exceeded
North Key will provide mental health and substance abuse services to families	15	36 Goal exceeded
NHA maintenance department will provide basic home maintenance	20	3
Participants will go through the NKU entrepreneurship center for small business	10	0
Participants will receive HUD mortgage counseling through BC	30	33 Goal exceeded
Participants will complete HUD mortgage counseling through BC	16	21 Goal exceeded
Families will receive budget counseling through the CSS worker	40	90 Goal exceeded
Families have credit reports pulled	40	47 Goal exceeded
Families will resolve credit issues	20	31 Goal exceeded
Families will receive transportation assistance	31	48 Goal exceeded
Families will be given information about TANK routes and increase usage of public transportation	20	46 Goal exceeded

Abbreviations:
BC Brighton Center
CET Center for Employment Training
CSS Community Social Services
GED Graduate Equivalency Degree
HUD Housing and Urban Development
NHA Newport Housing Authority
NK Northern Kentucky
NKU Northern Kentucky University
TABE Test of Adult Basic Education
TANK Transit Authority of Northern Kentucky
YLD Youth Leadership Program

programs (94.1 percent) have met more than half of their participation goals; 10 of the 35 participation goals (28.6 percent) have been exceeded by more than 100 percent. CSS has added a monthly movie day to the activities, as well as workshops and office activities such as puzzle building that have proven to be popular with the residents. The success of meeting the participation goals is surprising in light of the decreases in families eligible for HOPE VI due to evictions or moving for other reasons.

A key component and aspiration of all HOPE VI programs is participant inclusion in the planning process and instilling a sense of program ownership in residents. Brighton Center's outreach program has been successful in increasing the attendance at town meetings through incentives and peer pressure. Town hall meetings have offered prizes and amenities and have become a popular meeting place for friends and neighbors. A total of 33 of the 34 scheduled supportive services programs (97 percent) have been utilized. The only class that has yet to be utilized is the Northern Kentucky University entrepreneurship program for potential small-business owners, and this is attributed to lack of interest among the residents in owning their own businesses.

Newport HOPE VI Relocation Data

By December 31, 2005, only 22 of the original 178 HOPE VI-eligible families remained on the site (Photos 6.1 and 6.2). Among those who had left, 18 had received Section 8 rental vouchers and leased units; 3 had used Section 8 homeownership vouchers and purchased homes in Newport; 15 had transferred to the South site; and 2 transferred to the public housing development for the elderly, Grand Towers Apartments. The remaining families either gave notice and moved or were evicted for various lease violations. Of the 3 families that purchased homes, 1 bought on Liberty Row and 2 bought elsewhere in Newport.

The City of Newport purchased the NHA site and planned to close it in mid-2006, raze the public housing, and replace it with highrises for high-end residential and office space. In the expectation that some residents would not have moved out by the deadline, NHA acquired three cottages to rehab (Photos 6.3 and 6.4).

In April 2005, the Newport Housing Authority began the Community Investment Partnership Program (CIPP). HUD allowed NHA to set aside approximately $1.6 million to finance this program, which was designed to close by the end of 2007. CIPP is a soft second mortgage program intended to assist low- and moderate-income homebuyers in purchasing existing non–HOPE VI

6.1 Public housing in Newport before HOPE VI

6.2 Boarded-up public housing in Newport

6.3 Historic cottages before renovation for overflow housing

homes within the City of Newport. The program offers non-interest-bearing soft second mortgage loans up to $35,000 to bridge the gap between the purchase price of the property and the sum of the required down payment plus the first mortgage financing package. The homebuyer makes no payments on the soft second mortgage as long as he or she owns the home and uses it as the principal residence for at least five years. The loan is forgiven at a rate of 20 percent per year over the five-year period. If the homeowner sells or rents out the property before the five years are up, the balance is due at the time of the sale or moving out.

NHA established eligibility requirements for a homebuyer to participate in CIPP that initially included a maximum purchase price of the home of $140,000. The homebuyer had to have a household income that was no greater than 80 percent of the Area Median Income (AMI) in Campbell County. The homebuyer could not have a history of criminal activity by any household member for five years preceding the date of the application. Homebuyers were required to be current on all lease obligations for at least the previous six months. The homebuyer had to participate in Yes You Can! or another approved homebuyer training course.

The homebuyer was required to make a minimum down payment on the home of 1 percent or $500, whichever was greater, and this down payment would come from the homebuyer's own funds. Finally, the homebuyer had

6.4 Historic cottages renovated for overflow housing

to be employed full-time (an average of thirty hours per week) for at least one full year prior to the execution of the sales agreement; the elderly and disabled were exempt from this requirement.

CIPP was well received in its first year. The soft second mortgages it offered attracted young people from surrounding areas. Real estate agents and area lenders were enthusiastically involved in the program. From April through December 2005, CIPP closed on thirty mortgages and spent $792,083 of available funds. The average mortgage amount was $26,400.

One requirement to participate in the CIPP was revised. The buyer's income, not the purchase price of the home, dictated the eligibility amount. After nine months, NHA administrators felt that income was a more equitable way to determine a fair amount for the buyer. This way, a family earning 80 percent of AMI would be eligible for less than a family earning in the 30–40 percent range. All other CIPP eligibility requirements remained the same. NHA administrators expected this revision to enable approval of approximately thirty more mortgages before closing the program by the end of 2007. All houses that were built have sold.

A profound result of the CIPP has been the restoration of house pride and clean neighborhoods in Newport. For a house to be eligible for purchase with CIPP funds, it had to pass HUD's minimum property standards test, the Housing Quality Standards (HQS). If people expected to sell their homes to CIPP participants, they had to have their houses in an above-par state of appearance and structural integrity. These standards have had an impact on the homes that were prepared for potential CIPP sales. In turn, the restoration and maintenance of these homes has had an impact on neighbors, who began to show more pride in the appearance of not only their homes but also their yards and the areas surrounding their homes.

Business Startups

One of the criticisms often cited against HOPE VI projects is the lack of economic and commercial incubation they have offered. Newport HOPE VI has enjoyed a consistent growth in business startups since its inception in June 2001 (Table 6.3). The City of Newport covers only 5.6 square miles, so the creation of more than sixty businesses a year is very apparent to the residents. The area flourishing most over the past five years has been the space known as Newport on the Levee, a $170 million, 408,000-square-foot, mixed-use family entertainment complex that includes a million-gallon aquarium as well as shops, restaurants, offices, and a hotel. From a geographic standpoint, Monmouth Street (Photo 6.5) has been the ripest area for business development outside of the Levee. In 2005, slightly over 19 percent of all business startups occurred on Monmouth Street.

Initiating Work on the Newport Sites

The initial developers, Philadelphia-based Penrose Properties Inc., signed the development agreement with NHA on September 30, 2002. Shortly thereafter, Cole and Russell Architects was hired to design the development. Changes to the development plan and new market studies delayed work, and HUD approved a new schedule submitted in August 2003, as well as occupancy for housing units on five properties: the Marx Building, Corpus Christi Apartments, Trixie's, Liberty Row II, and Saratoga-Roberts.

NHA applied to HUD in Washington to replace Penrose and become the developer through its subsidiary Newport Millennium Housing Corporation (NMHC) of the remaining 160 rental units. HUD approved this request. Through an agreement also approved by HUD, Brighton Properties, a subsidiary of Brighton Center, would develop the remaining 54 homeownership units.

TABLE 6.3. *Business Startups in Newport Since June 2001*

Year	Count	Percent Change
(June) 2001	66	
2002	85	28.8
2003	76	10.6
2004	91	19.7
2005	84	7.7

SOURCE: Newport Economic Development Office, from Gilderbloom and Hanka 2006

One homeownership site, Liberty Row Phase I (Photos 6.6, 6.7, and 6.8), is available for occupancy. This project is owned by NMHC and includes fourteen homeownership units—thirteen newly constructed and one rehabilitated.

The Corpus Christi Apartments project (Photo 6.9) is an iconic church built in 1844 and was sold to the city for developing mixed-income contemporary housing units. All the units are expected to be sold or rented. HOPE VI-eligible families had first priority on the waiting list for occupancy at Corpus Christi. Nonetheless, NHA developed a marketing plan in collaboration with local churches, banks, and organizations such as Brighton Center to notify the target populations. The site has twenty total units—ten for tax credit (60 percent of AMI) and ten for public housing (80 percent of AMI). The apartments vary in size, the smallest measuring 628 square feet (Figures 6.1 and 6.2) and the largest 767 square feet (Figure 6.3).

NHA and Brighton Center are collaborating on an exciting project for housing in the Newport area for people with disabilities. Brighton Center received an 811 Grant through the Kentucky Housing Corporation (KHC), a grant allocated specifically for developing housing for families that have a disabled member, not solely for families that have a disabled head of household. The homes will be developed using KHC's Universal Design Standards.

POLICY IMPLICATIONS AND CONCLUSION

The strength of the HOPE VI program rests in the goal of remaking neighborhoods from agglomerations of extremely poor people into communities with a mixture of low-, middle-, and upper-income households. Ideally HOPE VI also provides previously under-resourced communities with access

6.5 A historic building on Monmouth Street in Newport's Central Business District

6.6 New HOPE VI houses on Liberty Row

6.7 Closer view of new HOPE VI houses on Liberty Row

6.8 Front view of new HOPE VI houses on Liberty Row

6.9 Abandoned Catholic church that was converted to HOPE VI apartment units

to greater social, organizational, and economic capital for revitalizing and developing successful neighborhood schools, social and community organizations, businesses, and other institutions that are the necessary building blocks of stable, attractive, and livable communities (Brazley 2002).

The HOPE VI Newport program could be the best program of its kind in the nation. It is much better executed than many other highly praised HOPE VI programs. Compared to the Park DuValle program in Louisville, which has received a tremendous amount of national recognition, Newport clearly stands out as the superior of these two Kentucky HOPE VI projects (Gause 2002).

First, Park DuValle was placed on the same site as the old public housing project with problems of access to public transportation, shopping amenities, and good schools persisting after HOPE VI implementation. On the other hand, Newport's HOPE VI aims to spread and integrate public housing residents throughout the city using infill housing sites.

Second, Park DuValle's housing is located in the middle of historic West Louisville's black community, presumably resulting in whites having purchased only 2 of the more than 1,200 housing units. In comparison, Newport's housing was never segregated, and the program aims to integrate a

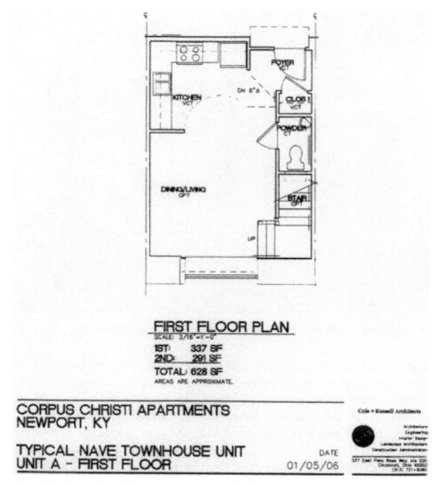

FIRST FLOOR PLAN
SCALE: 3/16"=1'-0"

1ST: 337 SF
2ND: 291 SF

TOTAL: 628 SF
AREAS ARE APPROXIMATE.

**CORPUS CHRISTI APARTMENTS
NEWPORT, KY**

Cole + Russell Architects

**TYPICAL NAVE TOWNHOUSE UNIT
UNIT A - FIRST FLOOR**

DATE
01/05/06

Figure 6.1 Corpus Christi floor plan, townhouse first floor

mixture of poor white and black residents into Newport's working-class and middle-class neighborhoods.

Third, Park DuValle has failed to develop new businesses around its development, and those businesses that had opened are now closed. Several urban experts (including these authors) fear that Park DuValle will decline in the near future unless businesses are generated, racial diversity is increased, and more convenient services are added. In contrast, business startups in Newport have ranged from sixty-six to ninety-one a year near the HOPE VI sites.

Ironically, HUD's biggest problem with the Newport HOPE VI was that it did not replicate the Park DuValle formula of demolishing the old project-like housing and replacing it with middle-class-style housing in the same location. Today, most experts agree that Newport has the right formula for urban revitalization, and Louisville's Park DuValle might become a disaster waiting to happen.

HOPE VI in Newport is working better than most programs around the nation. Here is what we have found in Newport:

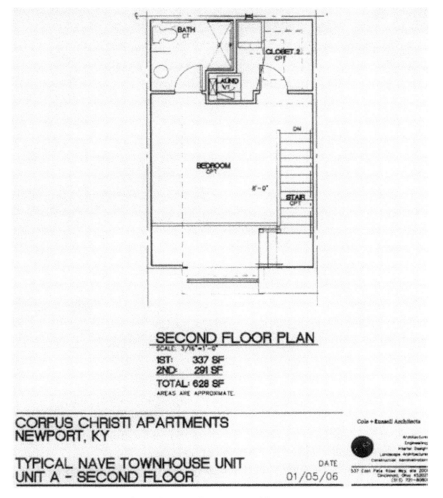

Figure 6.2 Corpus Christi floor plan, townhouse second floor

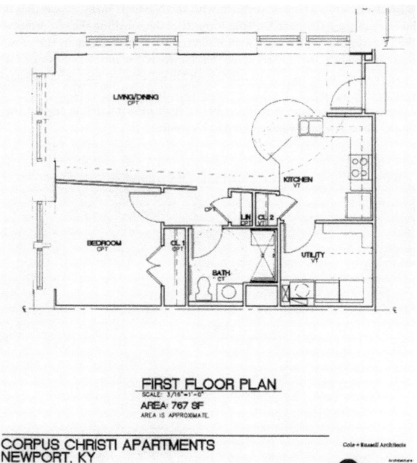

FIRST FLOOR PLAN
SCALE: 3/16"=1'-0"
AREA: 767 SF
AREA IS APPROXIMATE

CORPUS CHRISTI APARTMENTS
NEWPORT, KY

TYPICAL THIRD FLOOR CLASSROOM UNIT   DATE
UNIT F - FLOOR PLAN   01/05/06

Cole + Russell Architects

6.3 Corpus Christi floor plan, third-floor classroom unit

· The number of residents who are maintaining long-term jobs is growing.

· Homeownership is becoming a realistic vision for growing numbers of residents, especially with the inception of the CIPP.

· Despite the decreasing population of HOPE VI-eligible families on site, Brighton Center's CSS goals are being met and exceeded. Brighton Center is taking a bold new perspective on not only developing the skills of CSS participants but also developing the lives of participants. With the introduction of professional counseling and a partnership with a dentist, residents stand to gain in skills, health care, and self-esteem.

• Business startups and transfers have remained at a consistently positive pace. One encouraging sign is the diversification of business development, as expansion is no longer just occurring in concentrated areas of Newport. The viability of Newport as a location for businesses opens potential for many entrepreneurs and business owners.

• CIPP brings the community obvious direct and indirect benefits including perhaps unintended benefits from the Housing Quality Standards that homes had to pass to be eligible for CIPP.

The strength of the HOPE VI program is its ability to help residents on both physical and social levels. In this comparison we have seen that the Newport effort is succeeding, while its better-known counterpart in Louisville is not living up to the hype.

CHAPTER 7

RENEWING AND REMAKING NEW ORLEANS

WITH RICHARD LAYMAN

INTRODUCTION

In this chapter we explore how historic preservation can be a tool for creating affordable housing. Oddly, there has been a disconnect between historic preservation and housing affordability, but as we showed in Chapter 3, older housing stock provides a large array of affordable housing. In this chapter, we show how small inner-city lots with shotgun-style housing provide affordable housing and should be preserved.

There is at least one upside when a monumental disaster strikes a great city. With a disaster comes hope that the city can be rebuilt so that it is even better than before. The San Francisco earthquake of 1906 and the Great Fire in Chicago in 1871, while utterly destroying both cities, provided the opportunity for planners, architects, and municipal officials to resolve many of the physical problems the cities suffered prior to their respective catastrophes (Boehm 2004; Fradkin 2005). Historians often compare such situations to an artist with an empty palette. Without the encumbrance of having to consider the context of existing elements of the built environment, planners have the chance to avoid the ineffective and inequitable use of land. Water damage and the toxic sludge left behind by the floodwaters in New Orleans lamentably necessitate the demolition of thousands of structures, the majority of them in the city's poorest neighborhoods. Whole areas of New Orleans will have to be completely rebuilt. To a large degree the new physical form of these neighborhoods will be defined by the basic building block of the city: housing.

Building inspectors in New Orleans have estimated the total number of

7.1 Historic shotgun houses in New Orleans. Photo by Jerry Kase.

homes that will be demolished is 50,000 (Moe 2005). Currently, planners
and officials in New Orleans are considering their options for the rebuilding of entire neighborhoods. In the politically, economically, and racially
sensitive post-Katrina environment, there is the possibility that planning
initiatives for the "new" New Orleans could shun the traditional, authen-
tic, and historical residential housing type that particularly defines New
Orleans, shotgun houses (Photo 7.1), in favor of more suburban-style dwellings. Along these lines New Orleans Mayor Ray Nagin announced that his
model for redevelopment for New Orleans' devastated neighborhoods was
River Garden, a vaguely traditional but suburban-looking HOPE VI public
housing replacement project in the Lower Garden District (Knack 2006). In
the reconstruction of poor neighborhoods in New Orleans, traditional design principles such as smaller lot sizes, shallower setbacks, and the use of
indigenous architectural styles would perform well, but New Urbanist planners need to work with preservationists and community members to ensure
that the cultural capital of the neighborhoods of New Orleans is not lost to
what Southworth (1997) calls the sanitizing, suburban-like result of some of
the new "traditional" developments.

The prominence of shotgun houses throughout the various neighborhoods of New Orleans is impressive (Table 7.1). While New Orleans features
a great diversity of historic-style building types, including the well-known

TABLE 7.1. *Shotgun Houses in New Orleans Neighborhoods*

Neighborhood	Number of Shotguns	Percent of Total Buildings	Number of Total Buildings
Broadmoor	120	14	860
Bywater	1,249	61	2,051
Carrollton	2,339	45	5,198
Upper CBD	0	0	473
Lower CBD	6	2	293
Central City	2,809	70	4,013
Esplanade Ridge	1,782	43	4,146
Garden District	116	n/a	n/a
Gentilly Terrace	51	8	665
Holy Cross	479	56	857
Irish Channel	1,024	45	2,300
Lower Garden District	224	21	1,180
Mid City	2,063	46	4,489
New Marigny	2,154	61	3,533
Parkview	520	39	1,349
South Lakeview	48	29	164
Uptown	534	56	954
Vieux Carré	261	13	2,011
Total	15,779	46	34,536

Adapted from data provided by the Preservation Resource Center of New Orleans

Italianate, French Colonial, Spanish Colonial, Queen Anne, Victorian, the most prominent is the shotgun style, which represents nearly half of the city's building types. If you look at all building types, including commercial, in seventeen out of New Orleans' nineteen historic districts (data for two historic neighborhoods were unavailable), shotgun-style houses range from a low of 8 percent to a high of 70 percent, with a mean of 46 percent of all building types being shotgun style. When considering variations of the shotgun houses—camelback and double shotgun—more than 50 percent of the housing stock would be part of this classification.

Nearly three-fourths of the housing in New Orleans was damaged, even though an exact count does not exist for the kind of housing that was damaged from Katrina. Logan (2006) estimates that 73 percent of the housing stock was damaged and most of these units were occupied by the poor, minorities, and renters. Social scientists define "damaged" as ranging from the total house being destroyed to parts of the roof or floor being damaged. It is unclear how much of the housing can be saved, but preservationists argue that historic housing units can overcome water and wind damage, so all is not lost here. Renovation of housing stock can sometimes be an alternative to building new. Roofs can be replaced, water damage can be fixed with chemicals, and mold can be removed by replacing sheetrock.

Further evidence that New Orleans can be rebuilt by restoring and renovating historic housing is supported by Louisville's Great Flood of 1937, which resulted in 175,000 residents being displaced when the Ohio River rose 30 feet above flood levels (Bell 2007a, H-1). Flooding covered an area of 12 square miles in the downtown neighborhoods, hitting everyone in Louisville, rich and poor, black and white (Bell 2007b). Some buildings were completely engulfed by water, with approximately 32,000 housing units flooded by at least several inches of water.

After the flood, every house was inspected by a group of architects hired by the city to determine the structural safety of the housing affected by the flood and whether the housing units should be torn down. The building inspectors condemned only thirty-five housing units. Today throughout Louisville's neighborhoods (Russell, Smoketown, Old Louisville, Butchertown, Germantown, Central Louisville, Shawnee, Phoenix Hill along with a small tip of the Highlands) stand as reminders of how durable, strong, and sustainable these houses can be. Many of these shotgun units were made of not only brick but wood as well. The history of Louisville's Great Flood of 1937 and restoration of nearly all of its housing refutes the notion that historic homes in New Orleans need to be torn down.

Table 7.2 powerfully illustrates the numerous neighborhoods, both historic and non-historic, damaged by Katrina. Table 7.2 also shows the large numbers of poor and minority residents who live in New Orleans' older housing units and historic neighborhoods. By implication and observation, a large number of the poor live in shotgun housing in New Orleans.

Preserving, restoring, and building new shotgun houses is an effective, affordable, energy-efficient, and culturally important approach that could aid in the redevelopment of socially and economically challenged neighborhoods. Cities with strong ties to the shotgun house should strongly consider employing this housing type, whether rehabilitating historic structures, constructing new, modern shotguns, or rebuilding or revitalizing distressed neighborhoods from Louisiana to Louisville.

For New Orleans and the Gulf Coast specifically, similar building forms such as the Creole cottage and Camelback shotgun, which are small, one-and-a-half-story houses, also maintain these characteristics. The following sections illustrate how such small-footprint housing is a solution to some of the contemporary problems of providing affordable housing and housing ownership opportunities to low-income, inner-city neighborhoods in the

TABLE 7.2. *Social Characteristics of Districts Damaged by Hurricane Katrina*

Planning Districts	Percent in Damaged Areas	Population in Damaged Areas	Total Population	Percent Black	Percent Renter	Percent Poor
Algiers	1.2	612	51,110	56.6	48.3	24.1
Bywater	85.4	35,139	41,163	83.4	58.4	38.7
Central City/ Garden District	46.8	22,599	48,327	67.8	73.6	39.7
French Quarter/CBD	12.2	739	5,970	13.3	76.4	16.9
Gentilly	96.5	42,597	44,133	69.5	28.2	15.3
Lakeview	89.8	23,259	25,897	2.3	33.8	6.3
Lower Ninth Ward	92.6	18,077	19,515	95.7	46.0	34.4
Mid-City	100.0	79,438	79,441	82.9	72.9	44.4
New Aurora	1.1	62	5,672	68.2	27.0	24.8
New Orleans East	91.2	79,192	79,808	86.8	44.7	18.9
Uptown-Carrollton	68.9	40,850	67,083	46.6	53.3	24.3
Viavant/Venetian Island	78.6	11,270	14,342	47.8	48.3	33.1
Village de L'est	10.0	222	2,213	83.2	54.3	7.8
City of New Orleans	73.0	354,045	484,674	67.2	53.5	27.9

Logan 2006

South. The compact size of shotguns provides for a much higher degree of affordability as costs in material and land are reduced. The smaller dimensions of the shotgun house drastically reduce heating and cooling costs. The shotgun house was important to the cultural development of Southern cities including New Orleans and Louisville. "Smart growth" initiatives including affordable homeownership opportunities and denser residential development can be achieved through implementation or revitalization of neighborhoods that effectively incorporate shotgun houses. A potential stumbling block is the stigma often associated with living in a shotgun house. If issues of social acceptability and other obstacles can be overcome, this housing type could be integral to the rehabilitation of disinvested neighborhoods in

Louisville and key to the successful rebuilding of urban communities along the Gulf Coast.

THE EVOLUTION OF SHOTGUN HOUSING

In its most basic form, the shotgun house is a one-story, rectangular structure, only one room wide (usually twelve to fifteen feet wide) and three to four rooms deep (Preservation Alliance of Louisville and Jefferson Co. 1980). The versatility of shotgun housing has allowed for design innovations over the decades that have resulted in structures such as the camelback shotgun, a basic shotgun-house configuration with a second story added to the back, and the double shotgun, which is two shotguns side by side under the same roof. The city of New Orleans played a pivotal role in the evolution of the vernacular shotgun house. John Michael Vlach (1986) traces the emergence of the shotgun from its rudimentary origins in West Africa to self-built slave housing in colonial Haiti to New Orleans in the early nineteenth century. The Preservation Resource Center of New Orleans (2005) names the shotgun house the predominant house in New Orleans from the mid-nineteenth century to 1910. By the mid-nineteenth century the shotgun house had spread from Louisiana to other southern cities including Memphis and Louisville (Hopkins and Oates 1998). The cost-effectiveness of the shotgun allowed for large numbers of newly arriving immigrants to enjoy single-family units in neighborhoods near the industrial core. As a testament to their ubiquity in Louisville, a 1980 survey shows that shotgun houses comprise more than 10 percent of the city's housing stock (Preservation Alliance of Louisville and Jefferson Co. 1980).

SHOTGUN HOUSING IS AFFORDABLE

Many planners and housing researchers and some city officials have worn themselves thin advocating affordable housing. As students of urban housing we know what policies and programs would work to make quality housing available to people with low incomes. However, getting the financial institutions and the real estate developers to play along is markedly more difficult. Often, then, the middle class will stand in the way of affordable housing development through sheer NIMBYism (Not In My Back Yard). Rolf Pendall, planning professor at Cornell University, argues it as a problem of perception. He argues that we need to look at affordable housing as part of the city's vital infrastructure, just as important as water, sewers, and parks (in Goodno 2005).

Even in questioning studies that associate homeownership with community stability, researchers generally agree that homeowners have a large financial stake in their communities and therefore may invest more in their neighborhoods (Aaronson 2000). The key is to ensure that homeownership for low-income families is supported by the availability of affordable and quality units. Encouraging low-income families to purchase dwelling units that they may not be able to maintain at a reasonable standard can be harmful (Rohe and Stewart 1996). Therefore, increased homeownership rates through the availability of shotgun housing that is less costly and easier to maintain than other styles could bolster the revitalization of distressed neighborhoods.

The shotgun house is a solution that can form the basis of an affordable housing infrastructure in New Orleans. Community housing nonprofits have built new shotgun housing units in inner-city Louisville with much success (Garr 2005). In *Promise and Betrayal: Universities and the Battle for Sustainable Urban Neighborhoods* (Gilderbloom and Mullins 2005), we outline an urban rehabilitation program implemented in a once-decaying inner-city area of Louisville. Through a university-community partnership, the team was able to build shotgun housing with all new appliances for a construction cost of approximately $45,000 for a three-bedroom, one-bathroom house on land donated by the city. The relatively low construction cost of these houses provided homeownership opportunities for people who had never dreamed they were capable of owning property. Assuming a thirty-year mortgage, home payments would equal roughly $246 a month after an initial $5,000 down payment.

In terms of economics, it is not the government paying for the housing but the residents. In an environment in which scant federal housing support for lower-income residents is dwindling to nothing, the development of affordable housing may become possible only when housing types and development financing models are synchronized and driven primarily by homeowner payments rather than federal and private subsidies. With quality units to be constructed at a low cost, shotgun housing may be the solution to the dilemma of how to bring about affordable housing development. Post-Katrina New Orleans is an appropriate starting point, especially considering that much of the infrastructure, although damaged, is already in place.

In terms of rent, however, there is evidence that rehabilitating historic shotgun houses can help maintain affordable rents. Normally, as Rypkema (2002) argues in *Historic Preservation and Affordable Housing: The Missed Connection,* "there is one fact-of-life in real estate development that must be reckoned with—you can't build new and sell (or rent) cheap—it can't be done. At least it can't be done without either massive subsidies or very low-

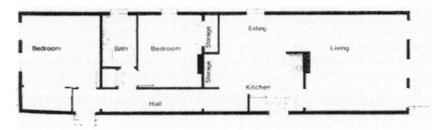

Figure 7.1 Rehabilitated shotgun floor plan. Courtesy Preservation Alliance of Louisville and Jefferson County Inc.

quality units." Similarly, a study of 140 U.S. cities (Gilderbloom and Appelbaum 1988) found that preservation of older housing stock causes rents to be lower. Moreover, we found that replacing older housing with newly constructed housing caused rents to sharply increase. Neighborhoods that contain a stock of historic shotguns could look toward rehabilitating these structures to provide more affordable single-family rental units. Figure 7.1 presents a floor plan for such a structure. Preservation, conservation, and rehabilitation of older housing can be dramatically less expensive than new construction, barring extraordinary requirements such as earthquake protection or environmental remediation (Millennial Housing Commission 2002).

SHOTGUN HOUSING IS ENERGY-EFFICIENT

While multi-family housing units can offer savings in energy consumption, they do not provide for the same feeling of privacy garnered from single-family dwellings. Shotgun housing is more energy-efficient than other forms of single-family housing due to its compact size. The smaller and narrower footprint of the shotgun allows for energy savings at the individual unit level by requiring less energy for heating and cooling. At the neighborhood scale, less urban land is consumed. This translates to denser communities that would diminish transport-related energy consumption and require less energy to maintain. Since 1970 the size of the average new home has ballooned by 50 percent (Fox 2005).

From a design standpoint, shotguns expend far less energy than many other types of housing. Gary Watrous (2005), an architect specializing in energy conserving designs, points out that the shotgun house was designed to stay cool without using electricity or gas by utilizing cross-ventilation. Structural orientation, windows on all four sides, and relatively high ceilings allow air to circulate freely through the house (Watrous 2005). Not only does this design allow for better temperature control in the summer, but the windows on all sides allow natural sunlight in to help decrease heating costs in the colder months. Moreover, shotgun housing can be constructed on piers, which also allows for ventilation underneath the house and a modicum of protection from floods for neighborhoods along the Gulf Coast or in areas with an unpredictable watershed. Shotgun housing is more efficient from a construction-cost standpoint, given that smaller amounts of material are used to shelter households of equal size.

Lower urban densities generate proportionally higher levels of energy consumption (Riddell 2003). Suburban-style growth consumes at least four times more land area and approximately three times more energy per household than urban living patterns (Edwards and Turrent 2000). Therefore, we must look to housing types that maximize the use of urban land and drastically decrease unnecessary and unsustainable energy consumption. Shotgun houses are far less land-intensive than the typical single-family home and can easily be incorporated into the fabric of a highly urbanized area. The compact footprint of shotgun housing makes it possible to concentrate desirable single-family housing on smaller tracts in close proximity to services, near employment centers, and on existing public transport lines.

CULTURAL IMPORTANCE

Dating from as early as 1810, shotgun houses have been an integral part of the architectural fabric of New Orleans. Undeniably, they contribute a great deal to the distinctiveness of the city's urban form and vitality. With French, Spanish, and Caribbean influences, New Orleans is truly unique in the United States, and neighborhoods that are dominated by the shotgun house comprise a key element of this uniqueness. Such neighborhoods of shotgun houses have been central to the development of a substantive and distinctive Afro-Caribbean "Creole" culture in Louisiana.

Therefore, shotguns are an important component of the architecture that makes cultural heritage tourism such a large segment of the total tourist mix visiting New Orleans (Judd and Fainstein 1999). While "archi-tourism" is a term often used to refer to Frank Gehry's Bilbao and its imitators, the term generally is used in connection with heritage tourism or cultural heritage tourism in places such as London, Amsterdam, Paris, Rome, Havana, Athens, Chicago, San Francisco, Charleston, and New Orleans (for example see National Trust for Historic Preservation 2007).

Preserving historic and symbolic buildings is important to retaining community identity (Petterson 1999). The historic preservation-sensitive reconstruction of Charleston, South Carolina, after the devastation wrought by Hurricane Hugo in 1989 demonstrates the success of asset-based urban revitalization and disaster recovery policies (Nelson 1991). Along the Gulf Coast a consortium of preservationists and universities has initiated "the Shotgun Project." This initiative is an attempt to revitalize and rebuild hurricane-affected neighborhoods through the preservation of historic shotguns and by promoting the construction of new shotguns in destroyed areas through a "modern" shotgun housing design competition (Architecture for Humanity 2005).

OVERCOMING THE STIGMA

In many gentrifying or historic neighborhoods, various shotgun housing types are highly valued. In other communities, however, there seems to be a prevailing sentiment that shotgun housing is "poor-people housing" that is ugly and out of date and that a better house is something on a wider lot. Similar to public housing, some see shotgun housing, primarily wooden structures, as associated with feelings of shame and rejection. Joyce Marin (2005), a former Knight Fellow in Community Building, notes the challenges of renewing, preserving, and revitalizing shotgun houses in South Carolina:

> There is apparently a big stigma associated with them in the South. Many people involved in the process articulated that they wouldn't live in a shotgun, ever, no matter what. There definitely is quite a bit to overcome in attitude. We heard repeatedly, "That is what I'm trying to move away from."[1]

In Marin's experience, there was a consensus that changing the name from "shotgun" to something else could help alleviate some of the stigma. However, the greater goal is to produce housing that is a symbol of self—a symbol that will evoke pride, safety, and well-being (Cooper-Marcus 1997).

In New Orleans, the shotgun house is viewed positively. People see shotguns differently when the original and problematic floor designs are renovated for more modern living arrangements. More often, residents of the city identify with the cultural capital associated with the structures. The director of the Preservation Resource Center of New Orleans explains:

> The shotgun house defines the city of New Orleans as much as jazz and Creole cuisine, complementing perfectly its earlier counterpart, the

Creole cottage, and larger, more imposing structures. Beautiful street-scapes and culturally rich neighborhoods were the result, with block after block evolved throughout the city, full of shotgun houses. The shotgun house provides an ideal house type—a house type that can be modest or grand, versatile in size and in adaptability as styles and living requirements changed over the years. The shotgun house has endured and is treasured in New Orleans, in large part thanks to its simplicity, irreplaceable materials, variety of styles, adaptability, and, indeed, its large numbers throughout the city. (Gay 2006)

Likewise, Louisville has had some success in promoting the shotgun as a desirable residential choice. For quite some time, Louisville preservation-ists have looked to the city's large historic shotgun housing stock as a viable solution for providing housing and homeownership opportunities to people with low incomes (Preservation Alliance of Louisville and Jefferson Co. 1980). Physical evidence of success is apparent, as well-maintained strips of shotguns are present in many Louisville neighborhoods of dramatically different socioeconomic compositions.

In Louisville, newly constructed shotgun housing targets only lower-income residents and poorer neighborhoods. Historically, shotgun houses were homes for European immigrants, especially Germans, who turned the wood-framed homes into brick shotguns (Photo 7.2). The style can run from vernacular to Italianate, Queen Anne, and Classical Revival (Weeter 2004). Luhan, Domer, and Mohney (2004) point out that "by the turn of the [twen-tieth] century, shotgun houses, many of them camelback, became the pre-dominant house type." Solidly working-class Louisville areas with shotgun homes near downtown are neighborhoods that some real estate investors believe will be the next places of gentrification in the city.

Louisville's African-American neighborhoods with shotgun houses tend to be a mixture of both poor and middle-class residents. The Russell neigh-borhood is undergoing gentrification, and the shotgun houses are being rep-licated (Photo 7.3). The shotgun is undergoing a rebirth by being constructed in the New Urbanist community of Norton Commons, designed by promi-nent architecture and planning firm Duany Plater-Zyberk for the suburbs of Louisville. Duany Plater-Zyberk has incorporated what the firm calls the "Traditional Louisville Shotgun" (Photo 7.4) into its pattern book of housing types for the development. Norton Commons will have more than 2,000 houses when completed. Stylish and attractive, these new homes, selling for a minimum of $260,000, are the last thing to be called "ghettoized" housing.

7.2 Historic shotgun houses in Louisville. Photo by Patrick Smith.

7.3 Single-family homes designed by SUN, University of Louisville

7.4 Shotgun home in Norton Commons created by New Urbanist Andres Duany. Photo by Patrick Smith.

UTILIZING THE SHOTGUN HOUSE IN THE RECONSTRUCTION OF NEIGHBORHOODS

Many urban housing projects, including those sponsored through HUD's HOPE VI program, implement the principles of New Urbanism in the revitalization of distressed inner-city neighborhoods. In the reconstruction of neighborhoods in New Orleans, these principles, such as smaller lot sizes, shallower setbacks, and the use of indigenous architectural styles could perform equally well, especially in respect to the shotgun. The question is how to make them a reality. Here are a few ideas:

• Ensure that narrow lot zoning is maintained where it previously existed
• Design for shotgun or Creole cottage neighborhoods with private backyards and alley access
• Recommend that shotgun housing be built using masonry where possible to mitigate the effects of natural hazards
• Provide density bonuses to developers that maximize use of land for shotgun housing
• Instate zoning that mandates maximum lot widths of thirty to thirty-five feet in target areas
• Raise structures off the ground for ventilation and flood mitigation

CONCLUSION

Newly constructed "traditional neighborhood design" projects as well as broader housing and regional land-use planning and development policies should embrace shotgun houses, their architectural history, and their adaptability. The style should be embraced not because the houses are charming and distinctive, but because this housing might be the most affordable and sustainable way to shelter those presently poor while providing a means to build stronger, more stable, and economically viable neighborhoods.

The stated mission of New Urbanism is about being inclusive, which must mean providing housing for the poor and working class. The Russell neighborhood of Louisville, a "poor, black neighborhood," was revitalized, remade, and renewed in large part due to the projects and programs of the University of Louisville's Sustainable Urban Neighborhoods program. We were able to retain many of the shotgun lots while also accommodating middle- and upper-class African-Americans who wanted to remain in the neighborhood, but with the option of residing in a larger, more contemporary, house. By increasing the diversity of housing types, including those that appealed to people of higher incomes, we were able to re-create a neighborhood of greater economic diversity, which further contributed to neighborhood stabilization and improvement. So maybe some flexibility is in order.

It is important to remember that you cannot rebuild a neighborhood with just housing. We found that you need to have places of worship, good schools, grocery stores, recreational opportunities, a positive police presence that works with the residents rather than against them, and location near jobs (Gilderbloom and Mullins 2005).

As we showed in the previous chapter, a sometimes unrealized yet worthy expectation of the HOPE VI program is to remake poor neighborhoods into viable, mixed-income communities. Shotgun-type housing can be a valuable component of successful and affordable communities. The significant architectural history and success of the shotgun house, along with the more contemporary lessons from successful HOPE VI projects across the United States, make the shotgun an important element in any rebuilding effort in New Orleans and elsewhere.

CHAPTER 8

UNIVERSITY PARTNERSHIPS TO RECLAIM AND REBUILD COMMUNITIES

In this chapter we show how universities can play a vital role in helping to address the housing crisis. This crisis impacts seniors, the disabled, and the working poor. Yet only a handful of the 3,650 higher education institutions are allocating resources of faculty, staff, and students to meet this urgent task. This is the story of one university that made a major effort to reclaim, rebuild, revitalize, and restore one of the nation's most historic black neighborhoods, which had fallen into neglect and despair. The childhood neighborhood of Muhammad Ali, West Louisville was once a proud middle-class neighborhood.

Since 1994, the University of Louisville Sustainable Urban Neighborhoods (SUN) program has worked to great acclaim, helping to facilitate the necessary resources that support the aspirations of resident families in West Louisville. The predominant focus of the SUN activities is in the historic, predominantly African-American neighborhood of Russell, with 10,000 residents. Russell is one of the most economically disadvantaged areas in the City of Louisville and is characterized by excessive poverty, unemployment, crime, and homelessness, along with relatively low levels of education and training. West Louisville's Russell neighborhood was a familiar portrait of inner-city American poverty, unemployment, crime, and despair.

Surveys of Louisville citizens have shown that housing affordability is among the most important issues confronting the city. In several Louisville neighborhoods, one out of every four housing units is substandard. This is in comparison to the national average of one out of every twenty. A majority of low-income renters in West Louisville paid more than 50 percent of their incomes for housing (Gilderbloom and Mullins 2005).

8.1 Boarded-up shotgun house in Russell neighborhood

Russell was a neighborhood of gangs, drugs, and prostitution. These vices paved the way for the heavy concentration of funeral homes, liquor stores, and pawnshops. Engineers turned the neighborhood into a four-lane, one-way freeway so downtown office workers could race to their suburban homes. One-way streets helped kill the neighborhood spirit—reducing housing appreciation, creating greater opportunities for criminal activity, and turning streets into no-play zones for kids.

While these were considered neighborhood liabilities, I also discovered neighborhood assets: a high concentration of churches, an eight-story historic YMCA, a public technical college, the first library open to blacks, several parks and cemeteries that give the neighborhood residents green spaces to use, and good-paying downtown jobs within walking distance. I was particularly struck by the large collection of historic buildings (Federal style, shotgun, Queen Anne, Arts and Crafts) dating back over a hundred years. The *Louisville Guide* by noted architecture professors Luhan, Domer, and Mohney (2004) describes at least twelve buildings of architectural distinction.

In many ways, this neighborhood had the potential to be developed as a New Urbanist neighborhood (Mohney and Easterling 1991; see also Duany,

Plater-Zyberk, and Speck 2000 and the compilation of articles of Leccese and McCormick 2000). Lot sizes were about one-third smaller than their suburban counterparts, allowing homes to be built more cheaply. Small lot sizes also caused new houses to occupy a large portion of the lots, with front porches extending out to touch the sidewalks. I saw Russell in West Louis-

8.2 Abandoned brick historic house in Russell neighborhood

ville as having the potential to become the first moderate-income, or for that matter, only predominantly black New Urbanist development.

I do not believe that all poor neighborhoods can be revitalized (especially suburban ones built in the 1960s), but Russell seemed like a good candidate, especially with the leadership of nonprofit organizations and city officials. I was also inspired by New Urbanist efforts in Seaside, Florida (Mohney and Esterling 1991), and in Santa Monica, California (Capek and Gilderbloom 1992). Numerous meetings were held with organizations and individuals in West Louisville to examine how SUN could help make more affordable housing. Many recognized leaders and organizations were consulted in the development of SUN. As a result of this process, our collective proposal was circulated to more individuals and organizations and received a positive reaction. The SUN proposal received letters of support from the mayor, nonprofit organizations, four institutions of higher education, various government agencies, numerous businesses, Realtors, banks, builders, and charities. The participation of these individuals and organizations molded SUN into an innovative and pragmatic partnership. SUN was developed as a realistic approach to create self-sufficiency among the economically challenged. This program can change hopelessness into hope for a poor neighborhood and help weave together the fabric of the community.

All plans to "do good" stir opposition. Despite the efforts to do grassroots planning, the program also had some major opposition. This is not surprising, but what was disappointing was where this opposition came from. It was not from black community leaders, city hall, and real estate interests but rather from top majority-based housing leaders who claimed it was wasteful, untested, and a failure from the start. A letter signed by heads of predominantly white organizations that provided a significant amount of affordable housing called for the proposal to be withdrawn. They demanded that a free-market economist from the University of Louisville who believed in less government (e.g., repeal of zoning, historic preservation, environmental regulations) be allowed to draw up a downtown enterprise plan and abandon black West Louisville. The letter was delivered to my boss, a top university official, who quietly said No to their demands.

But this was not the end. Once the grant was awarded, they demanded that "one of their own" help manage the project. But these persons were generally unable to relate to the optimism, brashness, idealism, spirit, and energy of the students, faculty, and black community leaders. The students saw opportunity where the "old guard" saw hopelessness.

The old guard was relentless in attacking the project—spreading gossip and going to the news media. The local newspaper, the *Courier-Journal,* came out with a negative news story claiming we were "way short" of our goals with too much money wasted on administration. What the newspaper failed to note was that the goals were for the life of the grant, which turned out to be ten years, not just the twelve to sixteen months on which they were reporting. It takes years, not months, to successfully renovate or build affordable housing. Moreover, many of the claims made by the newspaper were false and the grants evaluator, Reg Bruce, found that most of the goals of the grant were accomplished (Gilderbloom and Mullins 2005; see also Evans-Andris 1999). Mid-course corrections did eliminate some goals because of cost, lack of staff, or opportunities to invest resources elsewhere.

While they masked their actions under the guise of concerned civic leadership, the real reason for their opposition was fear of competition over scarce housing dollars and their self-appointed role as housing gatekeepers being put into jeopardy (Gilderbloom and Appelbaum 1988; Pahl 1975).

SUSTAINABLE URBAN NEIGHBORHOODS

Learning from lessons of the past, a fresh, innovative, bold, and pragmatic partnership of business, government, a local university, a junior college, and community-based groups was organized. The Russell partnership represented a multifaceted effort committed to helping a low-income black neighborhood lift itself from dependency to self-sufficiency.

This partnership was built on the belief that the problems of low-income neighborhoods can only be remedied by a combination of programs involving job development, home repair, homeownership, community planning, entrepreneurial training, and loans. Federal money from the U.S. Department of Education and HUD helped stimulate the development of this partnership. These funds were partially matched by local churches, nonprofit organizations, industries, businesses, local foundations, and community groups. SUN's goal is to make operational the concept of public-private partnerships in order to succeed in urban renovation and rehabilitation where many others have failed. As Marilyn Melkonian, president of Telesis Corporation, has observed, SUN's vision goes "beyond just the physical improvements of the bricks and mortar" (Gilderbloom and Mullins 2005, 194). SUN carries out its vision through outreach-orientated partnerships with community development organizations, business firms, government agencies, community groups, and universities. SUN promotes human and economic development in the impoverished neighborhoods of West Louisville, with a resulting impact on the entire city.

THE SUN DIRECTIVE

The mission of SUN is to explore all strategies that foster a sense of community while empowering individuals in the community and promoting neighborhood revitalization, individual self-sufficiency, and self-reliance. These goals are achieved through community partnerships. Former University of Louisville President John Shumaker remarked in 1996 that "SUN, through its sheer tenacity, helped turn an eyesore of blocks and blocks of boarded-up buildings into a development that the entire city can be proud of" (Gilderbloom and Mullins 2005, 60). To help end this decline and create the dynamics for revitalization, the partnership's goals and strategies focus on four functional categories: housing, economic development, community organizing, and neighborhood revitalization.

As part of its comprehensive approach, SUN provides oversight, monitoring, technical assistance, and advocacy for low-income residents of West Louisville. SUN works closely with local officials on budgetary and policy issues affecting the community. Revitalization of old urban neighborhoods is crucial to preserving Louisville's cultural heritage. Strengthening existing neighborhoods helps reduce sprawl, safeguard green spaces, and create healthier environments. SUN also works to identify, evaluate, preserve, and protect significant historic sites, structures, cultural landscapes, cultural artifacts, and tangible West Louisville community traditions.

SUN offers assistance to housing developers and small business owners in locally designated revitalization areas, stimulates community revitalization activities that protect and enhance historic resources, and improves existing residential and commercial structures. SUN and its partners support initiatives to revitalize neighborhoods through programs such as redevelopment assistance, business training for individuals, education, and community crime prevention.

COMMUNITY OUTREACH PARTNERSHIP CENTER

The goal of University of Louisville's SUN program is to develop partnerships that succeed in urban renovation and rehabilitation. SUN's successful programs illustrate the impact that university and community, public and private partnerships can have on target areas. The processes that have developed and that are being utilized are tools to successful urban rehabilitation. SUN celebrates its successes and learns from its mistakes.

The Community Design and Planning Program focuses on cooperation with neighborhood leaders and generating a shared community and neighborhood vision through "bottom-up" participation by residents. A master plan and detailed site-development plans for housing as well as commercial, recreational, and light industrial uses, guide development efforts. The quality of the plan rests in the feasibility of its implementation.

SUN provides direct assistance to the neighborhoods and institutions through community design work such as architectural services and helping developers adhere to Louisville's Urban Renewal Commission's rules and regulations. SUN also provides technical assistance ranging from resurveying lots and redesigning houses to creating design plans and providing site visits to oversee nonprofit developers' construction. SUN's assistance has the objective of improving the availability, affordability, and quality of housing in the Russell neighborhood and surrounding enterprise zones. The actual number of units that have been completed within the target neighborhood illustrates results.

In partnership with the Neighborhood Development Corporation (NDC), SUN has identified two housing priorities: increased homeownership opportunities for low-income households and preservation of the current housing stock through renovation of older housing. Pursuit of these goals involves acquiring vacant decayed buildings and rehabilitating and reselling them. Infill housing can also be created, resulting in new housing units on vacant city-owned land.

H. TEMPLE SPEARS ELDERLY HOUSING

One of the best examples of this partnership is H. Temple Spears elderly housing, which was started as a SUN project in 1994 (Photos 8.3 and 8.4). A graduate student came up with a 300-page plan to create sixty-five units of affordable senior housing in West Louisville, where the vast majority of residents are African-American. The need was great, as West Louisville had very little senior housing. The initial effort was to build a brand-new housing development in the neighborhood, but this was abandoned when NDC saw the economics and sentimentality of rehabilitating a historic, 100-year-old school. This architectural landmark, which was located on one city block with plenty of surrounding green space, won the hearts and minds of residents and city officials.

The student who came up with the proposal was Bill Friedlander, an active member of the American Planning Association who left SUN with a Ph.D. to revive and resurrect Louisville's defunct Neighborhood Development Corporation. H. Temple Spears has become one of its most important successes. Ten years later, Neighborhood Development Corporation has helped revive,

8.3 Abandoned historic school before conversion to H. Temple Spears Center senior housing

build, and save more than 150 housing units, and it manages roughly 300 units in West Louisville. Many of these housing units are historic and represent the fabric of the neighborhood.

LOUISVILLE CENTRAL COMMUNITY CENTER

sun worked hand in hand with the nonprofit Louisville Central Community Center (LCCC) to help provide drawings, designs, planning, and help with getting approvals. Ten years later, LCCC has helped develop seventy-six units, of which forty-six houses and seventeen apartment buildings have been built in Russell. Nearly all of the apartment units have three bedrooms and two bathrooms and range from about 1,120 to 1,800 square feet. All the units sold for between $49,500 and $115,000. For the earliest units, a monthly mortgage estimated at $395 a month was $100 less than nearby apartments. These housing units look attractive and fit within the historic character of the neighborhood of hundred-year-old shotgun homes. Many of the shotgun houses were renovated to maintain the historical character of the city.

A team of student architects, planners, lawyers, and engineers (most notably Rob Mullins, Mark Wright, Michael Brazley, and Scot Ramsey) helped to create architectural renderings and house plans for West Louisville. These students interacted with city leaders to help them understand the approval process of various private and public agencies and the economics of preservation and new housing construction. The students were edgy, energetic, and inventive. I gave them a long leash to "make it hap-

8.4 Garden view of H. Temple Spears Center

8.5 New home in West Louisville designed by the SUN team

8.6 Row of new housing in West Louisville designed by the SUN team

8.7 Renovated historic shotgun house developed by nonprofit Louisville Central Development Corporation

pen." Of special note was that many of the houses were pre-built before they even got to the lots—roofs, walls, kitchens, and bathrooms. The parts were fitted together on site similarly to modular housing. The lots were provided to Louisville Central Development Corporation (LCDC) for $1 (that is not a typo!) with sewers, electrical connections, paved roads, and some sidewalks. The leader of LCDC, the largest black social service agency in Russell, was Sam Watkins Jr., who opened the gate for us to come into the neighborhood. He was critical to our success; he was honest, charismatic, and smart. While embracing our grit and idealism, Mr. Watkins had the political clout to keep the naysayers at bay.

SUN worked with Telesis Development Corporation and neighborhood leaders such as Deborah Todd and Sam Watkins Jr. to help save Village West from demolition. The demolition of Village West would have resulted in the loss of 653 family housing units and exacerbated the housing crisis for blacks. Many of these housing units had been abandoned and boarded up. SUN helped introduce the idea of crime prevention through environmental design (see Jacobs 1961; Newman 1980). This resulted in the creation of 550 new units out of the 653 original units so that every unit had good views—

8.8 Telesis' 550-unit renovation of a boarded-up housing project at City View Park

eyes on the streets. The brick units had a total makeover, with front doors going out to the streets, public/private space demarcation, and attractive and varied roof lines with gables. Faux front porches were added, and small, personalized backyards were fenced off with short three-foot-high fences. Village West, the flat-roofed, barrack-like project was gone. It was renamed City View Park. These units are a mix of market-rate and Section 8 units.

Despite the history of these units as a place of rampant crime and vice, rents are nearly as high as in predominantly white middle-class neighborhoods—$707 for a four-bedroom unit; $594 for a three-bedroom unit; $496 for a two-bedroom unit; and $373 for a one-bedroom unit. Plans are in the making, by 2009, to sell the units off as affordable condominium units in a range of around $30,000 per unit, which would put the monthly payment of principal and interest at around $250.

Telesis is a highly respected Washington, D.C., developer with a track record of success, originality, common sense, and good economics. Telesis combines the architectural theory of Jane Jacobs' (1961) "eyes on the street" and Oscar Newman's (1980) "crime prevention through environmental design," along with a host of social programs that SUN provided, such as job training, drug and alcohol programs, counseling, educational advancement programs, computer Internet access, health, and leadership training. Moreover, Telesis' "new style" of management is a model that advocates hiring activists who live on the property to manage, market, maintain, and police the property. Thus the traditional friction between management and resident associations is eased. Finally, Telesis was able to convince prominent landscape architect James Van Sweden (1995, 1998)—known for the highly visible Nelson A. Rockefeller Park at Battery Park City in New York, the National World War II Memorial in Washington, D.C., and Oprah Winfrey's Northern Indiana mansion—to "give back to the community." Sweden's firm had the challenge of turning a bleak, depressing landscape into an uplifting, low-maintenance, tree-lined development that creates a sense of place. In 2004, Princeton University Press' *Louisville Guide* declared City View Park a place of "noteworthy architecture" (Luhan, Domer, and Mohney 2004). This is an important achievement, as very few architectural guides, including the *Louisville Guide*, can point to affordable housing developments as having design merit.

SUN also collaborated with the National Manufactured Housing Association to create a historic-looking manufactured house that would fit within a historic neighborhood. Ten years later, the manufactured house (Photo 8.9, left) has fit into the neighborhood well, with few folks knowing that the house was manufactured.

SUN was retained as a consultative and mediator partner in the proposed development of a HUD Section 232-backed project to construct a 156-unit retirement residential center for the underserved, which will be replicated in other parts of Louisville. A for-profit limited liability company anchors the project. The company is made up of three cooperative partners: the landowner, the builder, and a local labor organization, which is providing pre-development financing. The project would demonstrate how unions can realize superior investment returns by investing in housing. The project was expected to yield units that rent profitably at approximately 30 percent below current market rents for similar housing as a result of HUD financing and the limited-liability partnership. Financing, land, and construction-cost savings are pooled to create a long-term investment opportunity for the company and needed housing for the elderly. The project might have been built on leased land.

Unfortunately, this development stalled because of infighting among partners over how much of a slice of pie each partner would get. Hopefully, this model will be replicated by other labor organizations, nonprofits, and faith-based organizations in the future. A similar project was developed for the University of Louisville that was estimated to cost around $7 million on

8.9 Manufactured shotgun house (left) that fits into the neighborhood

land leased from the university for $1 a year. The three-story development would have sixty-five rooms to accommodate a peak capacity of 130 nursing home patients. After fifteen years, the nursing home would be given back to the university for $1, and the university would have a dormitory for 130 students at an appreciated value of $12 million to $15 million. However, the university said No to this proposal.

With a new president and chair, university support for SUN was cut dramatically, forcing us to stop providing planning, economic, and architectural services to West Louisville. Ego, power, and jealousy at the university were the main culprits. This was done despite community pleas for SUN to continue its revolutionary work. Universities have a great deal of promise but more often betray community interests (see Gilderbloom and Mullins 2005 for a much longer account of this soap opera).

SUN now works as a consultant to universities and neighborhood groups. As a result of our efforts, several university-community partnerships have been established using the SUN model to develop sustainable neighborhoods.

CONCLUSION

As a result of its successes, Sustainable Urban Neighborhoods was recognized by Harvard University. Harvard's John F. Kennedy School of Government chose SUN as a semi-finalist in its 2001 Innovations in American Government Awards Program. The University of Louisville's outreach community partnership initiative through SUN and me, the program's principal investigator, received the Sierra Club's National Best Practices Award. The SUN program also was given positive coverage in *Planning Magazine*, the *New York Times*, and the *Atlanta Journal-Constitution*. Even the local newspaper that had run a critical story in the beginning ran several positive stories on the accomplishments of SUN.

SUN's successful programs illustrate the positive impact that a university can have on a distressed neighborhood. SUN's programs involve local housing, economic development, community organizing, and neighborhood revitalization. The SUN project was designed to serve as a change agent in promoting revitalization in the federally designated West Louisville Enterprise Community. The overall mission of SUN is to improve the quality of life for residents of the Enterprise Community. SUN's East Russell, an inner-city Louisville neighborhood, has seized the nation's attention by creating a renaissance in the central city, bringing new life and vitality.

SUN's approach is holistic rather than piecemeal. SUN enhances problem-solving capacities by linking residents with systems that provide resources designed to increase productive self-sufficiency. Community education coordinated through partnerships with educational institutions, nonprofit organizations, and faith-based groups increases the depth and breadth of information available to the residents. These partnerships promote a positive outlook to overcome initial skeptical neighborhood attitudes. New business and investment in the neighborhood, vital to its redevelopment and growth, came about through the coordination of enterprises outside the neighborhood and those struggling within the neighborhood.

Today, the gangs, prostitutes, and drugs are invisible to the eye. Crime has fallen on a per person basis. The community looks like a safe and comfortable neighborhood. West Louisville has always been a distinct black neighborhood that was several blocks from the central business district and served as a western bookend for the center of the city. With the revitalization of Russell, there has also come a sudden revitalization in the center of the city, with new loft housing constructed and an entertainment district recently opening up. Universities do not need to be isolated in the ivory tower but can be an active agent of positive change. Imagine what a difference universities could make if programs like SUN were embraced by the other 3,650 higher education institutions.

Author's note: This is a revised and updated version of an article that was published in the Practicing Planner *in December 2004 (vol. 2, no. 4), titled "University Partnerships to House the Needy." Reprinted with permission from Practicing Planner (an e-journal of APA), copyright December 2004 by the American Planning Association. Our thanks to Sylvia Lewis.*

CHAPTER 9

HOUSING OPPORTUNITIES FOR EVERYONE

In the previous chapters we have investigated the limits of the supply-and-demand housing policy promoted mostly by conservatives and the "regulation" approach advocated by liberals. I argue that the best kind of affordable housing is homeownership—especially as a long-term strategy—as Steven Hornburg (2001, iii) also explains:

> Research surveyed shows that homeownership gives more control to owners over their physical surroundings and tenure, lowers real monthly payments over time, protects against unanticipated changes in rental costs, and helps build wealth. Homeownership also provides a ready mechanism for families to borrow money and get credit to, for instance, improve their home, make purchases, or invest in education or the financial markets. . . . Most of these benefits are available to all homeowners regardless of economic status.

Perhaps the best way to describe the multitude of benefits of homeownership is summarized in Table 9.1. The table indicates that there are positive and negative aspects attached to homeownership. But the positive aspects of control of space, fixed mortgage rates that are not subject to increases as a sort of radical rent control, and better physical and mental health outweigh the negatives.

TAX BENEFITS

At the forefront of economic advantages is the issue of taxation. Through the mortgage interest deduction and the capital gains exclusion, homeowners

TABLE 9.1. *Potential Impacts of Homeownership*

Potential Positive Impacts of Homeownership	Potential Negative Impacts of Homeownership
Neighborhood stability	Decreased residential mobility
Civic involvement/desirable social behavior	Exclusionary efforts
Improved psychological health	Decreased psychological health
Improved residential satisfaction	Residential dissatisfaction
Improved life satisfaction	Dissatisfaction
Improved physical health	Deteriorated health

Rohe, McCarthy, and Van Zandt 2001, 7

are able to generate sizeable financial gains. The total amount of federal tax expenditures for homeowners in 1990 was $70 billion. In 1989 the total expenditures for all low-income subsidized programs was $17.3 billion. Further highlighting this inequity is the fact that the tax expenditures for owners in the last two years of the 1980s ($107.4 billion) are comparable to the federal expenditure for low-income housing programs for that entire decade.

Even among homeowners, a disparate relationship exists between income and the amount of the mortgage interest deduction. The top 20 percent of income earners received about 60 percent of the homeownership deductions annually, yielding significant advantages for those with the highest incomes. A standard tax deduction for a single person or married persons filing jointly is the same amount regardless of how much each person makes. Changes introduced during the George W. Bush administration by the Republican-controlled Congress to overturn "the marriage tax penalty" would allow even higher deductions, proportionally, for married couples filing jointly than for singles or marital partners filing separately. This is one reason many people with low incomes do not receive a benefit for itemizing deductions (including mortgage interest) rather than taking a standard deduction. The significance of these tax breaks for homeowners is reflected in the 1992 Fannie Mae *National Housing Survey*, which reported that 78 percent of the respondents felt that lower income taxes were a convincing reason to own a home (7).

APPRECIATION

Another significant benefit that homeowners possess is that a home investment appreciates over time. This concept of appreciation is primarily a post–

World War II trend. Prior to the postwar federal programs, which extended homeownership opportunities to many who otherwise could not afford to buy homes, homeownership was often the sign or the result of wealth. However, in the past forty to fifty years, homeownership has increasingly become a vehicle to prosperity for many Americans. By 1986, owner-occupied homes were valued at $3.8 trillion, and the average homeowner held equity in excess of $50,000 (Stegman 1981). The 1992 Fannie Mae *National Housing Survey* confirms this belief in value appreciation among homeowners—77 percent of the respondents said their residence would yield more at that time than they had paid for it (20). For sure, what people paid in mortgage payments they got back in appreciation that many times equaled or exceeded mortgage payments. For many Americans, then, homeownership equals housing at virtually no cost.

Closely related to value appreciation is the appeal of equity. In the 1992 Fannie Mae *National Housing Survey*, 37 percent of the homeowners reported that the profits made from selling their prior residences aided their purchase of new homes (12). Moreover, 90 percent of the respondents conjectured that building equity to put toward a better house was a "convincing reason to own" a home (7). In discussing wealth, 1988 figures show that home equity contributes over 50 percent of the average homeowner's net wealth. This figure takes on even greater dimensions when minorities are isolated: 80 percent of African-American homeowners' net wealth and nearly 100 percent of Hispanic homeowners' net wealth was in the form of home equity.

A further advantage for many homeowners is the ability to refinance their mortgages at lower percentage rates of interest. Refinancing can substantially lower mortgage payments and save considerable sums of money for owners over the full length of their payments. Refinancing also cuts down substantially on capital gains taxes when the owner sells the home.

For example, an owner buys a duplex for $130,000, and six years later, with renovations, an improved neighborhood, and rising rents, the value of the home goes to $250,000. The owner, as a landlord, can refinance the loan at a lower rate and "cash out" by getting $80,000 without paying any taxes. Assuming the mortgage has been paid down to $115,000 and the landlord decides to sell it at $250,000, he or she would only owe capital gains taxes on about one-third of the total appreciation, or pay taxes on only $40,000, after the real estate commission is paid, instead of paying taxes on $120,000.

Meanwhile, the monthly mortgage payment after refinancing has only increased an additional $150. Along with this great tax shelter, landlords can also claim residency in the unit by receiving mail and "living there" for two years and never have to pay capital gains tax. Another way is to use a 1031 real estate exchange program, in which the appreciation is not taxed if the owner puts the money into a higher-value rental property.

The government might not ever tax you if you decide to refinance that property or allow your children to inherit your properties. The point here is that much of the profits of a landlord are hidden and have very little to do with "cash flow." This helps explain why rent control is a failure, because government seems to be ignorant when it comes to calculating a landlord's profit, often excluding appreciation, sheltered taxes, refinancing (which also can be used as an excuse to raise rents), and 1031 real estate exchanges. The real estate mantra that no other business has made more people millionaires than real estate certainly seems true.

An additional economic benefit of homeownership is revealed when home-owners are compared to renters. Tenants spend a larger proportion of their incomes on housing than owners do. Bearing in mind that "affordable" is defined as not exceeding 30 percent of a household's income, 35 percent of renters and 16 percent of homeowners said they paid more than 30 per-cent of their monthly incomes toward housing in the 1992 Fannie Mae *National Housing Survey* (16). This situation is exacerbated by the fact that the incomes of renters are generally lower than the incomes of owners. Given each of these economic advantages of homeownership, it is not surprising that 84 percent of those polled in a 1991 *New York Times* study affirmed this statement: "Buying a home is the best long-term investment in the United States" (in Fannie Mae 1992, 17).

NON-ECONOMIC BENEFITS OF HOMEOWNERSHIP

In addition to the numerous economic advantages of homeownership in the United States, many non-economic benefits should be considered. Chief among these is the importance of self-determination and control over one's dwelling space. Concerning the principle of dweller control, John Turner stated:

> When dwellers control the major decisions and are free to make their own contribution to the design, construction or management of their housing, both the process and the environment produced stimulate individual and social well-being. When people have no control over, nor have responsibility for key decisions in the housing process, on

the other hand, dwelling environments may instead become a barrier to personal fulfillment and a burden on the economy. (Quoted in Ward 1983, 7–8)

This notion of self-determination and control would be more significant if a home were seen as more than a roof and four walls. Turner observed that "the important thing about housing is not what it is but what it does in people's lives" (ibid.). Therefore, dweller control signifies more than regulating a residence—it means gaining authority over one's whole environment and significantly shaping the boundaries of the occupants' worldview and outlook on life. Ward argues that control over one's environment spawns a degree of optimism that cannot be replicated when residents are provided for rather than given the opportunity to provide for themselves. A strong link exists between dweller satisfaction and dweller control.

Western society, Ward (1983, 30) argues, has erased any chance for the poor to provide for themselves. The poor of the third world take pride and strive to make improvements in their dwellings, which may appear to be grossly substandard by Western lifestyles. Although they are impoverished, they still own their homes (79). Moreover, John Turner identifies three freedoms that the poor of the world's poor countries have that the poor of wealthier societies do not possess: "the freedom of community self-selection, the freedom to budget one's own resources, and the freedom to shape one's own environment" (in Ward 1983, 80).

Many of these ideas have received widespread attention as empowerment and self-help philosophies have become increasingly popular. Along these lines, Ward states that "property is inseparable from power, and rented property is inseparable from power over other people's lives" (142–143). Moreover, tenanthood spawns dependency while simultaneously withholding any chance for responsibility over the tenants' own affairs. These principles contain a clear message for many in the United States who believe that the national welfare system promotes a perpetual cycle of welfare dependency. Without increased homeownership and the sense of self-determination that accompanies it, the cycle will be that much more difficult to abolish.

The results reported in the 1992 Fannie Mae *National Housing Survey* echo the importance of the control and autonomy that homeownership allows. Throughout the report, the security that ownership promotes is highlighted. One statement reads: "Owning a home is not merely attractive because it connects a person to the community, but because it creates a fundamental feeling of safety and strength." In addition, 89 percent of those surveyed reported a sense of permanence generated through homeownership, and 92 percent of the respondents said that being able to make desired changes were convincing reasons to own a home.

Proponents argue that homeownership programs give low-income families a personal stake in their community. Former HUD Secretary Jack Kemp has stated:

> Only private property will be maintained, respected, and improved. . . . Publicly owned property is essentially owned by no one and will always be abused. . . . It promises to enhance community spirit, create pride of ownership, and provide greater stability of neighborhoods. (Quoted in Silver, McDonald, and Ortiz 1985, 215)

As the quality of life of former tenants is improved due to the increased housing quality, a number of psychological benefits will accrue to the new homeowners. Among these benefits are the enhancement of liberty and freedom of choice, the development of personal virtues such as independence and self-reliance, increased self-esteem, and a sense of control over their personal lives (Rohe and Stegman 1992, 145; Silver, McDonald, and Ortiz 1985, 214).

Data from the Public Housing Homeownership Demonstration (PHHD), which began in 1985, indicates that motivations for buying were both financial and psychological. The most frequently cited reason for buying a home was having a good financial investment (71 percent, cumulative). The second most cited reason was to have something to leave their children (43 percent, cumulative). Only 35 percent cited the ideology of ownership, or "something to call ours," as their reason for buying (Stegman 1991, 67).

COUNCIL HOUSING IN THE UNITED KINGDOM

The literature on the privatization of council housing in Britain, which began in the 1960s and accelerated in the 1980s under the Conservative government of Prime Minister Margaret Thatcher, has identified numerous and complex psychological and financial motives for council housing tenants to purchase their homes. One of the major reasons for purchasing was that residents liked the neighborhood. Despite its impoverished state, residents in the working-class area of Exeter, London, were comfortably familiar with the area, and many did not want to move away from family and friends (James, Jordan, and Kay 1991, 31–32).

The desire for control over their units was also a major reason for purchase. Residents complained about the lack of repairs and maintenance done by the housing councils and the lack of personal control as tenants. Many residents wanted the ability to "do what you want" to their homes (James, Jordan, and Kay 1991, 32). The work of Forrest and Murie (1991) also confirms this in their examination of the purchasers of council homes from 1968 to 1973, before the large-scale push by the Thatcher government to sell off the long-term public rental housing. They found that satisfaction in this area increased as tenants became homeowners.

The percentage of residents who experienced satisfaction with having repairs done after they bought homes increased from 64 percent as tenants to 80 percent as owners in London, and from 56 percent as tenants to 87 percent as owners in Birmingham. The percentage of residents who were satisfied that they had the freedom to do what they wanted with the property increased from 45 percent as tenants to 93 percent as owners in London and from 46 percent as tenants to 94 percent as owners in Birmingham (Forrest and Murie 1991, 1–25). Related to the desire for more personal control over their living environment, residents also expressed a desire to make their houses more "pleasant, convenient and convivial" (James, Jordan, and Kay 1991, 33).

Another reason for purchase was the ideology of ownership. Some residents wanted to own something of their own and move up the economic ladder (James, Jordan, and Kay 1991, 34). Once again, the empirical data of Forrest and Murie reinforce this sentiment. The feeling that "your home was your own" increased from 71 percent as tenants to 96 percent as owners in London and from 72 percent as tenants to 98 percent as owners in Birmingham (Forrest and Murie 1991, 1–25).

The literature also has identified certain financial reasons for purchase of council homes by former tenants. Forrest and Murie's 1968–1973 study of early privatization is revealing (Forrest and Murie 1991). The three most important reasons for tenants deciding whether to buy their homes were: it was a "good financial investment"; "it gives a sense of security"; and "you're getting a bargain" (624). Two other important reasons for purchasing included capital gains, appreciation, and having "spare money to invest" (ibid.). Clearly, the financial aspects of equity and capital appreciation are important factors in this context.

Many residents also had a fear of rising rents and of the instability of the public sector. As part of the Thatcher government's effort to encourage homeownership, rents were sharply increased in Britain (Kleinman 1990). This, coupled with the likelihood of the continued erosion of the importance of the public sector under a Conservative government, had the effect of substantially attenuating the difference between mortgage and rent payments.

Moreover, many residents wanted to protect their investment in their homes. Because residents of council homes in Exeter, London, were long-term tenants, many of them had made substantial improvements to their homes. Having spent money, time, and energy making structural improvements to their houses, many residents had a desire to protect these investments by purchasing their homes. Finally, purchasers expressed a desire to pass on their sacrifices and equity to their children (James, Jordan, and Kay 1991, 35).

NATIONAL ECONOMIC POLICY AND HOMEOWNERSHIP

From a national economic policy standpoint, homeownership provides some strong incentives. Homebuilding as an instrument to help spur economic growth is not a new idea. The post–World War II years witnessed a dramatic increase in the expansion of mortgage insurance through various federal lending institutions, allowing many first-time homebuyers the opportunity to acquire residences. The economic growth aspect of homebuilding was evidenced through its high multiplier effect. For example, as homes are built and bought, new appliances must also be purchased for these homes. As the United States emerged from the Cold War years with a sluggish economy, a shift toward homeownership served as a spark needed to "jump start" the economy.

President Jimmy Carter did as much to fuel the nation's housing crisis as Ronald Reagan by allowing interest rates to skyrocket and supporting accelerated depreciation allowances. These forces drove the rapid turnover of apartment ownership tied to higher interest rates (Gilderbloom and Appelbaum 1988). Moreover, Carter's support of the traditional Democratic supply-side approach was as ineffective as the Reagan-Bush demand-side programs of increasing housing vouchers. Calling for more government involvement also means having an honest government that provides oversight and accountability and participation, one that ordinary citizens watch over and participate in. Since the savings and loan and HUD scandals of the 1980s, it is clear that unmonitored government is bad government and that the economically disadvantaged are harmed the most by the misuse of funds.

BARRIERS TO HOMEOWNERSHIP FOR THE POOR

Despite the irrefutable benefits of homeownership, criticisms have been raised concerning its applicability as a concept for the poor. Many critics claim that there are too many barriers to homeownership for those below a certain income threshold. In the 1992 Fannie Mae *National Housing Survey*, some of these impediments were highlighted: 51 percent of the respondents listed the down payments and closing costs as significant barriers; 44 percent said that not having enough monthly income constituted a serious problem; 29 percent regarded security of employment as an obstruction; and 25 percent mentioned a poor credit record as a hindrance to obtaining homeownership.

Adding to these obstacles is that the poor are likely to encounter one or more of these barriers. Even if one of the problems is somehow reconciled, several more may still remain. A study by Michael Stegman (1981) produced findings that show this to be true. In attempting to purchase a home with a value of 75 percent of the median, a mere 16 percent of all U.S. renters were obstructed by mortgage notes that were too high. About 3 percent could not afford the down payment, and 14 percent were prevented because their installment debt was too large. The great majority—about two-thirds—were prevented from purchasing homes of modest value because they encountered difficulties in more than one of these areas.

One of the major concerns surrounding homeownership for the poor is the difficulty they have in maintaining a home even if they do have enough resources to make the purchase. Housing, like many other investments, may hold unforeseen and unpredictable costs (i.e., accidents may transpire, or the need for repairs may surface at any time). This is particularly true for older and less expensive housing with appliances no longer under warranty. The options for many of the poor may be limited to this segment of the housing stock.

Unanticipated costs do not prove to be an unbearable burden for the majority of homeowners of the middle and upper classes who can either pay for the expenses out of some type of savings or have enough net worth to successfully borrow the needed resources. For the poor, who may have little (if any) cash in reserve and an extremely limited borrowing capacity, these expenses may be beyond their means.

In this circumstance, lower-income households may be forced to choose between making a badly needed repair or paying the required monthly note on the house. If the household chooses to pay the monthly payment, the damage may worsen and may potentially require an even more expensive repair. If the household chooses to make the repair, they may be forced to move for subsequently falling behind in monthly payments.

Losing a home this way defeats the initiative of homeownership, and more importantly, it may demoralize the individuals who have had the American Dream pulled out from underneath them. Some would argue that owning a home has such a high value attached to it. Pursuing a homeownership program for those who are likely to default is not only a poor investment, but it also contributes to a tremendous sense of failure for individuals who might suffer with low levels of self-esteem.

The experience of the PHHD reflects the realities of the complex barriers to homeownership for the poor. Public housing authorities had problems attracting potential buyers who could afford to pay the full costs (mortgage, taxes, insurance, utilities, and maintenance) without HUD subsidies. Because of the relatively low income of persons in public housing, the percentage of this population that can afford to own homes is fundamentally and systemically limited.

The desire of the authorities to collect renovation and repair costs, in combination with the minimum required income to qualify to purchase, eliminates a substantial number of potential purchasers from the program (Rohe and Stegman 1992, 150). In Baltimore between 1987 and 1991, only 352 of its 2,500 total residents met the minimum income requirement of $10,000 per year (Rohe and Stegman 1992, 151). Only families or persons with relatively high incomes (the higher scale of low-income or poor persons) could participate in homeownership programs supported by a Philadelphia program in the late 1960s (Abrams 1970); by an experiment with two sites in the mid-1970s (Shanley and Hotchkiss 1979), and by the arguments of such scholars as Meehan (1988, 105).

TOWARD A PROGRESSIVE HOUSING PROGRAM

Homesteading involves residents providing "sweat equity" in the rehabilitation of an abandoned or foreclosed unit. Homesteading involves exerting physical labor to rehabilitate the housing unit and ranges from replacing or repairing major structural elements of the house to improving the plumbing, heating, electricity, and other necessities. The cost of bringing multi-family housing up to code through self-help rehabilitation can be 50 percent of the cost of conventional rehabilitation by private developers because homeowners spend no money on their own and use their free labor to improve their homes (Gilderbloom, Rosentraub, and Bullard 1987, 28). However, a major obstacle facing nonprofit housing organizations was state laws inhibiting homesteading programs.

Amsterdam, Rotterdam, New York, and Boston have been able to revitalize many declining neighborhoods by developing innovative homesteading programs. These programs result in greater housing opportunities for disadvantaged persons, an increase in tax revenue, more jobs, and the renewal of neighborhoods. When a landlord repeatedly refuses to fix housing code violations, tenants can ask the court under a statewide receivership program to apply their rent for needed repairs.

Housing receivership programs have worked well in New Jersey (Listokin with Allewelt and Nemeth 1985) and in Amsterdam. Our nation's poor neighborhoods could be dramatically turned around with the adoption of large-scale homesteading and receivership programs.

Not only can homeownership and homesteading laws improve the lives of poor people, they also give the elderly and disabled creative ways to use the equity they have built up by owning their homes. Creative solutions that continue to be rooted in homeownership are also preferable to assisted-living situations.

HOUSING POLICY OPTIONS

A large percentage of disabled and elderly persons own their homes. Our survey found that 75 percent of the disabled and 79 percent of the elderly lived in detached houses (Gilderbloom et al. 1987). This presents an important opportunity for providing housing to these special populations, regardless of whether they are owners or renters. Even if we examine disabled and elderly households in which total incomes are less than $10,000 a year, more than one-half of the disabled and two-thirds of the elderly own their homes. To rectify this, it is suggested that our cities promote three housing action projects: shared housing programs, congregate services, and equity conversion programs. These programs not only allow individuals to stay in their homes but to supplement their incomes.

The cost of operating these programs is small compared to traditional government programs. For example, a shared housing program could be run for the cost of building one apartment unit. For those who rent, shared housing and congregate housing services would produce more available housing at a lower cost.

Shared housing is a practical, non-bureaucratic program for promoting independence for seniors. Its potential for providing housing for elderly and disabled persons has not been fully realized. Four out of five elderly persons owned their homes in 1987, while seven out of ten disabled owned homes. Our data found that over 30 percent of the elderly and 21 percent of the disabled were "over-housed" (Gilderbloom et al. 1987). This means that an elderly or disabled household had more than two rooms for every person in their households.

SHARED HOUSING

Shared housing is a progressive housing alternative in which compatible people share a residence based on common needs and preferences. Shared housing can help reduce housing costs and household chores and provide companionship and in certain cases much-needed transportation services. Potential home sharers come from a range of backgrounds and have varied needs.

Houston's home-share program, under the auspices of Sheltering Arms, offered a housemate match-up service involving older adults or a younger and older adult together. Potential home sharers, those providing a residence to share and those seeking a residence to share, were screened and matched by Sheltering Arms. At least one of the pair seeking a home-sharing relationship was required to be sixty years of age or older, but all adults over the age of eighteen were encouraged to apply.

A detailed screening process was followed to assure reliable and compatible housemates. After a preliminary telephone screen to assure that the individual was suitable for the program, a personal interview was conducted. Potential home providers had their homes checked to determine their suitability. Special consideration was given to the location and design of the house. The interviews established the needs and desires of the potential home sharers, including the characteristics they were seeking in a housemate, such as the desired age, gender, ethnicity, and amount of housework or services they wanted to contribute.

Home sharers could provide or offer services in exchange for some portion or all of the living expenses. Some of the services that could be exchanged were yard work, laundry, transportation, shopping, cleaning, and cooking. References and doctors' statements were obtained from potential housemates. When all information was gathered, an attempt was made to match a home provider with a home seeker who appeared to have compatible characteristics and needs.

The next step was for the clients to make telephone contact with one another and decide whether to initiate personal contact. It was only after the two decided the match was desirable that a contract was negotiated with help from Sheltering Arms. A follow-up evaluation was made to determine the suitability of the relationship. Home sharers contributed financially to their housing expenses, with some sharers paying as little as $25 a month and others as much as $200 a month.

Unfortunately, this pragmatic and straightforward program was underutilized because few older citizens were aware of it. Our survey found that one out of four disabled and elderly persons favored this kind of program (Gilderbloom et al. 1987). This represented roughly 150,000 individuals who were potentially interested in this program. Of those who were disabled, most wanted to share a house with someone who was the same age.

CONGREGATE HOUSING PROGRAMS

A program related to shared home programs is the congregate housing program. Congregate housing programs are defined as places where residents are assisted in tasks such as cleaning their homes, working in the yard, and providing meals (Eckert and Murrey 1987; Lawton 1976). Congregate housing is for those individuals who can no longer live independently but need only a minimum amount of services. It is also an alternative to an institutionalized nursing home environment. Our survey found that 74 percent of the disabled and 59 percent of the elderly favored congregate housing services (Gilderbloom et al. 1987).

SALE LEASE-BACK ARRANGEMENTS

For elderly homeowners, home equity conversion allows them to unlock the monetary value of their homes and connect it to working capital or pay for services necessary for continuance of a set lifestyle (Trichillo 1987, 121). Of those persons who owned homes in 1987 and were sixty-five years of age or more, 80 percent owned their houses without any mortgage debt (Trichillo 1987). Consequently, the home equity conversion program could benefit two-thirds of the elderly who are poor. The elderly homeowner sells his or her home to an agency and then rents it back at a fair market value.

The program that has created the most interest among investors is the sale lease-back arrangement. An investor purchases the house and then guarantees the seller lifetime tenancy at a specific rent. This program provides numerous advantages for the seller, the investor, and the community at large. For the seller, a home equity conversion supplements existing income that often does not keep up with inflation. For the investor, a tax shelter is provided in the form of depreciation allowances and interest payments, along with appreciation of the property. The neighborhood benefits as well because needed repairs can finally be completed.

Another version of a home equity conversion involves a partnership with a public agency. This program originated in Buffalo, New York, and is called HELP (Home Equity Living Plan). According to Trichillo (1987, 124), the HELP program is a split-equity arrangement. The homeowner is guaranteed a lifetime tenancy estate to the property, while the public body becomes the owner of the remaining interest. The homeowner retains the title to the house until death (in the case of a couple, until both die). If the corporation fails to deliver the promised payments, it forfeits its right to the house. In essence, the monthly payments to the owner represent a long-term install-ment purchase of the property. Roughly two out of every five elderly and dis-abled households would support such a program (Gilderbloom et al. 1987).

A similar program, reverse annuity mortgage, started in San Francisco. Like the Buffalo program, senior citizens could transfer the equity in their homes into monthly income. Under this program, seniors retain the title to their homes and could borrow up to 80 percent of the assessed value of their homes (Park 1980). Up to 25 percent of the money borrowed would be made immediately available. The San Francisco Development Fund offered three programs: simple reverse mortgage, graduated-payment reverse-annuity mortgage (RAM), and adjustable reverse mortgages (ibid.).

COOPERATIVES

Community-based housing programs are a decentralized housing strategy that emphasizes empowerment of nonprofit community groups to produce, rehabilitate, manage, or own housing for low-income persons, where most of the decision making is done by people who reside in the housing. Restric-tions are placed on the resale price to ensure that the housing remains af-fordable. The government facilitates community-based housing programs by providing technical advice and funding. Bratt (1989) found that community-based housing is superior when compared to other kinds of low-income shelter programs.

Cooperatives are perhaps the most effective way to lower costs because interest rate payments are not subject to escalation, and developer fees are eliminated. Cooperatives, with resale restrictions, offer a useful example of attractive multi-family community-based housing, since they provide many of the guarantees ordinarily associated with homeownership. Such coopera-tives are operated through a nonprofit corporation with an elected board of directors that holds a single mortgage on the property.

Under a typical arrangement, each new owner purchases a share for a minimal down payment. In a limited-equity cooperative, a resident might pay a $500 initiation fee to become a member. Monthly payments include each owner's share of the common mortgage, plus a fee for maintenance and operating expenses. When an owner wishes to move, he or she sells the share back to the cooperative, which then resells it to a new owner. Since the whole process takes place within the cooperative corporation, no new financing or real estate fees are ever involved.

Community-based nonprofit housing organizations are increasingly responsible for a growing share of newly created low- and moderate-income housing. According to the Institute for Policy Studies (1989, 54):

> In Massachusetts about seventy-five nonprofit sponsors have created 7,000 affordable housing units since 1975, with another 2,000 in development. Total rehabilitation and construction by New York City neighborhood groups is estimated at 3,000 units annually. San Francisco's nonprofit developers, with a later start than many East Coast counterparts and an extremely speculative market, have produced 2,000 to 3,000 affordable units in recent years.

While little or no equity is earned, the cost of cooperative housing is substantially lower than market rate housing. Cooperative Services in Detroit has constructed housing at 25 percent below market cost and rent-out units 33 percent below comparable privately developed units.

The cooperative is term-limited equity because the appreciation in the value of each member's share is limited by common agreement at a low level. Cooperative members cannot sell their shares for what the market will bear. In this way, the sales price of units quickly falls below the market price for comparable housing. While a typical home or condominium is sold and refinanced many times over its life span, a limited-equity cooperative is never sold. The original mortgage is retained until it is fully paid off, at which time the monthly payments by the owners decrease to the amount necessary to operate and maintain the units.

The principal difference between a cooperative owner and a private owner is that under cooperatives, residents may change many times without the cooperative itself ever changing owners. Cooperative owners share the full rights and privileges of private owners, including the tax benefits that are not available to tenants in rental housing. Ownership can rest in the hands of residents, public agencies, or community organizations. In all instances, management would be structured to promote resident involvement and encourage resident control over the use of space. Numerous countries including Canada, Sweden, Finland, Netherlands, France, and Italy have enacted programs to create cooperative housing. These actions have led to a dramatic decrease in the percentage of income paid into housing. The overall cost of these programs is financed by taxpayers through a progressive income tax.

The passage of a cooperative housing program would result in a substantial reduction in housing costs for low- and moderate-income persons, resulting in an increase in money for savings. Cooperative housing would also result in substantially more control over the existing housing environment, which would lead to less crime. While it is difficult to predict the success of a community-based housing program, Ronald Lawson's (1984, 87) evaluation of low-income housing cooperatives in New York City indicated that the level of satisfaction was quite high.

Overall, the co-ops have proved successful across an array of key dimensions. Tenants were almost unanimous that the housing was better and cheaper than rental housing. This housing has saved many of them from displacement and has given them a sense of control that they had not previously known. They scored collectively well on other basic indicators of effective management, maintained low vacancy rates, experienced below-average turnover rates, and earned good marks on services provided. Moreover, the tenants stated overwhelmingly that they preferred living in a co-op to having a landlord. Therefore, the co-ops must be acknowledged as good for their tenants. Co-operative housing projects are increasingly popular with nonprofit organizations interested in serving as sponsors.

Co-ops are an effective way of reducing housing costs. This is made possible because the mortgage remains fixed, and it is never refinanced. Scott Franklin (1981, 393–394) has outlined the benefits of co-ops: protection against rising costs, homeownership, tax advantages, community interest, a sense of wellness, less crime, lower maintenance costs, less turnover, protection against eviction, equity accrual, and control and selection of incoming owners. The drawbacks to a co-op program, according to Franklin (1981, 393–394) are owner default, difficulty in financing, and restricted sovereignty.

The cost of cooperative ownership is low relative to private-market housing. Cooperatives have lower costs because interest rate payments are not subject to escalation and developer fees are eliminated. Moreover, when a non-equity cooperative is organized, units remain at their original cost. In a non-equity cooperative, a resident might pay a $500 initiation fee to become a member. When the member leaves the cooperative, he or she is refunded the membership fee but earns no equity from the rent paid. This arrangement is different from renting because no landlords get rich off their tenants. As cooperative wealth increases, cooperative owners benefit from their collective wealth, as shown by low monthly payments.

Our research found that close to one-half of the persons surveyed were interested in housing cooperatives (Gilderbloom et al. 1987). The greatest support was among low-income persons, followed by the disabled and then the elderly.

In Boston, the Methunio Manor, a 150-unit federally subsidized development, went into foreclosure in the 1980s and was sold to the residents as a limited-equity co-op for less than $100 per unit. The monthly payment for each household was $56 to cover insurance, maintenance, and other expenses (Institute for Policy Studies 1989, 49). Limited-equity cooperative housing provides the best hope for supplying decent and affordable housing for low- and moderate-income persons. While rent control is useful for organizing tenants politically and for eliminating the most blatant abuses, it is vulnerable to numerous forms of attack from landlords; thus, the immediate gains seem short-term. On the other hand, limited-equity cooperatives, while not so "sexy" an issue as rent control, provide a solution that will eventually result in even lower housing payments than under rent control.

This is dramatically illustrated by developments in Santa Monica, California. When tenants in a Santa Monica apartment complex rejected the conversion to a cooperative in 1987, they calculated that housing payments would increase by $65 to cover higher mortgage interest rates. They failed to anticipate that a gradual weakening of the Santa Monica rent control law, due to landlord attacks, would result in rent hikes that would eventually exceed projected co-op estimates. Moreover, the California State Assembly could ban strong rent control laws and allow only moderate regulations, resulting in catch-up rent increases between $200 and $400. Limited-equity cooperatives appear more stable and affordable than a rent control program that is becoming more of a gamble for tenants.

Land trusts also can be a valuable tool that promotes cooperative housing. The land is taken off the market and held by the government, which negotiates with a developer to build a certain amount of affordable and accessible housing that is friendly to the disabled and elderly (Bourassa 2006; Bourassa and Hong 2003). Such plans have been successful in western Europe in creating affordable housing. A major part of Holland's affordable housing strategy is public land leasing to housing developers with mandates for housing that is integrated, diverse economically, and sustainable.

HOUSING FOR THE DISABLED AND ELDERLY

The quality of housing for disabled and elderly persons needing certain design modifications to foster independent living was considered critical. Most important was the need for ramps and rails inside the homes.

The support for programs such as house sharing, congregate services, and equity conversions needs to be increased. Other programs that received support were cooperative housing programs and urban homesteading programs. First, we suggested that local officials could endorse and fund house sharing, sale lease-back programs, cooperatives, and homesteading programs. Community Development Block Grant (CDBG) funds could be used to support organizations that sponsor these important and vital programs.

Second, a number of housing vouchers could be issued for cooperatives, house sharing, and sale lease-back programs. This would further encourage the development of these programs, especially of cooperatives, which need these kinds of incentives. Third, it was suggested that prohibitions against in-law apartments should be abolished. These units offered a significant number of housing opportunities for elderly and disabled persons in middle-class neighborhoods. In-law apartments, whether located in the attic, garage, or basement, integrate individuals into good neighborhoods at a reasonable cost.

Local leaders should fund an independent housing service that would provide technical advice on the placement, design, and financing of homes to builders wishing to construct or convert housing for use by the elderly and disabled. An independent housing service could also provide architectural consultation free of charge to landlords interested in modifying housing units for disabled persons. The service could provide grants or loans to landlords to cover the costs of constructing barrier-free living environments. To make sure that these units remain affordable, certain stipulations could be suggested to regulate the rent of the units over a ten- to twenty-year period. The agency could also provide help in the issuance of housing vouchers. Finally, this organization could serve as an advocate for the disabled and elderly community.

Numerous cities have funded technical services that help disadvantaged residents to secure low-income housing while encouraging neighborhood development. San Francisco's Independent Housing Service funded by the Office of the Mayor provides loans and architectural services to modify housing for persons with disabilities. It also advises the mayor and Board of Supervisors on issues of concern to the elderly and disabled.

Planning should also be aimed at providing barrier-free environments. New multi-family housing units on the ground floor should be made accessible to wheelchair users. The cost of designing new housing units that are accessible is only an additional hundred dollars, compared to the thousands of dollars to modify a unit designed for an able-bodied user. All new housing developments must be required to provide bus shelters and sidewalks with curb cuts. Large housing developments should also be required to have a certain number of units that are accessible to disabled persons.

Finally, the city and county should appoint an individual to the local planning commission who is sensitive to the needs of the disabled. The planning staffs of the City of Houston, Harris County, and Metro were urged to hire at least one staff member who was familiar with the problems of disabled and elderly persons. Given the transportation needs and preferences of elderly and disabled individuals, government should increase user accessibility to specialized transit services through a supplemental taxi program designed to serve the spontaneous market trip of the elderly and disabled (ambulatory and wheelchair) users.

Cities should provide fixed-route bus lines that are accessible to disabled and elderly persons through the installation of special equipment (wheelchair lifts, tie-downs, kneel-downs) and other mobility-enhancing features (sidewalks, curb cuts, and shelter stops). The routes selected for the demonstration should also be accessible to medical facilities, shopping and retail centers, higher education institutions, community and cultural centers, low- and moderate-income housing, and various racial and ethnic neighborhoods.

OUTLAW HOUSING: ILLEGAL HOUSING CONVERSIONS

Another kind of affordable housing can be found with the illegal conversion of attics, basements, and garages into studio and one-bedroom apartments. These conversions occur mostly in older historic inner-city neighborhoods where large homes or mansions are divided into apartments or condominiums. Many of these neighborhoods have been in decline due to suburban flight of the 1960s and 1970s and are now coming back because of energy costs, a new cultural embrace of historic homes, and a desire to live in mixed-income neighborhoods. These conversions have planted the seeds for revitalization by increasing rent rolls and allowing for increased capital improvements. These conversions add a significant amount of affordable housing because the payback on these houses is relatively small. As we showed in Chapter 3, a large amount of older housing depresses urban rents. Reliable estimates of the illegal housing stock are unknown because residents are reluctant to discuss or admit it. There has been very little research in this area, and this section is based on my personal observations and talks with landlords who are members of a real estate investment association to which I belong.

The best kind of sustainable housing is the kind created within an existing home using recycled materials, which Chiras (2004, 16) says is

the epitome of conservation and is arguably one of the most sustainable forms of construction. . . . it uses existing resources such as lands, foundations, and walls. No new land must be bulldozed or cleared to make room for a new home: trees do not need to be cut down. Further benefits can be achieved if wastes generated from the project are recycled.

The American Association of Retired Persons (AARP) has reported that 65,000 to 300,000 outlaw units are created every year (Scott 2006). Over a ten-year period, this could average out to well over a million units. These units tend to be located in the older parts of the city. My own house (Photo 9.1) is an example of a recycled home that was once boarded up and faced the wrecking ball or arsonist's match. I bought it at a distress sale at which similar properties were worth twice as much. I was able to fully restore the home at a cost substantially below the market rate by using recycled doors and hardware, removing the unhealthy carpet and restoring the original floors, and using salvaged wood for trim. Moreover, I used passive solar principles by organizing space to maximize the sun rays to heat my home—since I spend most of my day writing and corresponding, I located my office in a room that faces south, and this allows me to significantly reduce my heating needs during the winter. I also used green housing principles to install compact fluorescent light bulbs, insulate the attic, add storm windows, install fans in every room, insulate the fireplace, purchase energy-efficient appliances, and collect water from the roof to recycle for the garden, aquarium, and consume. Not only was this a wise decision from an environmental viewpoint, but it also reduced the gas and electric costs by about one-half since I bought it two years ago.

As we have shown elsewhere in this chapter, a significant amount of housing is underused. Moreover, there are tremendous opportunities to convert basements and attics and second floors over garages into affordable housing. The cost of converting a basement or attic or garage is surprisingly low. An attic conversion of 900 square feet can cost around $15,000. Photos 9.3, 9.4, and 9.5 show how attractive these affordable units can look.

This conversion that would follow code and be attractive would need the following: (1) sanding and varnishing the floor ($500); (2) air and heat unit ($3,500); (3) bathroom plumbing including sink, shower, and toilet ($3,000); (4) kitchen cabinets and sink, stove, counter tops, dishwasher, refrigerator, and microwave ($3,500); (5) electrical wiring ($1,000); (6) drywalling and insulation ($1,000); (7) four skylights that open ($2,000); and (8) painting interior ($500). These are just round estimates, and the cost can be much lower.

I have seen a woman homeowner complete an attic conversion that cost $9,000 and met the sustainability test. She accomplished the conversion by doing much of the work herself and using recycled household items like toilets, cabinets, doors, sinks, and window units. The one variable cost would

9.1 Saved from the wrecking ball! Author's 110-year-old live/work place

be the fire exit ladder or stairs if the house has three floors or more, which would add to the cost another $3,000 to $7,000. Basements can be done between $10,000 and $15,000, and the variable would be a second egress needed to meet fire code. A garage conversion would be more expensive if it is unattached from the house, with extensions needed for plumbing and electrical work.

9.2 Unused attic before apartment conversion

9.3 Same attic converted to a living space

9.4 Kitchen of attic apartment

A rent payment of $250 per month would pay off these conversions within five years, or at $400 a month, the payments would be paid off in about three years. Once it is completed, the "additions" or "improvements" are rarely challenged by the government unless it violates building codes, such as not having a fire escape or having substandard electrical or plumbing work. Some conservative single-family homeowners have threatened these conversions of affordable housing, fearing a reduction in their house value and bringing in "poor people." These homeowners would like to see multi-family housing removed so that the value of their homes will increase—although evidence on this issue is mixed (Duany, Plater-Zyberk, and Speck 2000; Gilderbloom and Mullins 2005). These conversions also add to the value of the house. Using a rent multiplier approach, a $500-per-month basement or attic apartment would result in a $50,000 increase in the value of the property.

New Urbanism has reintroduced second-story garage apartments for grandparents, friends, adult children, or home-based offices to our neighborhoods (Duany, Plater-Zyberk, and Speck 2000). This kind of policy enables the disabled and elderly to have intimate home health care from caregivers, which would provide a better home environment than nursing homes. In

9.5 Attic conversion into an apartment

August 2006, Seattle City Council approved "backyard rental units," allowing detached apartments behind single-family homes in some neighborhoods (Langston 2006).

The outlaw housing units in the inner city provide five examples of affordable, attractive, and sustainable housing:

(1) As we have shown in Chapter 3, "mom and pop landlords" offer significantly lower rents and sometimes provide free rents to their children, out-of-work cousins, or friends. This arrangement can also provide a live/ work space that can reduce the usage of cars. A mom-and-pop landlord also can provide a quality apartment unit.

(2) Older housing units supply a disproportionate amount of the affordable housing stock. In other words, inner-city housing that was built for the upper class and abandoned during the 1960s and 1970s has provided a rich resource of sustainable housing with an existing infrastructure.

(3) Accessory units in the backyard garage, attic, or basement allow housing to be affordable for the owners, whether it is a rental unit at market rent, a unit for a senior relative, or a unit for a friend or relative who needs assisted living care. These units ultimately provide additional value for the home. If we use the rent multiplier formula, a $500 a month rental can mean an additional $50,000 in value, or a $750 a month rental might add $75,000—as is the case in Louisville. The cost of adding an accessory unit in an empty basement or attic is significantly less than the cumulative average monthly rent on a unit over time.

(4) Energy costs from an attic or basement can be significantly lower if

9.6 Basement converted to an apartment

one uses passive solar design. In addition, car usage can be reduced because a unit may be closer to a person's place of employment or a person works from home using the accessory unit. This kind of outlaw housing allows people to live in the city and be closer to work and entertainment opportunities and have a closer network of friends.

(5) Outlaw housing also addresses the problem of over-housing an older adult who might have too much space because of the loss of a partner or because children have grown up and left. Sociologists have argued that from infancy to old age, a human being is much better off living with someone close by than living alone.

Despite these sustainable, social, and affordable aspects, some gentrifying inner-city neighborhoods are working to eliminate outlaw housing units and enforce outdated zoning laws that prohibited splitting up homes with 2,000, 3,000, 4,000, or 5,000 square feet of living space. Homeowners in these neighborhoods fear that the added living accommodations will lower the value of their single-family housing. In some cases, they have prohibited three or more generations from living in one household. It is likely that the introduction of rental housing units might have "saved" many of these historic houses or mansions as well as supplied affordable housing in underused housing.

Another kind of outlaw housing is squatting in abandoned buildings. A large amount of affordable housing has been created in the Netherlands by squatting and laws that support squatting. According to Dutch law, a building can be occupied by a squatter if it has been empty for at least one year. More importantly, an empty building is often waiting to be demolished, and the squatting action is seen as saving an older historic building from the greed of a landlord. Neighborhood residents welcome squatters because many of the buildings are fixed up with new plumbing, paint, electrical wiring, and residents. Or another kind of outlaw housing could mean heading to the woods and building a treehouse to create affordable housing.

For the poor, an affordable housing strategy involves moving to another neighborhood, taking over an abandoned building, or outright buying it. We had one student who rebuilt the shell of a house that he bought for $37, turned it into a pleasant house for around $40,000, and later sold it for $175,000.

CONCLUSION

The private rental market alone cannot provide affordable housing for all citizens, and this is especially true for minorities, the disabled, the elderly,

9.7 Formerly a shell of a building, renovated at a fraction of its market price

and the poor. The conservative free-enterprise approach has worked against the economically disadvantaged. On the other hand, liberal programs such as rent control and vouchers attached to massive tax breaks and subsidies for builders and landlords have had a limited impact. New and bold measures must be used to combat the housing crisis. We need to attack the invisible city with an analysis of the needs of the invisible populations and develop a

9.8 Treehouses as a lower-cost alternative form of housing

perspective rooted in sustainable development, sociology, and New Urbanism. More involvement is needed to resolve the nation's housing crisis, and this greater involvement must be accompanied by an adoption of programs that have a proven track record.

Historically, housing policy in the United States has been shaped by landlords, builders, and bankers. Initially, housing activists were virtually invisible in this process, but by 2000, these activists, including tenants, had become key players in housing legislation and are demanding that the American Dream of homeownership should be made available to more people in this country instead of less.

In the end, the best kind of long-term affordable housing is homeownership. Clear-thinking leadership can provide the opportunity for attractive, accessible, and affordable homes for everyone. Opinion polls indicate that there is widespread national concern regarding the housing crisis, and there is support for spending taxpayer funds on innovative measures that get to the root of the housing problem. We hope that our leaders will have the vision and courage to shake up the old system and take decisive steps in support of progressive housing legislation.

WHY CITIES NEED AFFORDABLE HOUSING

A Case Study of Houston

WITH ROGER K. LEWIS AND STEVEN HORNBURG, HOUSING
STRATEGIES FOR HOUSTON TASK FORCE

Conservatives frequently argue that Houston—"the free enterprise city"—
has no housing crisis. Conservatives note that Houston's housing miracle
is the result of little or no government intervention in the housing market.
They argue that other cities facing a housing crisis should do away with zoning, historic preservation, planning, and community development.

Contrary to conventional wisdom, Houston has a significant housing
crunch. Parts of the city look like a third-world city, with shanties, dilapidated housing, and slums sprinkled throughout the city. Housing affordability for the poor and working class in Houston is a major problem. Houston has one of the lowest homeownership rates of any American cities.
Because neighborhood quality is poor relative to other cities, rents are lower
but in contrast to other large cities rank around the middle.

In many Houston neighborhoods, rising real estate values are reducing
housing affordability and forcing moderate-income families to move out to
fringe locations remote from employment. Without access to public transit,
such families depend completely on private automobiles, incurring burden-
some transportation costs and further contributing to sprawl, severe traffic
congestion, and air pollution. Houston also faces other serious, persistent
challenges, such as chronic flooding, fiscal imbalance, inadequately funded
schools, and governmental inefficiency.

Conducting business as usual in Houston may not work during the
twenty-first century. In the face of dramatic demographic changes, widening income gaps, rising living costs, growing demand for public services,
and greater need for enlightened environmental stewardship, Houston has
a choice. It can do little or nothing, which would jeopardize its future, or it

can craft a new vision for itself, adopting effective strategies to meet these interrelated challenges so that it remains dynamic, prosperous, and livable for all its citizens.

Achieving a new vision for Houston will require new thinking and new attitudes, inspired political leadership, and innovative policies. It also will require changes in government structure. New initiatives will not be effective and sustainable unless Houston eliminates its two-year election cycles and six-year term limits, which disrupt administrative continuity, dampen political creativity, weaken loyalty within city bureaucracies, and too frequently place agency leaders and their jobs in limbo.

"Housing Strategies for Houston: Expanding Opportunities" is a first step toward realizing a new vision. During the summer and fall of 2003, the American Institute of Architects and the Houston City Council identified a team of nationally respected professionals, experts in housing development, urban planning, architecture, public policy, housing agency administration, finance, economics, and sociology. The team was invited to Houston as volunteers to examine the city and recommend housing strategies. Focusing on research and reconnaissance during the first visit in November 2003, the team toured several Houston neighborhoods inside and outside the Loop and met with dozens of individuals representing civic and community organizations, the real estate and homebuilding industries, the business community, and city government. The team also heard from Houston-based transportation and demography experts. In January 2004, they returned to Houston to brainstorm and generate strategy options based on the first visit. The final report is available at http://www.aiahouston.org/housinghouston/downloads.html. The report won an American Institute of Architects Chapter Award and sparked the mayor to nominate a housing czar with a reporting line directly to the mayor.

WHY HOUSING STRATEGIES FOR HOUSTON?

Affordable Housing

As in most American cities, Houston's inventory, production, and availability of affordable housing is shrinking and is likely to continue to shrink for many reasons:

• Neighborhood gentrification—home prices and property taxes rising when affluent families move into and physically improve older, less affluent neighborhoods

• Rapidly rising land values in certain portions of Houston, particularly inside the 610 Loop and in the vicinity of the new 7.5-mile light rail line along the Main Street corridor
  • Conversion by property owners of subsidized rental housing to market-rate housing
    • Obsolescence, abandonment, and demolition of existing dwellings
    • Limited state and diminishing federal funding for housing subsidies
    • Lack of adequate economic incentives for investors and developers to build either new affordable units or to rehabilitate existing units

Paradoxically, despite the relatively low cost of market-rate housing, Houston has a low rate of homeownership, 44 percent, compared with the national average of 68 percent. In 2003, only about 5,000 homes for sale were built within the Houston city limits, while more than 30,000 were built in Harris County.

Neighborhoods, Sprawl, Mobility, and the Environment

The housing challenge in Houston is related to other challenges that face the city. Some of Houston's older residential neighborhoods are physically at risk, with both buildings and infrastructure in disrepair or blighted. These communities require preservation and revitalization, including condemnation and redevelopment of thousands of tax-delinquent properties. Mobility is compromised because transit options are limited, while traffic congestion intensifies, which contributes further to the city's air pollution. Throughout the city, poor stormwater drainage and chronic flooding remain one of Houston's most vexing problems. Low-density subdivision development, sprawling miles into the surrounding counties and countryside, increases upstream stormwater runoff that adds to environmental degradation of the area. With ever-greater commuting distances, suburban and exurban families typically must own, finance, insure, fill with gasoline, service, and repair two cars. Thus transportation costs take a big bite out of many household budgets in Houston.

Houston 2025: What Happens if Nothing Is Done to Address the Houston Housing Crisis?

Imagine two dramatically contrasting versions of Houston in 2025. The desirable version is the globally competitive, economically thriving, culturally vibrant city. Its positive attributes include expanded housing and employment opportunities for all segments of the population, good public schools, safe, stable, diverse neighborhoods throughout the city, state-of-the-art infrastructure, convenient multi-modal mobility, minimal air pollution and flooding, and the look and feel of an attractive, well-planned, urban metropolis with beautiful, tree-lined streetscapes, animated civic spaces, and outstanding architecture.

The undesirable version is a provincial, dysfunctional city plagued by a host of problems, such as lack of affordable housing, troubled neighborhoods, failing and overcrowded public schools, economic stagnation, disinvestment and high rates of unemployment, fiscal stress and high taxes, marginal public services, overloaded and deteriorating infrastructure, degraded urban ecology, severe traffic congestion and constrained mobility, and the look and feel of an endlessly sprawling, unattractive, urban-suburban agglomeration.

If Houston continues doing business as usual and continues to improperly manage future growth and development, the undesirable outcome is likely. This is the risk of doing little or nothing, of continuing past policies and practices no longer appropriate in the twenty-first century. Conversely, by taking bold steps now and embracing a feasible, comprehensive city vision for 2025, the chances of achieving a desirable outcome are greatly enhanced. With federal and state resources available to the city likely to continue diminishing in the future, creating the right vision today is even more critical. This vision must encompass strategies and tactics to expand housing opportunities for today's workforce as well as for the future city's additional two million inhabitants.

Housing Opportunities and the Broad Vision for Houston

Expanding housing opportunities and increasing the supply of affordable housing not only mean worrying about housing for the impoverished. Nor do they refer solely to public housing. In fact, Houston's profit-motivated, market-driven real estate industry will always be the primary producer and manager of most of the city's future housing inventory. Housing affordability is likely to become even more critical for the majority of Houston's population. A significant segment of the city's future population, part of the city's indispensable workforce, is expected to have household incomes too low to afford market-rate housing, given persistently upward trends in land and construction costs. While development of diverse housing across a broad market spectrum will continue, the marketplace alone is unlikely to meet the housing needs of much of Houston's workforce at the lower end of the economic spectrum. If low- and moderate-income workers cannot find homes in the city, they will move farther out, worsening sprawl and depriving the city of their skills, services, spending, and taxes. Therefore, Houston's housing challenge is not only about affordability for potentially hundreds of thousands of people not yet in the city, but also about sustaining the fiscal health of the city as a whole.

There are other reasons to make a serious public commitment to ensuring that affordable housing is available: economics and social justice. Like the economies of all American cities, Houston's economy relies on fully employed workers whose wages are relatively low. The price and affordability of goods and services, to which we all have access and from which we all benefit economically, depend on these workers and their willingness to sell their labor at market rates. The market price of most housing is a stretch for many of these workers. We cannot expect workers to impoverish themselves just so those for whom they work can maintain their standard of living. Therefore, it seems only fair that we attempt to bridge the gap between what low-income working families can pay and what a decent dwelling costs.

Housing strategies for a metropolis as large and dynamic as Houston require a broad vision for the city. Such a vision reflects and shapes public attitudes and public policy as well. Moreover, the vision can clearly illuminate sometimes subtle linkages between housing and the broader urban context of the city such as mobility, economic vitality, neighborhood preservation and revitalization, environmental health, cultural activity, and aesthetic attributes. The following are key elements of that urban vision.

• A city with a growing stock of diverse, affordable, well-designed housing developed and financed through concerted efforts of government, businesses, institutions, civic organizations, and citizens
• A city whose patterns of growth are based on sensible, comprehensive land use and transportation planning, at the scale of the city as a whole and of individual neighborhoods, with growth linked to existing infrastructure, school capacity, and other public facilities
• A city in which areas served by bus and rail transit are targeted for higher densities and developed to create mixed-use, mixed-income, pedestrian-friendly neighborhoods, including affordable housing
• A city meeting the housing needs of an increasingly diverse population, including the aging, singles, work-at-home couples, extended families, and low-income households
• A city in which affordable housing is *not* concentrated in selected neighborhoods but rather is available throughout the city
• A city whose existing neighborhoods are preserved, rendered safe,

and revitalized economically and socially, reflecting unique neighborhood needs and attributes and based on neighborhood-generated plans

• A city with practical but aesthetically inspired urban design and architectural design guidelines, including "green" building and environmental standards, critical to realizing the vision

Successfully pursuing the vision and achieving the desired outcome require forging a partnership between government, business, city-based institutions, universities, civic groups, and individual citizens. The implementation of these ideas into public policy and practice are a means by which Houston's desirable future will be assured.

Housing Strategies: Goals, Tools, and Resources

To foster beneficial development, especially affordable housing development, the government of the City of Houston must help establish the vision for the future city and then work with its key partners—the business, civic, and Community Development Corporation (CDC) communities—to achieve that vision. Government agencies need to be proactive rather than reactive, recognizing that market forces and free-enterprise initiative alone will not solve all the city's problems or provide for all of its needs. Achieving the vision requires changing how the city does business. However, it also requires that Houston's business interests, especially real estate developers, recognize their self-interest in fostering more sustainable growth. They must join in the effort to realize the vision and ensure that Houston's future citizens can find a decent place to live.

The key to this desired future of Houston is planning. However, planning is not zoning, and zoning is not planning. Throughout the United States, conventional zoning generally has failed as an effective planning tool for creating balanced growth, good urban design, beautiful cityscapes, or affordable housing. Primarily separating and restricting land uses while protecting existing property values, zoning regulations have impeded desirable urban development and redevelopment in many cities, making contemporary planning efforts in those cities ineffective. In many jurisdictions, the effect of zoning has been to exclude the less affluent and deny fair access to housing opportunities. Unburdened by zoning, well-conceived comprehensive urban plans can create a perceivable, functioning framework for growth, encourage mixed uses, and allow greater ranges of density; and unlike zoning maps, such plans can provide for flexibility and changing circumstances. Unconstrained by conventional zoning regulations, Houston has a unique opportunity that no other American city has: it can undertake effective planning not trumped or compromised by existing zoning.

An array of diverse tools and tactics can be used to steadily expand housing opportunities, increase affordable housing production, and revitalize existing communities. Some are already in place or available, while others need to be developed. Most entail city government initiatives coupled with private-sector and non-governmental organization activities. Even Houston's universities can contribute uniquely to this effort by establishing first-rate urban studies and planning programs with strong linkages to local communities.

Most of the team's recommended strategies are premised on or call for creating viable, integrated land use, transportation, and housing plans for the city. Properly conceived, such holistic plans neither curtail free enterprise nor reduce development opportunities. Instead, they provide a rational framework for enabling wisely managing future growth, for making prudent public and private investment decisions, and for coordinating capital spending for public infrastructure with private development. By helping shape the future form of the city in the interest of both the public and private property owners, sound planning creates predictability, opportunity, and above all, enduring value for Houston's businesses and citizenry.

Resources for affordable housing must be commensurate with existing and projected affordable housing needs. Implementing recommended strategies both near-term and long-term will entail costs but will ultimately create value exceeding those costs. Therefore, substantial new funding will be needed not only to provide subsidies for housing rented or sold at below-market rates, but also to provide incentives sufficient to motivate and enable the business community to build affordable housing. Furthermore, existing resources must be used more strategically and potentially available funds pursued more aggressively. All of these strategies will become even more critical in light of shrinking financial support and diminishing programs for housing at federal and state levels.

Recommended Strategies

The team proposed seven integrated, interdependent strategies. They are not optional items on a menu to pick and choose when some items are embraced and others rejected. Rather, they constitute a unified set of recommended policies and specific actions. With further study and elaboration, all of these policies and actions can be implemented in the near future. Some will yield results quickly, while others will require several years to bear fruit. All of the strategies will provoke debate, but only through public discussion and support can the city's political, civic, business, and institutional leaders carry out these recommendations to expand housing opportunities, strengthen communities, and ensure Houston's future vitality.

• **Houston's mayor and City Council should immediately appoint a cabinet-level housing "chief," equivalent to a deputy mayor, with authority both to shape city housing policies and to oversee, guide, coordinate, and energize the city's disparate housing efforts.** The housing chief's ultimate goal is to stimulate and facilitate both for-profit and nonprofit sector housing production while increasing the efficacy of public-sector investments. To optimize the use of resources and programs, Houston's housing chief and agency officials should evaluate existing housing programs, policies, and regulations; eliminate ineffective approaches; and strengthen those that work. The housing chief should also immediately mobilize the Land Assemblage Redevelopment Agency (LARA). LARA can use its property acquisition/disposition and land-banking powers to acquire and dispose of property in order to support neighborhood preservation and redevelopment, including properties acquired proactively in support of specific public goals, or reactively through condemnation of tax-delinquent or other distressed properties.

• **Under the leadership of the housing chief, the mayor, City Council, and appropriate agency officials, Houston should adopt an enforceable, comprehensive, and inclusive housing plan realistically tailored for Houston and persuasively developed through an open, transparent public process.** A comprehensive housing plan should set forth overall housing policies and identify long-range housing production targets and homeownership goals, including benchmarks for monitoring progress; public-sector funding needs and priorities; areas of the city intrinsically suited for increased housing density, as well as areas unsuited for higher densities; and residential neighborhoods and properties most in need of suitable revitalization and/or preservation. Viable, actionable housing policies and plans should be linked to comprehensive land use and transportation plans for the city as a whole and for specific city sectors and neighborhoods. This requires strengthening existing legislation and ordinances for generating, adopting, and enforcing such plans. It also requires surveying, precisely defining, and using consolidated Geographic Information System (GIS) mapping: specific neighborhood and citywide resources, such as delinquent properties and vacant or underutilized city land; sites where local problems and needs are most critical, such as especially weak schools or neighborhoods with inadequate public facilities, and potential housing development opportunities, such as Transit-Oriented-Development sites.

· **Houston should adopt a "fair share" housing ordinance to increase production of affordable housing, both for sale and for rent. Dispersing such housing equitably in neighborhoods throughout the city will avoid creating stigmatized "projects" or low-income ghettos.** The ordinance would require new residential developments or redevelopments exceeding a certain size—thirty or forty units—in locations designated in the housing plan to include a stipulated percentage of units. For example, 5 to 10 percent of the units should be set aside for moderate-income households. Percentages, below-market pricing, and household income levels would follow established, periodically updated city guidelines and would be negotiated by developers with the city's housing agencies, which must provide economic incentives for both nonprofit and for-profit developers of such projects. Incentives can take many forms, such as direct subsidies for land acquisition, infrastructure, site preparation, and building construction; real estate tax abatement; investment tax credits; density bonuses; write-down of city-owned land costs; below-market interest rates on construction and permanent financing; and reduction or waiving of municipal fees.

· **To provide economic incentives for developers and to bridge gaps between the price of housing and what some families can afford, Houston should increase locally generated funds devoted to affordable housing using a variety of methods.** Public financing mechanisms include city bond issues, dedicated tax revenue sources, allocations from the city's general funds, and the city's Housing Trust Fund, where the business and real estate communities can contribute. Investments by pension funds and tax credit project investments by local businesses, professional firms, and wealthy individuals should be vigorously pursued. Local financial institutions should increase support for affordable housing through fair lending and community reinvestment practices. For the benefit of their employees and in their own self-interest, Houston's business and institutional communities such as energy corporations, the Texas Medical Center, and universities should help finance and co-sponsor housing initiatives. These initiatives will recognize that adequate workforce housing will be indispensable to sustaining Houston as a world-class, economically competitive city. The city government should obtain Houston's fair share of dollars from competitively awarded state and federal funding sources through more aggressive "grantsmanship" on the part of city officials.

· **Houston should publicly finance or directly undertake infrastructure improvements in inner-city neighborhoods where existing streets and**

utilities are dysfunctional or obsolete and where housing development at higher densities is feasible and desirable. Planning and coordinating infrastructure and housing investments can measurably increase affordable housing production. At the same time, the city should enact an Adequate Public Facilities Ordinance (APFO) that allows higher densities and substantial new development only if existing or planned public facilities—roads, utilities, stormwater system, public schools, and police and fire services— will have adequate capacity to serve the additional population engendered by proposed development. Typically developers submit evidence that APFO standards will be met, usually through a mixture of public and private investments, when they apply for permits. A properly crafted and administered APFO, rather than obstructing growth, ensures that growth, public services, and infrastructure are reasonably synchronized.

  • **Houston's government should help improve the capacity of potentially effective Community Development Corporations to increase affordable housing opportunities**. The city should identify promising CDC organizations and provide them with entrepreneurship training, such as management, finance, marketing, and target public investments for worthwhile, CDC-sponsored projects in the neediest neighborhoods. Likewise, it should encourage partnerships between CDCs and motivated private developers who will continue to build and manage most of Houston's future housing. One of the CDC's partnership roles can be finding and advising qualified homebuyers or tenants within the community.

  • **Houston's government should encourage or undertake with private-sector and Community Development Corporation partners the development of several well-designed "model" projects in key locations linked to transit and infrastructure, schools, and other community resources**. Model developments at appropriate sites would demonstrate to Houstonians the viability, desirability, affordability, and profitability of alternative land use patterns, new types of architecture, mixed uses, higher densities, and demographic diversity. Such pilot projects can convincingly show the effectiveness of good design and the relationship between design quality and livability. Enabling citizens to see innovative, affordable development "in the flesh" is always more persuasive than asking them to believe what they hear someone say or what they see in renderings, photographs, and slick brochures.

Concluding Remarks

The team's recommended strategies were purposefully broad in scope and conceptual. Consequently, the next steps to be undertaken will be (1) more detailed research and analysis; (2) examining relevant precedents; (3) exploring fully the economic, social, and political implications of these strategies; and (4) formulating detailed plans for implementation, including legislative proposals. Setting forth these strategies is just the first step, the beginning of an effort requiring persistent hard work in the years to come. Nevertheless, it is a critical step on the road to creating the future that Houston's citizens deserve.

This report is a good example of how a coalition of progressives can get together and come up with innovative, bold, and brash housing and planning proposals. Although Houston has problems that mirror the nation's cities, these policy recommendations provide a good model for creating consensus on the importance of progressive housing and planning. The report also illustrates how the conservative approach of creating a housing market free of zoning, historic preservation, and planning will not solve the housing problem.

Note: John Gilderbloom was part of this task force, and the final report was written by team leader Roger K. Lewis, Fellow of the American Institute of Architects (FAIA), with assistance from team member Steven Hornburg. John Gilderbloom wrote the introductory paragraphs and edited and rearranged the final report for presentation here. The credit should still go to Lewis and Hornburg.

NOTES

1. For an in-depth discussion of the theories underlying the selection of variables and the expected direction of correlation, the interested reader may consult Gilderbloom and Appelbaum (1988).

2. A previous variable included in our original study (Gilderbloom and Appelbaum 1988) was the percentage increase in city population over the previous decade. This variable has been omitted from the current regression models due to the fact that there are 117 new cities in the 2000 data that are not included in the 1990 data. Yet another reason for omitting this variable was that it was not found to be a significant or consistent predictor of median rents in past studies. The climate score variable included in the previous research was also omitted due to computational difficulties when applying it to the larger sample of cities.

3. Utilities such as expenses for electricity, heat, water and sewer are sometimes included in base rents, especially when these services are not individually metered. We assume that such variations are consistent across all cities.

4. This is the same approach used in our earlier analysis (Gilderbloom and Appelbaum 1988).

1. Our thanks to Burt Pusch and Robert Bullard, who provided comments on the first draft. Special thanks to Mimi Hinnawi for her expert editing suggestions. We remain solely responsible for the entire content of this chapter. A more extensive discussion of the planning needs of disadvantaged Houstonians can be found in *Designing, Locating, and Financing Housing and Transportation Services for Low-Income, Elderly, and Disabled Persons* (Gilderbloom, Rosentraub, and Bullard 1987) from the University of Houston Center for Public Policy.

2. We would like to thank Zhenfeng "Terry" Pan and Lin Ye for their assistance on this section.

3. Burgdorf and Burgdorf (1975, 884) found that Western society for the most part has refused to treat handicapped persons differently from criminals, drunkards, or slaves.

4. Burgdorf and Burgdorf (1975, 863) document such legislation including one ordinance from Chicago that read, "No person who is diseased, maimed, mutilated or in any way deformed to be an unsightly or disgusting object or improper person to be allowed in or on the public ways or other public places in this city shall therein or thereupon expose himself to public view." The authors noted similar ordinances in cities including Columbus, Ohio, and Omaha, Nebraska.

5. Unemployment of disabled persons is a tremendous problem due largely to an inaccessible urban environment and prejudices of employers. Almost one-half of the paraplegics who are of working age are unemployed; more than 75 percent of working-age persons with epilepsy are without work; and a dismal 87.7 percent of disabled Vietnam veterans were unable to find jobs after returning from the war (Burgdorf and Burgdorf 1975). Studies have shown that when persons with disabilities are assigned an appropriate position, their job performance is comparable to non-disabled persons (Burgdorf and Burgdorf 1975, 864).

CHAPTER 6

1. Briggs 1997, 195–234; Briggs 1998, 177–221; Briggs, Darden, and Aidala 1999, 27–48; Carter 2001; Darden 1973, 62; Garvin, Berens, and Leinberger 1997, 127; Gilderbloom and Appelbaum 1988, 75–175; Goldsmith and Blakely 1992; Kasarda 1993, 123–157; Krumholz and Forester 1990, 17–210; Kunstler 1993; Phelan and Schneider 1996, 659–680; Rosenbaum 1995, 231–269; Rosenbaum and Harris 2001; Rosenbaum 1991, 179–213; Rosenbaum and Popkin 1991; Rosenbaum 1993; Popkin et al. 2000; Varady and Preiser 1998, 189–207.

CHAPTER 7

We appreciate the research and editing assistance of Patrick Smith and Matt Hanka in writing this chapter. Special thanks to Rick Bell, Joanne Weeter, and Tom Owen for their help in Louisville's history.

1. Marin elaborated on her observations during a 2005 interview:

The Knight Fellowship went to Macon, Georgia, for our charrette. There, we worked in the Beall's Hill neighborhood, a very poor, predominately African American neighborhood with many shotgun houses that is located adjacent to Mercer University and a regentrifying area of historic homes. In Macon, our discussion of shotguns was very interesting to me at the time.

As we were discussing in detail an area of about a square block, some of us supported the idea that the shotguns be converted to much-needed "Main Street" commercial space, perhaps to house funky coffee shops, bistros, and shops, a "Shotgun Alley." This would be the "make lemons out of lemonade" approach to community revitalization, highlighting this historic building type that seems to be so much a part of the psyche of the South. As a northerner, I found the topic of shotguns fascinating. As a visitor to the area, I want to know about the real South . . . how people lived, even, or especially, if they were of modest means.

In the discussion, it was pointed out that in Key West, Florida, many of the highly sought-after historic houses are basically shotguns and that we could try to repackage Macon's as something that would be perceived as more desirable. In the end, the Shotgun Alley Main Street idea didn't end up on the plan. Instead, they reformatted it into co-housing, another interesting adaptive reuse for shotguns. The shotgun buildings kept their form, and a central common courtyard area was planned to be built in the center of the block.

In the process of the discussion, I was surprised that so many locals still carried a fair amount of baggage about shotguns. I discovered that there is a big stigma associated with them in the South. Many people involved in the process articulated that they wouldn't live in a shotgun, ever, no matter what. There definitely is quite a bit to overcome in attitude. We heard repeatedly, "That is what I'm trying to move away from." I believe that shotguns are a building type of merit that should theoretically work for many reasons related to efficient land use and lower construction costs. However, they will need to be designed with careful attention and attractive detailing. They will need to be marketed as something notably different so that people can make the necessary leap forward.

REFERENCES

Aaronson, D. 2000. "A Note on the Benefits of Homeownership." *Journal of Urban Economics* 47, no. 3:356–369.

Abrams, Charles. 1970. *Home Ownership for the Poor: A Program for Philadelphia.* New York: Praeger.

Achtenberg, Emily P. 1975. *Critique of the Rental Housing Association Rent Control Study: An Analysis of the Realities of Rent Control in the Greater Boston Area.* Boston: Urban Planning Aid.

Adams, J. S. 1984. "The Meaning of Housing in America." *Annals of the Association of American Geographers* 74, no. 4:515–527.

Agnew, J. W. 1978. "Market Relations and Locational Conflict in Cross-National Perspective." In *Urbanization and Urban Planning in Capitalist Society,* edited by Kevin Cox, 457–480. New York: Methuen.

Albon, R. P., and D. C. Stafford. 1990. "Rent Control and Housing Maintenance." *Urban Studies* 27, no. 2:233–240.

Alford, R., and H. Scoble. 1968. "Sources of Local Political Involvement." *American Political Science Review* 62:1192–1205.

Alston, R. M., J. R. Kearl, and R. B. Vaughan. 1992. "Is There a Consensus Among Economists in the 1990s?" *American Economic Review* 82 (May): 203–209.

Angotti, Thomas. 1977. "The Housing Question." *Monthly Review* 29, no. 5 (October): 39–51.

Angrist, Shirley S. 1974. *Dimensions of Well-Being in Public Housing Families.* Pittsburgh: Carnegie-Mellon University.

Apartment and Office Building Association. 1977. "Fact Sheet: Deterioration and Abandonment in Rent Control." Report by National Association of Realtors. Chicago: Apartment and Office Building Association.

Appelbaum, R. P. 1986. "An Analysis of Rental Housing in Los Angeles, Santa Monica, Berkeley, and West Hollywood Under Current Rent Control and A.B. 483." Santa Barbara: Department of Sociology, University of California.

Appelbaum, R. P., P. Dolny, P. Dreier, and J. Gilderbloom. 1991. "Scapegoating Rent Control: Masking the Causes of Homelessness." *Journal of the American Planning Association* 57, no. 2:153–164.

Appelbaum, R. P., and J. I. Gilderbloom. 1983. "Housing Supply and Regulation: A Study of U.S. Rental Housing Market." *Journal of Applied Behavioral Science* 19, no. 1 (February): 1–18.

Appelbaum, R. P., and J. I. Gilderbloom. 1990. "The Redistributional Impact of Modern Rent Control." *Planning* 22, no. 5:601–614.

Appelbaum, R. P., and T. Glasser. 1982. *Concentration of Ownership in Isla Vista, California*. Santa Barbara: USCB Housing Office.

Architecture for Humanity. 2005. "The Shotgun Project: Preserving Hurricane Affected Neighborhoods and Creating a New Vernacular." http://www.aiany.org/eOCULUS/2005/2005-11-28.html.

Arnott, R. 1995. "Times for Revisionism on Rent Control?" *Journal of Economic Perspectives* 9, no. 1:99–120.

Ashford, D., and G. Salmonsen. 1978. "Property Rights Versus Personal Rights, and the Impact of Housing Opportunities for Children." *Fair Housing Forum* 1, no. 4:36–37.

Atlas, John. 1981. "Writing a Strong, but Legal Rent Control Law." In *Rent Control: A Source Book*, edited by John I. Gilderbloom, 121–126. Santa Barbara, CA: Foundation for Progress and Housing Information Center.

Atlas, John, and Peter Dreier. 1980. "Legislative Strategy: Fighting for Rent Control." *Shelterforce* 5, no. 4 (October).

———. 1981. "Making Tenant's Vote Count in New Jersey." *Social Policy* (May/June).

Baar, K. 1983. "Guideline for Drafting Rent Control Laws: Lessons of a Decade." *Rutgers Law Review* 35, no. 4:721–885.

Baar, K., and D. Keating. 1981. *Fair Return Standards and Hardship Appeal Procedures: A Guide for New Jersey Rent Leveling Boards*. Berkeley: National Housing Law Project.

Baldassare, Mark. 1979. *Residential Crowding in Urban America*. Berkeley: University of California Press.

Ball, Michael. 1973. "Recent Empirical Work on the Determinants of Relative Housing Prices." *Urban Studies* 10, no. 2:213–233.

———. 1976. "Owner-Occupation." In *Housing and Class in Britain*, edited by M. Edwards, F. Gray, S. Merrett, and J. Swann, 24–29. London: Political Economy of Housing Workshop of the Conference of Socialist Economists.

Barnes, J. 1989. "Preempting Local Rent Control." *Policy Review* 47 (Winter): 84–85.

Barnes, Peter. 1981. "Lamenting the Rent." In *Rent Control: A Source Book*, edited by John I. Gilderbloom, 16–20. Santa Barbara, CA: Foundation for National Progress and Housing Information Center.

Bartlet, David, and Ronald Lawson. 1982. "Rent Control and Abandonment: A Second Look at the Evidence." *Journal of Urban Affairs* 4:4.

Barton, Stephen E. 1998. "The Success and Factors of Strong Rent Control in the City of Berkeley, 1978 to 1995." In *Rent Control: Regulation and the Urban Housing Market*, edited by W. D. Keating, M. B. Teitz, and A. Skaburskis. New Brunswick, NJ: Center for Urban Policy Research, Rutgers University.

Bell, Rick. 2007a. "A Great Crisis, Followed by Great Change." *(Louisville) Courier-Journal*, January 28.

———. 2007b. *The Great Flood of 1937: Rising Waters—Soaring Spirits.* Louisville, KY: Butler Books.

Belsky, E. 1992. "Rental Vacancy Rates: A Policy Primer." *Housing Policy Debate* 3, no. 3:793–812.

Belsky, E., and J. L. Goodman. 1996. "Explaining the Vacancy Rate Paradox of the 1980s." *Journal of Real Estate Research* 11, no. 3:309–323.

Betz, J. 1981. "Rental Housing Crisis Called Calamity." *Los Angeles Times*, October 4.

Beyer, G. 1958. *Housing: A Factual Analysis.* New York: Macmillan.

———. 1966. *Housing and Society.* New York: Macmillan.

Blank, D., and L. Winnick. 1953. "The Structure of the Housing Market." *Quarterly Journal of Economics* 77, no. 2:181–208.

Blum, T., and P. Kingston. 1984. "Homeownership and Social Attachment." *Sociological Perspectives* 27, no. 2:159–180.

Blumberg, Richard, Brian Q. Robbins, and Kenneth Baar. 1974. "The Emergence of Second Generation Rent Control." *Clearinghouse Review* (August): 240–249.

Boehm, L. K. 2004. *Popular Culture and the Enduring Myth of Chicago, 1871–1968.* New York: Routledge.

Booher, D. E. 1990. "Who Gains Most Under Santa Monica's Rent Control?" *Journal of the American Planning Association* 56, no. 4:526–527.

Booth, Alan, and John N. Edwards. 1976. "Crowding and Family Relations." *American Sociological Review* 41, no. 2:308–321.

Boston Emergency Shelter Commission. 1983. *The October Project: Seeing the Obvious Problem.* Boston: Emergency Shelter Commission.

Bourassa, S. C. 2006. "The Community Land Trust as a Highway Environmental Impact Mitigation Tool." *Journal of Urban Affairs* 28, no. 4:399–418.

Bourassa, S. C., and W. Grigsby. 2000. "Income Tax Concessions for Owner-Occupied Housing." *Housing Policy Debate* 11, no. 3:521–546.

Bourassa, S. C., and Y. H. Hong. 2003. *Leasing Public Land: Policy Debates and International Experiences.* Cambridge, MA: Lincoln Land Institute.

Bradbury, K., and A. Downs, eds. 1981. *Do Housing Allowances Work?* Washington, DC: Brookings Institution.

Bratt, Rachel G. 1989. *Rebuilding Low-Income Housing Policy.* Philadelphia: Temple University Press.

Brazley, Michael. 2002. "An Evaluation of Residential Satisfaction of HOPE VI: A Study of the Park DuValle Revitalization Project." Ph.D. dissertation, University of Louisville.

Brazley, Michael, and John I. Gilderbloom. 2007. "Hope VI Housing Program: Was It Effective?" *American Journal of Economics and Sociology* 66:2.

Brenner, J., and H. Franklin. 1977. *Rent Control in North America and Europe.* Washington, DC: Potomac Institute.

Briggs, Xavier de Souza. 1997. "Moving Up Versus Moving Out: Neighborhood Effects in Housing Mobility Programs." *Housing Policy Debate* 8, no. 1:195–234.

———. 1998. "Brown Kids in White Suburbs: Housing Mobility and the Many Faces of Social Capital." *Housing Policy Debate* 9, no. 1:177–221.

Briggs, Xavier de Souza, Joe T. Darden, and Angela Aidala. 1999. "In the Wake of Desegregation: Early Impacts of Scattered-Site Public Housing on Neighborhoods in Yonkers, New York." *Journal of the American Planning Association* 65, no. 1:27–48.

Bruss, Robert J. 1979. "Real Estate Mailbag." *Philadelphia Inquirer*, August 4.

Burby, Raymond J., and William M. Rohe. 1989. "Deconcentration of Public Housing: Effects on Residents' Satisfaction with Their Living Environments and Their Fear of Crime." *Urban Affairs Quarterly* 25, no. 1:117–141.

Burgdorf, Marcia Pearce, and Robert Burgdorf. 1975. "A History of Unequal Treatment: The Qualifications of Handicapped Persons as a Suspect Class Under the Equal Protection Clause." *Santa Clara Lawyer* 15:855–910.

Burton, Larry, Heather Handle, and Saty Patrabansh. 2001. Interim Memo on HOPE VI Tracking (Retrospective) Study. April 27. Washington DC: ABT Associates.

California Department of Housing and Community Development. 1977. *California Statewide Housing Plan*. Sacramento: California Department of Housing and Community Development.

California Housing Task Force. 1979. *Major Housing Legislation for 1979: Recommendations to the Governor and Legislature*. Sacramento: Office of Planning and Research.

Capek, Stella M. 1985. "Urban Progressive Movements: The Case of Santa Monica." Ph.D. dissertation, Department of Sociology, University of Texas.

———. 1989. *Missing Social Actors: Tenants and Collective Organizing in Arkansas*. Paper presented at the annual meeting of the Southwest Social Science Association, Little Rock, March 31.

Capek, Stella M., and John I. Gilderbloom. 1992. *Community Versus Commodity: Tenants and the American City*. Albany: SUNY Press.

Carter, Darla. 2001. "Park DuValle Gets Housing for Seniors, Apartments." *(Louisville) Courier Journal*, April 14.

Castells, Manuel. 1977. *The Urban Question*. London: Edward Arnold

———. 1983. *The City and the Grassroots*. Berkeley: University of California Press.

Center for Housing Policy. 2005a. *Housing Landscapes for America's Working Families*. Washington, DC: Center for Housing Policy.

———. 2005b. "Something's Gotta Give: Working Families and the Cost of Housing." *New Century Housing* 5, no. 2 (June 1).

Centers for Disease Control and Prevention/National Center for Health Statistics (CDC/NCHS). 1999. *National Nursing Home Survey: Trends from 1973 Through 1999*. http://www.cdc.gov/nchs/data/nnhsd/NNHSTrends1973to1999.pdf.

Centers for Medicare and Medicaid Services. 2002. *Report to Congress: Appropriateness of Minimum Nurse Staffing Ratios in Nursing Homes Phase II Final Report.* Prepared by ABT Associates Inc. At http://www.frontline pub.com.

Cherry, R., and E. J. Ford. 1975. "Concentration of Rental Housing Property and Rental Housing Markets in Urban Areas." *American Real Estate and Urban Economics Association Journal* 3, no. 1:7–16.

Chiras, Daniel D. 2004. *The New Ecological Home: A Complete Guide to Green Building Options.* White River Junction, VT: Chelsea Green Publishing.

Clark, W., A. Heskin, and L. Manuel. 1980. *Rental Housing in the City of Los Angeles.* Los Angeles: Institute for Social Science Research, University of California.

Clark, William, Marinus Devloo, and Frans Dieleman. 2000. "Housing Consumption and Residential Crowding in the US Housing Markets." *Journal of Urban Affairs* 22, no. 1:49–63.

Clark, William, and Allan Heskin. 1982. "The Impact of Rent Control on Tenure Discounts and Residential Mobility." *Land Economics* 58, no. 1:109–117.

Clavel, Pierre. 1987. *The Progressive City: Planning and Participation, 1969–1984.* New Brunswick, NJ: Rutgers University Press.

Clemer, Richard B., and John C. Simonson. 1983. "Trends in Substandard Housing, 1940–1980." *Journal of American Real Estate and Urban Economics Association* 10:442–464.

Coalition for Housing. 1977. *Rent Control and the Housing Crisis in Southern California.* Los Angeles: Coalition for Economic Survival.

Cockburn, Alexander, and James Ridgeway. 1981. "Tenant Coalition Sweeps Local Elections." *Village Voice,* April 22–28.

Consortium for the Homeless (CFTH). 1983. *The Homeless of Phoenix: Who Are They? And What Should Be Done?* Phoenix: CFTH.

Consumer Reports. 1998. "Dream Home . . . or Nightmare?" February, 30–35.

Consumers Union. 2002. *In Over Our Heads: Predatory Lending and Fraud in Manufactured Housing.* February. http://www.consumersunion.org/other/mh/over1.htm.

Cooper, Clare. 1971. *The House as a Symbol of Self.* Working Paper No. 120. Berkeley: Institute of Urban and Regional Development, University of California.

Cooper-Marcus, C. 1997. *Housing as a Mirror of Self.* Berkeley: Conari Press.

Cox, Kevin. 1981. "Capitalism and Conflict Around the Communal Living Space." In *Urbanization and Urban Planning in Capitalist Society,* edited by Michael Dear and Allen Scott, 431–455. London: Methuen.

———. 1982. "Housing Tenure and Neighborhood Activism. *Urban Affairs Quarterly* 18, no. 1:107–129.

Cronin, Francis J. 1983. "Experts Predict Rent Will Climb." *Green Bay Press Gazette,* August 2.

Cummings, Scott, and Michael Price. 1997. "Race Relations and Public Policy in Louisville: Historical Development of Urban Underclass." *Journal of Black Studies* 27, no. 5 (May): 615–649.

Darden, Joe T. 1973. *Afro-Americans in Pittsburgh: The Residential Segregation of a People.* Lexington, MA: D.C. Heath.

Daugherbaugh, Debbie. 1975. *Anchorage Rent Review Program.* Mimeograph. Anchorage: Alaska Public Interest Group.

de Jouvenel, Bertrand. 1948. *No Vacancies.* Irvington-on-Hudson, NY: Foundation for Economic Education.

Devine, Richard J. 1986. *Who Benefits from Rent Control?* Oakland, CA: Center for Community Change.

Dolbeare, Cushing N. 1983. "The Low-Income Housing Crisis." In *America's Housing Crisis: What Is to Be Done?*, edited by Chester Hartman, 29–75. Boston: Routledge and Kegan Paul.

Domhoff, G. William. 1978. *Who Really Rules? New Haven and Community Power Re-Examined.* Santa Monica, CA: Goodyear Publishing.

Downs, A. 1983. *Rental Housing in the 1980s.* Washington, DC: Brookings Institute.

Dreier, P., R. P. Appelbaum, M. Dolny, and J. Gilderbloom. 1991. "Scapegoating Rent Control: Masking the Causes of Homelessness." *Journal of the American Planning Association* 57, no. 2 (Spring): 153–164.

Dreier, Peter. 1982. "Dreams and Nightmares." *Nation*, August 21, 141–146.

Dreier, Peter, and John Atlas. 1980. "The Housing Crisis and the Tenants' Revolt." *Social Policy* 10, no. 4:13–24.

Dreier, Peter, John I. Gilderbloom, and Richard P. Appelbaum. 1980. "Rising Rents and Rent Control: Issues in Urban Reform." In *Urban Planning in an Age of Austerity*, edited by Pierre Clavel, John Forrester, and William Goldsmith, 154–176. New York: Pergamon Press.

Dreier, Peter, John H. Mollenkopf, and Todd Swanstrom. 2004. *Place Matters: Metropolitics for the 21st Century.* Lawrence, KS: University Press of Kansas.

Duany, Andres, Elizabeth Plater-Zyberk, and Jeff Speck. 2000. *Suburban Nation: The Rise of Sprawl and the Decline of the American Dream.* New York: North Point Press.

Early, D. W., and E. O. Olsen. 1998. "Rent Control and Homelessness." *Regional Science and Urban Economics* 28, no. 6:797–816.

Eckert, Joseph. 1977. "The Effect of Rent Control on Assessment Policies, Differential Incidence of Taxation, and Income Adjustment Mechanisms for Rental Housing in Brookline, Massachusetts." Ph.D. dissertation, Department of Economics, Tufts University.

Eckert, Kevin J., and Mary Ittman Murrey. 1987. "Alternative Housing Models." In *Housing the Elderly*, edited by Judith Hancock, 57–80. Piscataway, NJ: Center for Urban Policy Research, Rutgers University.

Edwards, B., and D. Turrent. 2000. *Sustainable Housing: Principles and Practice.* London: E and FN Spon.

Edwards, L., and P. Torcellini. 2002. *A Literature Review of the Effects of Natural Light on Building Occupants.* Golden, CO: National Renewable Energy Laboratory.

Engels, Friedrich. 1970. *The Housing Question*. Moscow: Progress Publishers.

Epple, D. 1998. Rent Control with Reputation: Theory and Evidence. *Regional Science and Urban Economics* 28, no. 6:679–710.

Evans-Andris, Melissa. 1999. *Sustainable Urban Neighborhoods: Project Evaluation*. Department of Sociology, University of Louisville.

Expatica News. 2005. "Dutch Citizens Told to Avoid Riot Trouble Spots in France." November 8.

Fallis, G., and B. Smith. 1985. "Price Effects of Rent Control on Controlled and Uncontrolled Rental Housing in Toronto: A Hedonic Index Approach." *Canadian Journal of Economics* 18, no. 3:652–659.

Fannie Mae Foundation. 1992. *National Housing Survey*. June. Washington, DC: Government Printing Office.

Feagin, Joe. 1983. *The Urban Real Estate Game*. Englewood Cliffs, NJ: Prentice-Hall.

———. 1988. *Free Enterprise City: Houston in Political and Economic Perspective*. New Brunswick, NJ: Rutgers University Press.

Ferguson, C. E., and S. C. Maurice. 1974. *Economic Analysis*. Homewood, IL: Richard D. Irwin.

Fisch, O. 1983. "The Impact of Rent Control on Effective Tax Bias and on Structural Changes of Residential Buildings." Paper delivered at the colloquium on rent control, Lincoln Institute of Land Policy, Cambridge, MA, November.

Fischer, Claude S. 1982. *To Dwell Among Friends*. Chicago: University of Chicago Press.

Fischer, Paul B. 1991. *Is Housing Policy an Effective Anti-Housing Strategy?* Cincinnati: Stephen H. Wilder Foundation.

Flandez, Raymund. 2004. "First-Time Home Buyers Contribute to High Sales." *Wall Street Journal Online*, December 8. http://www.realestate journal.com/buysell/markettrends/20041208-flandez.html.

Flanigan, William H., and Nancy H. Zingale. 1979. *Political Behavior of the American Electorate*. Boston: Allyn and Bacon.

Florida, R. 2002. *The Rise of the Creative Class*. New York: Basic Books.

Forrest, Ray, and Alan Murie. 1991. "Transformation Through Tenure? The Early Purchasers of Council Houses, 1968–1973." *Journal of Social Policy* 20, no. 1:1–25.

Fox, N. 2005. "This New House." *Mother Jones*, March/April, 26–27.

Fradkin, P. L. 2005. *The Great Earthquake and Firestorms of 1906: How San Francisco Nearly Destroyed Itself*. Berkeley: University of California Press.

Francescato, G., S. Weidemann, and J. R. Anderson. 1987. "Residential Satisfaction: Its Uses and Limitations in Housing Research." In *Housing and Neighborhoods, Theoretical and Empirical Contributions*, edited by W. van Vliet, H. Choldin, W. Michelson, and D. Popenoe. New York: Greenwood Press.

Franklin, Scott. 1981. "Housing Cooperatives: A Viable Means of Home Ownership for Low-Income Families." *Journal of Housing* 38, no. 7:392–398.

Freeman, Richard, and Brian Hall. 1986. *Permanent Homeless in America?* Working Paper No. 2013. August. Cambridge, MA: National Bureau for Economic Research.

Fried, Marc. 1963. "Grieving for a Lost Home." In *The Urban Condition,* edited by L. J. Duhl. New York: Basic Books.

Friedland, Roger. 1982. *Power and Crisis in the City.* London: Macmillan.

Friedman, M., and G. Stigler. 1946. "Roofs or Ceilings? The Current Housing Problem." *Popular Essays on Current Problems* 1:2.

Gabriel, S. A., and F. E. Nothaft. 1988. "Rental Housing Markets and the Natural Vacancy Rate." *AREUEA (American Real Estate and Urban Economics Association) Journal* 16, no. 4:419–429.

Galster, George C., and Sean P. Killen. 1995. "The Geography of Metropolitan Opportunity: A Reconnaissance and Conceptual Framework." *Housing Policy Debate* 6, no. 1:7–43.

Garr, R. 2005. *Groups That Change Communities: New Directions Housing.* Louisville, KY: New Directions Housing Corp. http://www.grass-roots.org/usa/newdir.shtml.

Garrigan, Richard. 1978. "The Case for Rising Residential Rents." *Real Estate Review* 8, no. 3:36–41.

Garvin, Alexander, Gayle Berens, Christopher B. Leinberger. 1997. *Urban Parks and Open Space.* Washington, DC: Urban Land Institute and Trust for Public Land.

Gause, Jo Allen. 2002. *Great Planned Communities.* Washington, DC: Urban Land Institute.

Gay, P. 2006. Director, Preservation Resource Center of New Orleans. Telephone interview with the author, March 1.

Gertner, Jon. 2005. "Chasing Ground." *New York Times,* October 16.

Gilderbloom, John I. 1976. Report to Donald E. Burns, Secretary of Business and Transportation Agency, on the Validity of the Legislative Findings of A.B. 3788 and the Economic Impact of Rent Control. Sacramento: Department of Housing and Community Development.

———. 1978. *The Impact of Moderate Rent Control in the United States: A Review and Critique of Existing Literature.* Sacramento: California Department of Housing and Community Development.

———. 1980. *Moderate Rent Control: The Experience of U.S. Cities.* Washington, DC: National Conference on Alternative State and Local Public Policies.

———, ed. 1981. *Rent Control: A Source Book.* Santa Barbara, CA: Foundation of National Progress and Housing Information Center.

———. 1982. "Toward an Understanding of Inter-City Rent Differential: A Sociological Contribution." Ph.D. dissertation, University of California, Santa Barbara.

———. 1983. "The Impact of Moderate Rent Control in New Jersey: An Empirical Analysis of 26 Rent Controlled Cities." *Urban Analysis* 7, no. 2:135–154.

———. 1984. "Redistribute Impacts of Rent Control in New Jersey." Paper presented at the American Sociological Association meeting, San Antonio, TX, August.

———. 1985. "Social Factors Impacting Landlords in the Determination of Rent." *Urban Life* 14, no. 2 (July): 155–179.

———. 1986. "The Impact of Moderate Rent Control on Rent in New Jersey Communities." *Sociology and Social Research* 71, no. 1:11–14.

———. 1989. "Socioeconomic Influences on Rentals for U.S. Urban Housing: Assumptions of Open Access to a Perfectly Competitive 'Free Market' Are Confronted with the Facts." *American Journal of Economics and Sociology* 48, no. 3 (July): 273–292.

———. 2000. "Rent Control." *Journal of the American Planning Association* 66, no. 1:99–100.

———. 2004. *An Evaluation of Newport's* HOPE VI *Program,* vol. 5. Louisville, KY: Sustainable Urban Neighborhoods, University of Louisville. www.louisville.edu/org/sun.

Gilderbloom, John I., and Richard P. Appelbaum. 1987. "Toward a Sociology of Rent: Are Rental Housing Markets Competitive?" *Social Problems* 34, no. 3 (June): 261–276.

———. 1988. *Rethinking Rental Housing.* Philadelphia: Temple University Press.

Gilderbloom, John I., Richard P. Appelbaum, M. Dolny, and P. Dreier. 1992. "Sham Rent Control Research: A Further Reply." *Journal of the American Planning Association* 58, no. 2 (Spring): 220–224.

Gilderbloom, John I., and W. P. Friedlander. 2003. "How Assessed Values Vary Between Manufactured and Site-Built Houses." *Housing and Society* 30, no. 2:189–206.

Gilderbloom, John I., and M. Hanka. 2006. *Hope VI Evaluation Report.* Volume IX. Louisville, KY: University of Louisville Center for Sustainable Urban Neighborhoods.

Gilderbloom, John I., and Dennis Keating. 1982. *An Evaluation of Rent Control in Orange.* San Francisco: Foundation for National Progress, Housing Information Center.

Gilderbloom, John I., and John P. Markham. 1993. "Hispanic Rental Housing Needs in the United States: Problems and Prospects." *Housing and Society* 20, no. 3:9–25.

———. 1995. "The Impact of Homeownership on Political Beliefs." *Social Forces* 73, no. 4 (June): 1589–1607.

———. 1996. "Moderate Rent Control: Sixty Cities over 20 Years." *Journal of Urban Affairs* 18, no. 4:409–431.

Gilderbloom, John I., and Rob Mullins, 2005. *Promise and Betrayal: Universities and the Battle for Sustainable Urban Neighborhoods.* Albany: SUNY Press.

Gilderbloom, John I., Zhenfeng Pan, and Lin Ye. 2005. "The Worsening National Nursing Home Crisis." *Practicing Planner* 3, no. 2 (June): 2.

Gilderbloom, John, Mark Rosentraub, and Robert Bullard. 1987. *Designing, Locating, and Financing Housing and Transportation Services for Low-Income, Elderly, and Disabled Persons.* Houston: Center for Public Policy, University of Houston.

Goldsmith, William W., and J. Blakely. 1992. *Separate Societies: Poverty and Inequality in U.S. Cities.* Philadelphia: Temple University Press.

Goodman, Paul. 1956. *Growing Up Absurd: Problems of Youth in the Organized System*. New York: Random House.

Goodno, J. B. 2005. "Getting to Yes." *Planning* 71, no. 9:12–19.

Gordon, D. 1977. *Problems in Political Economy: An Urban Perspective*. 2d ed. Washington, DC: Heath.

Gove, Walter, Michael Hughes, and Omar Galle. 1979. "Overcrowding in the Home: An Empirical Investigation of Possible Pathological Consequences." *American Sociological Review* 44 (February): 59–80.

Grant, Gary. 1976. "Speech to the Sacramento Apartment Owners' Association." In Report to Donald E. Burns, Secretary, Business and Transportation Agency, on the Validity of the Legislative Findings of A.B. 3788 and the Economic Impact of Rent Control, by John I. Gilderbloom. Sacramento: Department of Housing and Community Development.

Grigsby, W. 1973. "Housing Markets and Public Policy." In *Housing in America: Problems and Perspectives*, edited by Daniel Mandelker and Roger Montogomery. Indianapolis: Bobbs-Merrill.

Groller, Ingrid. 1978. "Kids Keep Out." *Parents Magazine*, August, 63.

Gruen, Claude, and Nina Gruen. 1977. *Rent Control in New Jersey: The Beginnings*. Sacramento: California Housing Council.

Gupta, D., and L. Rea. 1984. "Second-Generation Rent Control Ordinances: A Quantitative Comparison." *Urban Affairs Quarterly* 19, no. 3:395–408.

Guterbock, T. 1980. *Machine Politics in Transition: Party and Community in Chicago*. Chicago: University of Chicago Press.

Gyourko, J. 1990. "Controlling and Assisting Privately Rented Housing." *Urban Studies* 27, no. 6:785–793.

Hall, Peter. 1981. "Squatters' Movement Solidifies." *Rolling Stone*, September 17.

Halle, D. 1984. *America's Working Man: Work, Home and Politics among Blue Collar Property Owners*. Chicago: University of Chicago Press.

Harlow, Karen S., and Mark S. Rosentraub. 1984. *A Pilot Study to Develop a Methodology to Identify by Disability and Location Individuals in the General Population Who Have Disabling Conditions*. Arlington: Institute of Urban Studies, University of Texas at Arlington.

Hartman, Chester. 1983. *America's Housing Crisis: What Is to Be Done?* Boston: Routledge and Kegan Paul.

———. 1984. *The Transformation of San Francisco*. Totowa, NJ: Rowman and Allanheld.

———. 2002. *Between Eminence and Notoriety: Four Decades of Radical Urban Planning*. New Brunswick, NJ: Center for Urban Policy Research, Rutgers University.

Harvey, David. 1973. *Social Justice and the City*. Baltimore: Johns Hopkins University Press.

———. 1976. "Labor, Capital and Class Struggle Around the Built Environment in Advanced Capitalist Societies." In *Urbanization and Conflict in Market Societies, Politics, and Society*, edited by Kevin Cox, 625–695. Chicago: Maaroufa Press.

———. 1979. "Rent Control and a Fair Control." *Baltimore Sun*, September 20.

Hayden, Delores. 1984. *Redesigning the American Dream: The Future of Housing, Work, and Family Life.* New York: W. W. Norton.

Hayek, F. A. 1972. "Austria: The Repercussions of Rent Restrictions." In *Verdict on Rent Control*, edited by A. Seldon. Worthing, England: Cormorant Press.

Heffley, Dennis, and Rex Santerre. 1985. "Rent Control as an Expenditure Constraint: Some Empirical Results." Annual Meetings, Eastern Economic Association, Pittsburgh, PA, March 23.

Hendershott, Patric H. 1981. "The Rental Housing Crisis." In *Rental Housing: Is There a Crisis?*, edited by John C. Weicher, Kevin E. Villani, Elizabeth A. Roistacher. Washington, DC: Urban Institute Press.

Henretta, John C. 1984. "Parental Status and Child's Home Ownership." *American Sociological Review* 49, no. 1:131–140.

Herbers, John. 1985. "Housing-Aid Debate Focuses on Question of United States Duty to Poor." *New York Times*, May 4.

Heskin, Allan D. 1981a. "A History of Tenants in the United States: Struggle and Ideology." *International Journal of Urban and Regional Research* 5, no. 2 (special issue on housing): 178–204.

———. 1981b. Is a Tenant a Second Class Citizen? In *Rent Control: A Source Book*, edited by John I. Gilderbloom, 95–106. Santa Barbara, CA: Foundation for National Progress and Housing Information Center.

———. 1981c. *Tenants and the American Dream: The Ideology of Being a Tenant.* Mimeograph. Los Angeles: School of Urban Planning and Architecture, University of California.

———. 1983. *Tenants and the American Dream: Ideology and the Tenant.* New York: Praeger.

Ho, L. S. 1992. "Rent Control: Its Rationale and Effects." *Urban Studies* 29, no. 7:1183–1190.

Hohm, Charles F. 1984. "Housing Aspirations and Fertility." *Sociology and Social Research* 68:350–363.

Homenuck, H. P. M. 1977. *A Study of High Rise: Effects, Preferences, and Perceptions.* Toronto: Institute of Environmental Research.

Hoover, Herbert. 1923. Foreword to *How to Own Your Own Home.* Washington, DC: U.S. Department of Commerce.

Hopkins, John Linn, and Marsha R. Oates. 1998. "Shotgun Houses." *Tennessee Encyclopedia of History and Culture.* http://tennesseeencyclopedia.net/imagegallery.php?EntryID=H078.

Housing Authority of Louisville (HAL). 1998. Revitalization Plan, Existing Site Conditions, Predevelopment Activities, Revitalization, Self-Sufficiency and Community Building Workshop, and Homeownership Units. Louisville, KY: HAL.

Hubert, F. 1993. "The Impact of Rent Control on Rents in the Free Sector." *Urban Studies* 30, no. 1:51–61.

Igarashi, M. 1991. "The Rental-Vacancy Relationship in the Rental Housing Market." *Journal of Housing Economics* 1, no. 3:251–270.

Jacob, Mike. 1977. *Understanding Landlording.* Oakland: California Housing Action and Information Network.

———. 1979. "How Rent Control Passed in Santa Monica, California." Oakland: California Housing Action and Information Network.

Jacobs, Jane. 1961. *The Death and Life of Great American Cities*. New York: Vintage.

James, Simon, Bill Jordan, and Helen Kay. 1991. "Poor People, Council Housing, and the Right to Buy." *Journal of Social Policy* 20, no. 1:27–40.

Jones, Michael L. 1999. "The Rebirth of Park DuValle." *Louisville Magazine*, November.

Judd, D. R., and Fainstein, S. S., eds. 1999. *The Tourist City*. New Haven, CT: Yale University Press.

Kadushin, C. 1976. *Introduction to the Sociological Study of Networks*. New York: Columbia University Press.

Kain, J. 1975. Testimony on Rent Control, Local Affairs Committee of the Massachusetts Legislature, March 21. Boston.

Kasarda, John D. 1993. "Inner-City Concentrated Poverty and Neighborhood Distress, 1970–1990." *Housing Policy Debate* 4 (3): 253–302.

Katz, Biber, and Lawrence Inc. 1977. Report to Tax Assessor of Fort Lee. Tax Assessor's Office, Fort Lee, NJ.

Kearl, J. R., C. Pope, G. Whiting, and L. Wimmer. 1979. "A Confusion of Economists?" *American Economic Review* 69, no. 2:28–37.

Keating, D. W. 1976. *Rent and Eviction Controls: An Annotated Bibliography*. Chicago: Exchange Bibliographies, Council of Planning Librarians. October.

Keating, D. W., M. B. Teitz, and A. Skaburskis. 1998. *Rent Control: Regulation and the Rental Housing Market*. New Brunswick, NJ: Center for Urban Policy Research, Rutgers University.

Kelley, E. N. 1975. "How to Get Your Manager to Raise Rents." Reprinted from *Journal of Property Management*, March/April 1975. Chicago: Institute of Real Estate Management.

Kelley, Jonathan, Ian McAllister, and Anthony Mughan. 1984. "The Decline of Class Revisited: Class and Party in England, 1964–1979." Paper presented to the annual meeting of the American Sociological Association, San Antonio, TX, August 31.

Kemeny, Jim. 1977. "A Political Sociology of Homeownership in Australia." *Australian and New Zealand Journal of Sociology* 13:47–52.

———. 1980. "Homeownership and Privatization." *International Journal of Urban and Regional Research* 4, no. 3:372–387.

Kinchen, David M. 1982. "Real Estate Predictions Coming True?" *Los Angeles Times*, July 11, 30.

Kingsley, G. Thomas, and Peter Tatian. 1997. "Housing and Welfare Reform: Geography Matters." Paper presented at the Policy Research for Housing annual meeting, Washington, DC, July.

Kingston, Paul W., L. P. Thompson, and Douglas M. Eichar. 1984. "The Politics of Homeownership." *American Politics Quarterly* 12:131–150.

Kirschman, Mary Jo. 1980. "Winning Rent Control in a Working Class City." Mimeograph. Baltimore: Rent Control Campaign.

Kleinman, Mark. 1990. "The Future Provision of Social Housing in Britain." In *Government and Housing Development in Seven Countries*, edited by William van Vliet and Jan van Wesep. Newbury Park, CA: Sage Publications.

Knack, R. E. 2006. "Let the Rebuilding Begin." *Planning* 72, no. 1:6–11.

Knox, Noelle. 2006. "Apartment Rents Expected to Rise 5%." *USA Today*, May 30.

———. 2007. "Renters Will Dig Deeper in 2007." *USA Today*, February 5, 1A.

Koenig, Tom, and Robert Gogel. 1981. "Interlocking Corporate Directorships as a Social Network." *American Journal of Economics and Sociology* 40, no. 1:37–50.

Krantz, Matt. 2005. "Mobile Home Madness: Prices Top $1 Million." *USA Today*, July 5.

Krinsky, Steve. 1981. "Tenant Activist Wins City Council Seat." *Shelterforce* 6:2.

Krohn, Roger, Berkeley Fleming, and Marilyn Manzer. 1977. *The Other Economy: The International Logic of Local Rental Housing*. Toronto: Peter Martin Associates.

Krumholz, Norman, and John Forester. 1990. *Making Equity Planning Work: Leadership in the Public Sector*. Philadelphia: Temple University Press.

Kunstler, James Howard. 1993. *The Geography of Nowhere: The Rise and Decline of America's Man-Made Landscape*. New York: Touchstone.

Lake, Robert W. 2005. *Section 8 Housing Vouchers*. Washington, D.C.: National Low-Income Housing Coalition.

Langston, Jennifer. 2006. "Backyard Rental Units OK'd for Southeast Seattle." *Seattle-Post Intelligencer*, August 8.

Laverty, C. 1976. "Effect on Property Valuation and Assessed Valuations for Ad Valorem Taxation." Tax Assessor's Office, Cambridge, MA.

Lawson, Ronald. 1983. "A Decentralized but Moving Pyramid: The Evolution and Consequences of the Structure of the Tenant Movement." In *Social Movements of the Sixties and Seventies*, edited by Jo Freeman. New York: Longman.

———. 1984. *Owners of Last Resort: An Assessment of the Track Records of New York City's Early Low Income Housing Cooperative Conversions*. New York City: Department of Housing Preservation and Development, Office of Program and Management Analysis.

Lawton, M. P. 1976. The Relative Impact of Congregate and Traditional Housing on Elderly Tenants." *Gerontologist* 16, no. 3:237–242.

Leccese, Michael, and Kathleen McCormick. 2000. *Charter of the New Urbanism*. New York City: McGraw-Hill.

Leight, Claudia, Elliot Lieberman, Jerry Kurtz, and Dean Pappas. 1980. "Rent Control Wins in Baltimore." In *Moving On*. Chicago: New America Movement.

Lett, M. 1976. *Rent Control: Concepts, Realities, and Mechanisms*. New Brunswick, NJ: Center for Urban Policy Research, Rutgers University.

Levine, N. J., J. E. Grigsby III, and A. Heskin. 1990. "Who Benefits from Rent Control?" *Journal of the American Planning Association* 56, no. 2:140–152.

Lewis, T. J., and R. A. Muller. 1992. "Contracting Out of Rent Control." *Canadian Journal of Political Science* 25:557–572.

Lifchez, Raymond. 1987. *Rethinking Architecture: Design Students and Physically Disabled People*. Berkeley: University of California Press.

Lifchez, Ray, and Barbara Winslow. 1979. *Design for Independent Living*. Berkeley: University of California Press.

Lima, T. 1990. "Gray Ladies: Another Consequence of San Francisco Rent Control." *Challenge* 33:54–55.

Linson, Neal. 1978. "Concentration of Ownership in Santa Barbara." Mimeograph. Santa Barbara: Santa Barbara Tenants Union.

Lipsky, Michael. 1970. *Protest in City Politics: Rent Strikes, Housing, and the Power of the Poor*. Chicago: Rand McNally.

Listokin, David, with Lizabeth Allewelt and James J. Nemeth. 1985. *Housing Receivership and Self-Help Neighborhood Revitalization*. New Brunswick, NJ: Center for Urban Policy Research, Rutgers University.

Logan, J. R. 2006. "The Impact of Katrina: Race and Class in Storm-Damaged Neighborhoods." Working paper. Providence, RI: Department of Sociology, Brown University.

Logan, John, and Harvey Molotch. 1987. *Urban Fortunes: The Political Economy of Place*. Berkeley: University of California Press.

Los Angeles Community Development Department (CDD). 1979. *Rent Stabilization Study*. Los Angeles: CDD.

Los Angeles Rent Stabilization Division (RSD). 1985. *Rental Housing Study. The Rent Stabilization System: Impacts and Alternatives*. Los Angeles: RSD.

Los Angeles Times. 1979. "State Boosts Brown's Rent 36% to $375." May 2.

———. 2007. "Study Shows 744,000 Were Homeless in U.S. in 2005." January 11.

Louisiana Division of Historic Preservation. 2005. "A Report from New Orleans." New Orleans: Preservation Resource Center of New Orleans.

Lowe, Carey, and Richard Blumberg. 1981. "Moderate Regulations Protect Landlords, as Well as Tenants." In *Rent Control: A Source Book*, edited by John I. Gilderbloom, 72–75. Santa Barbara: Foundation for National Progress and Housing Information Center.

Lowry, D., and L. Sigelman. 1981. "Understanding the Tax Revolt: Eight Explanations." *American Political Science Review* 75:963–974.

Lowry, Ira S. 1981a. *Inflation Indexes for Rental Housing*. Santa Monica: Rand Corporation.

———. 1981b. "Rental Housing in the 1970s: Searching for the Crisis." In *Rental Housing: Is There a Crisis?*, edited by John C. Weicher, Kevin E. Villani, and Elizabeth A. Roistacher. Washington, DC: Urban Institute Press.

———. 1992. "Rent Control and Homelessness: The Statistical Evidence." *Journal of the American Planning Association* 58, no. 2:224–228.

Luhan, Gregory A., Dennis Domer, and David Mohney. 2004. *Citibase: Louisville Guide*. New York: Princeton Architectural Press.

Lyman, Stanford M., and Marvin B. Scott. 1967. "Territoriality: A Neglected Sociological Dimension." *Social Problems* 15, no. 2:236–248.

Malpezzi, S. 1996. "Housing Prices, Externalities, and Regulation in U.S. Metropolitan Areas." *Journal of Housing Research* 7 (2): 209–241.

Mandelker, D., and R. Montgomery. 1973. *Housing in America: Problems and Perspectives.* Indianapolis: Bobbs-Merrill.

Manzer, Marilyn, and Roger Krohn. 1973. "Private Redevelopment and Older Low Rent Housing: A Conflict of Economies." Mimeograph. Montreal: McGill University.

Marcuse, Peter. 1979. *Rental Housing in the City of New York: Supply and Conditions, 1975-1978.* New York: New York City Department of Housing Preservation and Development.

————. 1981a. *Housing Abandonment: Does Rent Control Make A Difference?* Washington, DC: Conference on State and Local Policies.

————. 1981b. The Strategic Potential of Rent Control. In *Rent Control: A Source Book,* edited by John Gilderbloom, 86–94. Santa Barbara, CA: Foundation for National Progress.

————. 1986. "The Uses and Limits of Rent Regulations: A Report to the Division of Housing and Community Renewal." Albany: State of New York Division of Housing and Community Renewal.

Marin, Joyce. 2005. Telephone interview with John I. Gilderbloom, October 10.

Marks, D. 1984. "The Effect of Rent Control on the Price of Rental Housing: A Hedonic Approach." *Land Economics* 60, no. 1:81–94.

————. 1991. "On Resolving the Dilemma of Rent Control." *Urban Studies* 28, no. 3:415–431.

Marquez, Sandra. 2002. "California Leads Nation in Number of People per Household." Associated Press, June 15.

Martin, Phillip. 1976. "The Supreme Court's Quest for Voting Equality on Bond Referenda." *Baylor Law Review* 28, no. 1:25–37.

Massachusetts Department of Corporations and Taxation. 1974. *A Study of Rent and Eviction Controls for the Commonwealth of Massachusetts.* Boston: Joint Legislative Committee on Local Affairs, State of Massachusetts.

McComb, David G. 1969. *Houston: A History.* Austin: University of Texas Press.

McKee, Cindy. 1981. "Tenants Help Elect Progressive Mayor." *Shelterforce* 6, no. 2:8.

Meehan, Eugene. 1988. "Low-Income Housing: The Ownership Question." *Journal of Housing* 45, no. 3:105–109.

Millennial Housing Commission. 2002. *Meeting Our Nation's Housing Challenges.* Washington, DC: Bipartisan Millennial Housing Commission.

Mills, C. Wright. 1959/1976. *The Sociological Imagination.* Reprint 1976, New York: Oxford University Press.

Miron, J. R. 1990. "Security of Tenure, Costly Tenants and Rent Regulation." *Urban Studies* 27, no. 2:167–184.

Moe, R. 2005. "Historic Preservation vs. Katrina: What Role Should Federal, State and Local Governments Play in Preservation of Historic Properties Affected by These Catastrophic Storms?" Testimony before the U.S. House of Representatives Committee on Government Reform Subcommittee on Federalism and the Census, November 1. http://www.national trust.org/hurricane/testimonies.html.

Mohney, David, and Keller Easterling, eds. 1991. *Seaside: Making a Town in America*. New York: Princeton Architectural Press.

Mollenkopf, John, and Jon Pynoos. 1973. "Boardwalk and Park Place: Property Ownership, Political Structure and Housing Policy at the Local Level." In *Housing Urban America*, edited by Jon Pynoos, Robert Schaffer, and Chester Hartman, 56–74. Chicago: Aldine.

Molotch, Harvey L. 1976. "The City as Growth Machine: Toward a Political Economy of Place." *American Journal of Sociology* 82, no. 2:309–332.

Moon, C. G., and J. G. Stotsky. 1993. "The Effect of Rent Control on Housing Quality Change: A Longitudinal Analysis." *Journal of Political Economy* 101, no. 6:1114–1148.

Morris, Earl W., Mary Winter, and Mary Ann Sward. 1984. "Reporting Error and Single-Family Home Ownership Norms and Preferences." *Housing and Society* 11, no. 2:82–97.

Morrissy, Patrick. 1987. "Housing Receivership: A Step Toward Community Control." *Shelterforce* 10:8–10.

Murray, M. P., C. P. Rydell, C. L. Barnett, C. Hillestad, and K. Neels. 1991. "Analyzing Rent Control: The Case of Los Angeles." *Economic Inquiry* 29:601–625.

Muth, Richard. 1969. *Cities and Housing*. Chicago: University of Chicago Press.

Myers, Dowell, and Katherine Baillargeon. 1985. "Deriving Place-Specific Measures of the Rental Housing Crisis from the 1980 Census: An Application from Texas." *Journal of Urban Affairs* 7, no. 3:63–74.

Mortgage Bankers Association of America (MBAA). 2002. *State of the Real Estate Finance Industry Report*. Washington, DC.

Nader, Ralph. 1973. *Politics of Land*. New York: Grossman.

Nash, C., and A. Skaburskis. 1998. "Toronto's Changing Rent Control Policy." In *Rent Control: Regulation and the Rental Housing Market*, edited by Keating, Teitz, and Skaburskis, 169–192.

National Association of Realtors (NAR). 2002. *Real Estate Outlook*. Washington, DC, April.

———. 2005. *Housing Affordability Index*. Washington, DC, August.

National Low Income Housing Coalition. 2004. *Up Against a Wall: Housing Affordability for Renters*. Washington, DC.

National Trust for Historic Preservation. 2007. "Heritage Tourism." http://www.nationaltrust.org/heritage_tourism/index.html?cat=2.

National Urban League and the Center for Community Change. 1971. *The National Survey of Housing Abandonment*. New York: National Urban League.

Navarro, P. 1985. "Rent Control in Cambridge, Mass." *Public Interest* 78:83–100.

Navarro, Mireya. 2006. "Families Add 3rd Generation to Households." *New York Times*, May 25.

Nelson, C. L. 1991. *Protecting the Past from Natural Disasters*. Washington, DC: Preservation Press and National Trust for Historic Preservation.

New Jersey Department of the Treasury. 1970–1977. *Summary: New Jersey Residential Permits and Demolitions.* Trenton: New Jersey Department of Labor and Industry.

New Jersey Tenants Organization (NJTO). 2003. *Rent Control Survey.* Hackensack, NJ.

New York Temporary State Commission on Living Costs and the Economy. 1974. *Report on Housing and Rents.* New York.

Newman, Oscar. 1980. *Community of Interest.* Garden City, NY: Anchor/Doubleday.

Nursing Home Abuse Resource Center. 2002. *Nursing Home Facts.* http://www.nursinghomeabuseresourcecenter.com/facts.

O'Connor, James. 1981. "Rent Control Is Absolutely Essential." In *Rent Control: A Source Book,* edited by John I. Gilderbloom. Santa Barbara, CA: Foundation for National Progress and Housing Information Center.

Olkowski, Thomas. 1993. *Moving with Children.* New York: Gylantic Publishing.

Olsen, E. O. 1973. "A Competitive Theory of the Housing Market." In *Housing in Urban America,* edited by Jon Pynoos, Robert Shafer, and Chester Hartman. Chicago: Aldine.

———. 1998. Economics of Rent Control. *Regional Science and Urban Economics* 28, no. 6:673–678.

Orbell, J. M., and T. Uno. 1972. "A Theory of Neighborhood Problem Solving: Political Action vs. Residential Mobility." *American Political Science Review* 61:471–489.

Pahl, Ray E. 1975. *Whose City?* Middlesex, England: Penguin.

Paish, F. W. 1950. *The Economics of Rent Restriction.* London: Lloyds Bank Review.

Park, Walter. 1980. *Access to Housing in the 80s.* San Francisco: Independent Housing Services.

Pennance, F. G. 1969. *Housing Market Analysis and Policy.* London: Simon-Wherry Press.

———. 1972. Introduction to *Verdict on Rent Control,* edited by A. Seldon. Worthing, England: Cormorant Press.

Pentifallo, N. 1977. "An Argument for the Equating of Local Property Taxes Among All the Classes of Properties." Tax Assessor's Office, Fort Lee, NJ.

Petterson, J. 1999. *A Review of the Literature and Programs on Local Recovery from Disaster.* Working Paper No. 102. Fairfax, VA: Public Entity Risk Institute.

Pew Research Center for People and the Press. 2005. "Economic Concerns Fueled by Many Woes: Gas Prices, Jobs, Housing, Debt Burden, and the Stock Market." June 1.

Phelan, Thomas J., and Mark Schneider. 1996. "Race, Ethnicity, and Class in American Suburbs." *Urban Affairs Review* 31, no. 5 (May): 659–680.

Phillips, D. 1974. *Analysis and Impact of Rent Control Program in Lynn.* Mayor's office, Lynn, MA.

Popkin, Susan, Diane Levy, Laura Harris, Jennifer Comey, Mary Cunningham, and Larry Buron. 2004. "The HOPE VI Program: What About the Residents?" *Housing Policy Debate* 15, no. 3:715–751.

Preservation Alliance of Louisville and Jefferson Co. 1980. *The Shotgun House: Urban Housing Opportunities.* Louisville, KY.

Preservation Resource Center of New Orleans. 2005. *Architecture: Types and Styles.* http://prcno.org/arch.html.

Proxmire, William. 1978. "The Destructive Folly of Rent Control." *Congressional Record* 124 (September 18), pt. 22:29735.

Pusch, Burton D. 1987. "Point of View." (Houston Center for Independent Living) *Spectrum* 2, no. 2:4–5.

Pynoos, Jon, Robert Schafer, and Chester Hartman. 1973. *Housing Urban America.* Chicago: Aldine.

Quigley, J. 1990. "Does Rent Control Cause Homelessness?: Taking the Claim Seriously." *Journal of Policy Analysis and Management* 9, no. 1:89–93.

Raiford, Regina. 2002. "Solar Gains." *Buildings.* http://www.buildings.com/articles/detail.asp?offset=25&ArticleID=663.

Rapaport, C. 1992. "Rent Regulation and Housing-Market Dynamics." *American Economic Review* 82:446–451.

Retsinas, Nicholas P., and Eric S. Belsky, eds. 2002. *Low-Income Homeownership: Examining the Unexamined Goal.* Joint Center for Housing Studies and Brookings Institution Press. Washington, DC.

Revenue and Rent Study Committee. 1974. Minutes of meeting, April 19. Brookline, MA.

Rich, Jonathan M. 1984. "Municipal Boundaries in a Discriminatory Housing Market: An Example of Racial Leapfrogging." *Urban Studies* 21, no. 1:31–40.

Riddell, R. 2004. *Sustainable Urban Planning: Tipping the Balance.* Oxford, England: Blackwell.

Rohe, W. H., and L. S. Stewart. 1996. "Homeownership and Neighborhood Stability." *Housing Policy Debate* 7 (1): 37–81.

Rohe, William, George McCarthy, and Shannon Van Zandt. 2001. *The Social Benefits and Costs of Homeownership: A Critical Assessment of the Research.* Working Paper LIHO-01.12. Cambridge, MA: Joint Center for Housing Studies, Harvard University.

Rohe, William, and Michael Stegman. 1992. "Public Housing Homeownership: Will It Work and for Whom?" *Journal of the American Planning Association* 58, no. 2:144–157.

———. 1994. "The Effects of Homeownership on the Self-Esteem, Perceived Control, and Life Satisfaction of Low-Income People." *Journal of the American Planning Association* 60, no. 2:173.

Roistacher, Elizabeth. 1972. "The Distribution of Tenant Benefits Under Rent Control." Ph.D. dissertation, University of Pennsylvania, Philadelphia.

Ropers, Richard H. 1986. *Living on the Edge: The Sheltered Homeless, an Empirical Study of Los Angeles Single Room Occupancy Residents.* Cedar City, UT: Department of Behavioral and Social Sciences, Southern Utah State College.

Rosen, K. T. 1996. "The Economics of the Apartment Market in the 1990's." *Journal of Real Estate Research* 11, no. 3:242–265.

Rosen, K. T., and L. B. Smith. 1983. "The Price Adjustment Process for Rental Housing and the Natural Vacancy Rate." *American Economic Review* 73: 779–786.

Rosen, Marvin, Gerald R. Clark, and Marvic S. Kivitz. 1977. *Habilitation of the Handicapped*, Baltimore: University Park Press.

Rosenbaum, Emily, and Laura E. Harris. 2001. "Low Income Families in Their New Neighborhoods: The Short-Term Effects of Moving from Chicago's Public Housing." *Journal of Family Issues* 22, no. 2:183–210.

Rosenbaum, James E. 1991. "Black Pioneers—Do Their Moves to the Suburbs Increase Economic Opportunity for Mothers and Children?" *Housing Policy Debate* 2, no. 4:179–213.

———. 1993. "Closing the Gap: Does Residential Integration Improve the Employment and Education of Low-Income Blacks?" In *Affordable Housing and Public Policy: Strategies for Metropolitan Chicago*, edited by L. B. Joseph, 223–228. Chicago: Center for Urban Research and Policy Studies, University of Chicago.

———. 1995. "Changing the Geography of Opportunity by Expanding Residential Choice: Lessons from the Gautreaux Program." *Housing Policy Debate* 6, no. 1:231–269.

Rosenbaum, James E., and Susan J. Popkin. 1990. *Economic and Social Impacts of Housing Integration: A Report from the Charles Stewart Mott Foundation*. Evanston, IL: Center for Urban Affairs and Policy Research.

———. 1991. "Employment and Earnings of Low-Income Blacks Who Move to Middle Class Suburbs." In *The Urban Underclass*, edited by Christopher Jencks and Paul Peterson. Washington, DC: Brookings Institution.

Rosentraub, Mark S., Pamela A. Holcomb, Lester Salamon, and James C. Musselwhite Jr. 1987. *Human Service Spending in Dallas: The Changing Roles of Government and Private Funders*. Washington, DC: Urban Institute.

Rosentraub, Mark, and Robert Warren. 1986. "Tenant's Associations and Social Movements: The Case of the United States." Paper presented at Urban Affairs Association meeting, Fort Worth, March 8.

Rosofsky, Ira. 2007. "Escape from the Nursing Home." Op-ed. *New York Times*, January 17.

Rothblatt, Donald, Daniel J. Garr, and Jo Sprague. 1979. *The Suburban Environment and Women*. New York: Praeger.

Rydell, C. Peter. 1981. *The Impact of Rent Control on the Los Angeles Housing Market*. Santa Monica, CA: Rand Corporation.

Rydenfelt, S. 1949. "Rent Control Thirty Years On." In *Human Action: A Treatise on Economics*. New Haven, CT: Yale University Press.

Rypkema, D. D. 2002. *Historic Preservation and Affordable Housing: The Missed Connection*. Washington, DC: National Trust for Historic Preservation.

Saegert, Susan. 1981. "Masculine Cities and Feminine Suburbs: Polarized Ideas, Contradicting Realities." In *Women and the American City*, edited by Catherine Stimpson et al. Chicago: University of Chicago Press.

Samuelson, P. 1967. *Economics: An Introductory Analysis.* New York: McGraw-Hill.

San Francisco Chronicle. 1985. "A Rent Bill Deserves Support," editorial, May 5.

Santa Barbara News Press. 1978. "Raise Rents," editorial, December 3.

Santa Monica Rent Control Board. 1979. Proposed General Rent Adjustment. Santa Monica, CA: Rent Control Office.

Santerre, R. 1986. "The Effect of Rent Control on the Price of Rental Housing: Comment." *Land Economics* 62:104–105.

Sarason, Seymour B., and John Doris. 1979. *Educational Handicap, Public Policy, and Social History.* New York: Free Press.

Saulny, Susan. 2006. "A Legacy of the Storm: Depression and Suicide." *New York Times,* June 21.

Saunders, Peter. 1978. "Domestic Property and Social Class." *International Journal of Urban and Regional Research* 2:233–251

———. 1984. "Beyond Housing Classes: The Sociological Significance of Private Property Rights in a Means of Consumption." *International Journal of Urban and Regional Research* 8, no. 2:202–227.

Schorr, Alvin. 1963. *Slums and Social Insecurity.* Washington, DC: Government Printing Office.

Scott, Janny. 2006. "The Granny Flat is Back—and Not Just for Grannies." *New York Times,* December 2.

Seldon, A., ed. 1972. *Verdict on Rent Control.* Worthing, England: Cormorant Press.

Selesnick, Herbert L. 1976. *Rent Control: A Case For.* Lexington, MA: Lexington Books.

Shanley, Michael, and Charles Hotchkiss. 1979. *How Low-Income Renters Buy Homes.* A Rand Note. Santa Monica, CA: Rand Corporation.

Shipnuck, Leslie, Dennis Keating, and Mary Morgan. 1974. *The People's Guide to Urban Renewal.* Berkeley: A Community Defense Manual and Community Development Programs.

Shlay, Ann. 1983. "Castles in the Sky: Measuring Housing and Neighborhood Ideology." Paper presented at American Sociological Association annual meeting, Detroit, September 3.

Shulman, David. 1980. "Real Estate Valuation Under Rent Control: The Case of Santa Monica." Mimeograph. Los Angeles: Business Forecasting Project, University of California.

Silver, Hilary, Judith McDonald, and Ronald Ortiz. 1985. "Selling Public Housing: The Methods and Motivations." *Journal of Housing* 42, no. 6: 213–228.

Simmons, Patrick A. 2002. *Patterns and Trends in Overcrowded Housing: Early Results from Census 2000.* Washington, DC: Fannie Mae Foundation.

Smith, W. F. 1973. "Filtering and Neighborhood Change." In *Housing in America: Problems and Perspectives,* edited by Daniel Mandelker and Roger Montogomery. Indianapolis: Bobbs-Merrill.

Solomon, Arthur P., and K. D. Vandell. 1982. "Alternative Perspectives on

Neighborhood Decline." *Journal of American Institute of Planners* 45, no. 1:81–91.

Sorenson, Baerbel. 1983. "The Alaska Emergency Residential Rent Regulation and Control Program." Paper presented at Lincoln Land Institute Colloquium on Rent Control, Cambridge, MA, November.

Southworth, M. (1997). "Walkable Suburbs?" *Journal of the American Planning Association* 63 (1): 25–44.

Squires, Gregory. 1981. "Housing in America: Shelter or Social Control." *Contemporary Sociology* 10, no. 6:755–757.

Stegman, M. A. 1981. "The President's Commission Calls for Vouchers: Some Reflections and Concerns." Comments prepared for delivery at the National Association of Housing and Redevelopment Officials (NAHRO) Housing Policy Forum. Washington, DC: Urban Institute.

Stegman, Michael. 1991. *More Housing. More Family.* New York: Twentieth Century Fund Press.

Stegman, Michael A., and H. Sumka. 1976. *Nonmetropolitan Urban Housing: An Economic Analysis of Problems and Policies.* Cambridge, MA: Ballinger.

Steinberger, P. 1981. "Political Participation and Community: A Cultural/Interpersonal Approach." *Rural Sociology* 46, no. 1:7–19.

Sternlieb, George. 1966. *The Tenement Landlord.* New Brunswick, NJ: Rutgers University Press.

———. 1974. *The Realities of Rent Control in the Greater Boston Area.* New Brunswick, NJ: Center for Urban Policy Research, Rutgers University.

———. 1975. *Fort Lee Rent Control.* New Brunswick, NJ: Center for Urban Policy Research, Rutgers University.

Stone, Lorene Hemphill. 1986. "Shelters for Battered Women: A Temporary Escape from Danger or the First Step Toward Divorce?" In *Housing for the Homeless*, edited by Jon Erickson and Charles Wilhelm. New Brunswick, NJ: Center for Urban Policy Research, Rutgers University.

Stone, Michael. 1980. "Housing and the American Economy: A Marxist Analysis." In *Urban Planning in an Age of Austerity*, edited by Pierre Clavel, John Forster, and William W. Goldsmith, 81–116. New York: Pergamon Press.

———. 1983. "Housing and the Economic Crisis: An Analysis and Emergency Program." In *America's Housing Crisis: What Is to Be Done?*, edited by Chester Hartman. Boston: Routledge and Kegan Paul.

Stoner, Madelaine R. 1986. "The Plight of Homeless Women." In *Housing for the Homeless*, edited by Jon Erickson and Charles Wilhelm. New Brunswick, NJ: Center for Urban Policy Research, Rutgers University.

Strassman, W. P. 1991. "Housing Market Interventions and Mobility: An International Comparison." *Urban Studies* 28:759–771.

Struyk, R. J., and M. Bendick Jr., eds. 1981. *Housing Vouchers for the Poor: Lessons from a National Experiment.* Washington, DC: Urban Institute.

Surowiecki, James. 2003. "Leave No Parent Behind." *New Yorker*, August 18 and 25.

Suttles, Gerald. 1972. *The Social Construction of Communities.* Chicago: University of Chicago Press.

Sykes, G. 1951. "The Differential Distribution of Community Knowledge." *Social Forces* 29:376–382.

Teitz, Michael B. 1998. "Rent Stabilization in Los Angeles: A Moderate Approach to Regulation." In *Rent Control: Regulation and the Rental Housing Market*, edited by Keating, Teitz, and Skaburskis. New Brunswick, NJ: Center for Urban Policy Research, Rutgers University.

Treskon, Mark, and Danilo Pelletiere. 2004. *Up Against a Wall: Housing Affordability for Renters: An Analysis of the 2003 American Community Survey*. Washington, DC: National Low-Income Housing Coalition.

Trichillo, Vincent. 1987. "Home Equity Conversions." In *Housing the Elderly*, 121–128. Piscataway, NJ: Center for Urban Policy Research, Rutgers University.

Tucker, William. 1987. "Where Do the Homeless Come From?" Associates Memo No. 5, November 20. New York: Manhattan Institute for Policy Research.

———. 1991. "Scapegoating Rent Control: A Reply." *Journal of the American Planning Association* 57:485–489.

Turner, Margery. 1988. "Rent Control and the Availability of Affordable Housing in the District of Columbia." Report prepared for the District of Columbia's Department of Consumer and Regulatory Affairs. Washington, DC: Urban Institute.

Twohey, Megan. 2000. "Chicago Hope." *National Journal*, April 22.

Urban Institute. 2000. *A New Look at Homelessness in America*. http://www .urban.org/url.cfm?ID=900366.

Urban Land Institute. 1976. "Prospects for Rental Housing Production Under Rent Control: A Case Study of Washington D.C." Research Report 240. Washington, DC.

———. 2002. "Engaging the Private Sector in HOPE VI." Washington, DC.

Urban Planning Aid. 1975. *Critique of the Rental Housing Association Rent Control Study: An Analysis of the Realities of Rent Control in the Greater Boston Area*. Cambridge, MA.

U.S. Census Bureau. 1970. Census of Housing in New Jersey. Washington, DC: Government Printing Office (GPO).

———. 1979. *Voting and Registration in the Election of November 1978*. Current Population Reports, Series P. 20, 344. Washington, DC: GPO.

———. 2000. 2000 Census of Population and Housing. Washington, DC: U.S. Census Bureau. http://www.census.gov/prod/cen2000/index.html.

———. 2003. *American Housing Survey*. Washington, DC: US Census Bureau. http://www.census.gov/hhes/www/housing/ahs/ahs03/ahs03.html.

———. 2004. Housing and Household Economic Statistics Division. "Historical Census of Housing Tables, Gross Rents." Revised December 2.

———. 2005. *Homeownership Tables*. U.S. Department of Housing and Urban Development (HUD). 1983. *Annual Housing Survey: General Housing Characteristics for the United States and Regions*. Washington, DC: GPO.

———. 1984. *A Report to the Secretary on the Homeless and Emergency Shelters*. U.S. House of Representatives. Joint Hearing before the Subcommittee on Housing and Community Development and the Subcommittee on Manpower and Housing, May 24. Washington, DC: GPO.

———. 2001. HOPE VI Revitalization Grant Program. Quarterly Project Progress Report. Washington, DC.

U.S. General Accounting Office (GAO). 1978. *Housing Abandonment: A National Problem Needing New Approaches.* Washington, DC: GAO.

U.S. League of Savings Associations. 1982. *Homeownership: The American Dream Adrift.* Chicago: League of Savings Associations.

U.S. President's Commission on Housing. 1982. *Report of the President's Commission on Housing.* Washington, DC: GPO.

———. 1983. *Report of the President's Commission on Housing.* Washington, DC: GPO.

USA Today. 1985. "USA's Homeless Face More Health Problems," December 16.

Van Sweden, James. 1995. *Gardening with Water.* New York City: Random House.

Van Sweden, James, with Susan Rademacher. 1998. *Bold Romantic Gardens.* Washington, DC: Spacemaker Press.

Varady, D. P., and W. F. E. Preiser. 1998. "Scattered-Site Public Housing and Housing Satisfaction." *Journal of the American Planning Association* 64, no. 2 (Spring): 189–207.

Varady, David P., Carole C. Walker, and Xinhao Wang. 2001. "Voucher Recipient Achievement of Improved Housing Conditions in the US: Do Moving Distance and Relocation Services Matter?" *Urban Studies* 38, no. 8: 1273–1304.

Vaughan, Roger. 1972. "Landlord-Tenant Relations in a Low-Income Area." In *Tenants and the Urban Housing Crisis,* edited by Stephen Burghardt, 77–88. Dexter, MI: New Press.

Vitaliano, Donald F. 1983. "The Economic Consequences of Rent Control: Some Evidence from New York State." Paper presented at the Lincoln Land Institute Colloquium on Rent Control, Cambridge, MA, November.

———. 1985. "The Short-Run Supply of Housing Services Under Rent Control." *Urban Studies* 22, no. 6:535–542.

Vlach, J. M. 1986. "The Shotgun House: An African Architectural Legacy." In *Readings in American Vernacular Architecture,* edited by D. Upton and J. M. Vlach. Athens: University of Georgia Press.

Walsh, Joan. 1985. "Are City Shelters Now Open Asylums?" *In These Times* 9:9.

Ward, Colin. 1983. *Housing: An Anarchist Approach.* London: Freedom Press.

Warren, Elizabeth, and Amelia Warren Tyagi. 2003. *The Two-Income Trap.* New York: Basic Books.

Watrous, G. 2005. President, Watrous Associates Architects. Interview with John I. Gilderbloom, University of Louisville, October 11.

Watson, K. 2002. "A Solution to the Affordable Housing Crisis." *Journal of Housing and Community Development* 59, no. 3:22–25.

Wechsler, H. 1961. "Community Growth, Depressive Disorders, and Suicide." *American Journal of Sociology* 67, no. 1:9–16.

Wedner, Diane. 2006. "To Live and Buy in Los Angeles." *Los Angeles Times*, June 4.

Weeter, J. 2004. *Louisville Landmarks: A View of Architectural and Historic Landmarks in Louisville, Kentucky.* Louisville: Butler Books.

Weicher, J. C. 1990. "Comment on William Apgar's 'Which Housing Policy Is Best?'" *Housing Policy Debate* 1 (1): 33–39.

Weicher, John C., Kevin E. Villani, and Elizabeth A. Roistacher. 1981. *Rental Housing: Is There A Crisis?* Washington, DC: Urban Institute Press.

Williams, J. A. 1971. "The Multi-Family Housing Solution and Housing Type Preference." *Social Science Quarterly* 52:543–559.

Willis, J. 1950. "Short History of Rent Control Laws." *Cornell Law Quarterly* 36:54–92.

Wingo, L. 1973. "The Quality of Life: Toward a Microeconomic Definition." *Urban Studies* 10, no. 1:3–18.

Winograd, Kenneth. 1982. *Street People and Other Homeless: A Pittsburgh Study.* Pittsburgh: Emergency Shelter Task Force.

Wirth, Louis. 1947. "Housing as a Field of Sociological Research." *American Sociological Review* 12, no. 2:137–142.

Wolfe, Marian F. 1983. "An Empirical Examination of Landlord Behavior and Implications for Rental Housing Policies." Paper presented at the Annual Conference of the Association of Collegiate Schools of Planning, San Francisco, October 21.

Wolkoff, M. 1990. "Property Right to Rent Regulated Apartments: A Path Toward Decontrol." *Journal of Policy Analysis and Management* 9, no. 2:260–265.

Women's City Club of New York. 1977. "The Cities: Empty Homes." Report. New York: Women's City Club Publications.

Wubneh, Mulatu, and Guoqiang Shen. 2004. "The Impact of Manufactured Housing on Nearby Residential Properties: A GIS Approach." *Review of Urban and Regional Development Studies* 16, no. 1:56–73.

Yousem, J. 1977. "Rent Controls Destructive in Principle and Practice." In *Rent Control Report*, National Association of Realtors, 220–230. Chicago: Institute of Real Estate Management.

Zito, Kelly. 2005. "Housing Unaffordable, Gas Is Heading That Way: San Francisco Leads List of Most Expensive Regions for Buyers and Renters." *San Francisco Chronicle*, August 10.

Zola, Irving. 1979. Prologue to *Design for Independent Living*, by Ray Filches and Barbara Winslow. Berkeley: University of California Press.

ABOUT THE AUTHORS

John I. Gilderbloom is a professor of urban and public affairs in the Graduate Program in Urban and Public Affairs at the University of Louisville, where he also directs the Center for Sustainable Urban Neighborhoods. Since 1992 his competitive federally funded grants have totaled nearly $4 million, and from non-federal sources he has brought in more than $1 million from private foundations, churches, and local government. Since he earned his Ph.D., Dr. Gilderbloom's economic policy research has appeared in thirty peer-reviewed journals, twenty chapters in edited books, eleven monographs, and twenty-five opinion pieces in newspapers and magazines. He has written or edited four other books and has published opinion pieces in the *Wall Street Journal, Washington Post, Los Angeles Times,* and *USA Today Magazine.* In the Clinton administration he worked as a consultant on several items including the State of the Union Speech, Section 108 programs, HOPE VI, and Community Outreach Partnership Programs. His work has won recognition and honors from the U.S. Senate and House of Representatives, President Clinton, Sierra Club, American Institute of Architects, and the mayor of Houston, as well as an American Planning Association Chapter Award and as a Harvard Innovations in Government semi-finalist. He has been featured in the Sunday *New York Times,* the *Atlanta Journal-Constitution,* and various other international newspapers. In 2005 Planetizen called *Encyclopedia of 20th-Century Architecture* one of the ten best planning and architecture books—Dr. Gilderbloom's contribution was a chapter on modern Cuban architecture. His website is www.louisville.edu/org/sun.

Richard P. Appelbaum is a professor of sociology and global and international studies at the University of California at Santa Barbara. He heads the Center for Global Studies, directs Graduate Studies in Global and International Studies, and serves on the Executive Committee of the Center for Nanotechnology and Society. Dr. Appelbaum's research focuses on the outsourcing of low-wage labor and its impact on workers in the United States and abroad; housing markets and policy; the economic rise of China; and the globalization of high-technology research, development, and commercialization.

Michael Brazley is an assistant professor in the School of Architecture and Interior Design at Southern Illinois University, where he teaches architectural design, urban design, Kid Architecture, and in the Le Petit Grand Tour d'Architecture Program. Professor Brazley has received awards including Who's Who in U.S. Executives, Professional Service Firm of the Year Award, Emerging Minority Enterprise Award, Minority Service Firm of the Year Award, and the Sierra Club's Smart Growth Award. Dr. Brazley is a registered architect in Illinois, Kentucky, Indiana, and Ohio and has owned and managed an architectural company for seventeen years. His areas of specialized interest include interior design, diversity, architecture, and housing.

Michael Anthony Campbell served as a graduate research assistant in the School of Urban and Public Affairs at the University of Louisville and collaborated with Dr. John Gilderbloom on several publications and the government-sponsored assessment of HOPE VI projects in Newport, Kentucky. Mr. Campbell has held internships with the nonprofit Project Vote Smart and with the city manager's office in Tamarac, Florida.

Steven Hornburg is a national housing strategist and founding principal of Emerging Community Markets who works to fairly expand opportunity for people and communities not well served by housing and mortgage finance markets. Working with associations, nonprofits, businesses, and governments, Mr. Hornburg provides research and strategic guidance on program development and outreach on affordable and subprime lending, counseling, smart-growth finance, and workforce housing.

Richard Layman is a historic preservation and urban revitalization advocate and consultant in Washington, D.C., and a blogger on urban affairs (http://urbanagenda.blogspot.com and http://urbanplacesandspaces.blogspot.com, among others). Mr. Layman is interim director of the Citizens Planning Coalition, a grassroots organization that works to protect, enhance, and extend the livability of Washington, D.C., by linking historic preservation, urban design, transportation, and asset-based community development.

Tom Lehman is an associate professor of economics at Indiana Wesleyan University, where he teaches macroeconomics and microeconomics courses. Dr. Lehman's specialized areas of teaching, research, and publication include public policy and administration, public finance and budgeting, urban economics and government, urban housing markets, urban economic growth, inequality, and statistics and social science research methods. His dissertation research at the University of Louisville focused on the relationships of urban economic growth, technological change, and rising urban inequality in metropolitan areas during the 1990s.

Roger K. Lewis, FAIA, is a practicing architect and planner, educator, and author. He writes a biweekly column, "Shaping the City," for the *Washington Post* while continuing project design work, consulting, lecturing, and pro bono service activities. He is a professor emeritus at the University of Maryland School of Architecture, Planning, and Preservation, which he helped to initiate in 1968, and he co-authored the widely disseminated *Growth Management Handbook*. Professor Lewis' articles on architecture, planning and urban design, historic preservation, housing, zoning, and public policy affecting the built environment appear regularly in national journals, periodicals, anthologies, and encyclopedias.

Zhenfeng "Terry" Pan is an associate research scientist at the Pacific Institute for Research and Evaluation Louisville Center conducting research in the area of substance abuse and prevention. He is project manager for the Thailand Treatment Community Followup Evaluation Study funded by the International Bureau of Narcotics and Law Affairs within the U.S. State Department and has served as lead analyst for various other projects. Dr. Pan holds a doctorate from the School of Urban and Public Affairs at the University of Louisville and collaborated with colleagues there in research and publications.

Stephen A. Roosa is an expert in delivering energy-efficiency projects for buildings and processes. He has extensive experience in performance contracting, mechanical systems, control systems, architectural modifications, and financial analysis for performance-based projects. Dr. Roosa and his projects have received national recognition. He is a Certified Energy Manager and a LEED-Accredited Professional who was accepted into the Energy Engineers Hall of Fame in 2006. Dr. Roosa holds a doctorate in public and urban affairs from the University of Louisville.

Mark S. Rosentraub is the dean of and a professor at the Maxine Goodman Levin College of Urban Affairs at Cleveland State University. The college is committed to the advancement of cities and to sustainable and equitable economic and social development. Dr. Rosentraub specializes in economics and politics of professional sports teams and their relationships with cities; the financing of sports facilities; the financing, organization, and delivery of urban services; and economic development issues. His many journal articles and books often have focused on people with disabilities, the elderly, and the economics of arenas and ballparks.

Lin Ye is an assistant professor of political science and public administration at Roosevelt University in Chicago. Professor Ye has published several public affairs articles in peer review journals and recently got his Ph.D. at the University of Louisville Department of Urban and Public Affairs.

INDEX

Lightning Source UK Ltd.
Milton Keynes UK
UKHW021910220520
363694UK00009B/67